RICHARD III
England's
Black Legend

RICHARD III
England's
Black Legend

Desmond Seward

Country Life Books

Published by Country Life Books
and distributed for them by
The Hamlyn Publishing Group Limited
London · New York · Sydney · Toronto
Astronaut House, Feltham, Middlesex, England

First published 1983
ISBN 0 600 36850 5

Set in 10pt Palatino by Input Typesetting Limited, London
Printed and bound in Great Britain by
Hazell, Watson & Viney Limited
Aylesbury

For
Reresby and Penelope Sitwell

ACKNOWLEDGEMENTS

Illustration number 13 is reproduced by gracious permission of Her Majesty the Queen. Number 34 is reproduced by permission of His Grace the Archbishop of Canterbury and the Trustees of Lambeth Palace Library; number 25 the Dean and Chapter of Westminster, numbers 16, 18, 27 and 41 the Dean and Canons of Windsor; number 6 the Provost and Fellows of King's College, Cambridge and number 3 the President and Fellows of Queens' College, Cambridge. The manuscript reproduced as illustration number 37 is owned by Bristol City Council and is kept at the Bristol Record Office.

PHOTOGRAPHS

British Library, London 12, 17, 30; Centrale Bibliotheek, Rijksuniversiteit, Ghent 9; Leonard and Marjorie Gayton 28; Gemäldegalerie, Staatliche Museen Preussischer Kulturbesitz, Berlin 8; Glasgow Museum and Art Gallery 44; Hamlyn Group Picture Library 14; A. F. Kersting, London 5, 15; Mansell Collection, London 20, 35; Musées Nationaux, Paris 7; National Portrait Gallery, London 22, 33; Order of Saint John, London 29; Photographie Giraudon, Paris 26, 40; Pierpont Morgan Library, New York 36; Society of Antiquaries of London 1; Victoria and Albert Museum, London 2; Weidenfeld and Nicolson, London 32; Geoffrey Wheeler, London 4, 11, 19, 21, 23, 24, 31, 38, 39, 42, 43; Yorkshire Museum, York 10.

'It is necessary for a prince who wishes to survive to know how to do wrong.'
Machiavelli, Il Principe

'Lo, ye all Englishmen, see ye not what a mischief here was?'
Sir Thomas Malory, Morte d'Arthur

CONTENTS

LIST OF PLATES

20. Minster Lovell.
21. Richard as King.
22. Signature of Richard as King.
23. Brass of Dr John Argentine.
24. Brass of Dr Christopher Urswick.
25. Margaret Beaufort.

Following page 116

26. Henry Tudor.
27. Anne, Duchess of Exeter and Sir Thomas St Leger.
28. Bodiam Castle.
29. Fra John Kendall.
30. Page from *The Book of the Order of Chivalry*.

Following page 148

31. Tomb and effigy of Edward of Middleham, Prince of Wales.
32. Richard and his wife, Anne Neville.
33. Elizabeth of York.
34. Richard's prayer book.

Following page 164

35. Nottingham Castle.
36. A gentleman arming himself for battle.
37. A King of England rides forth to war.
38. Brass of Sir Gervase Clifton.
39. Brass of William Catesby.

Following page 196

40. Bernard Stuart, Signeur d'Aubigny.
41. Garter plate of Thomas, Lord Stanley.
42. Brass of John Sacheverell.
43. Sir John Cheyney.
44. Battleaxe or 'battle hammer'.

HOUSES OF LANCASTER, BEAUFORT AND TUDOR

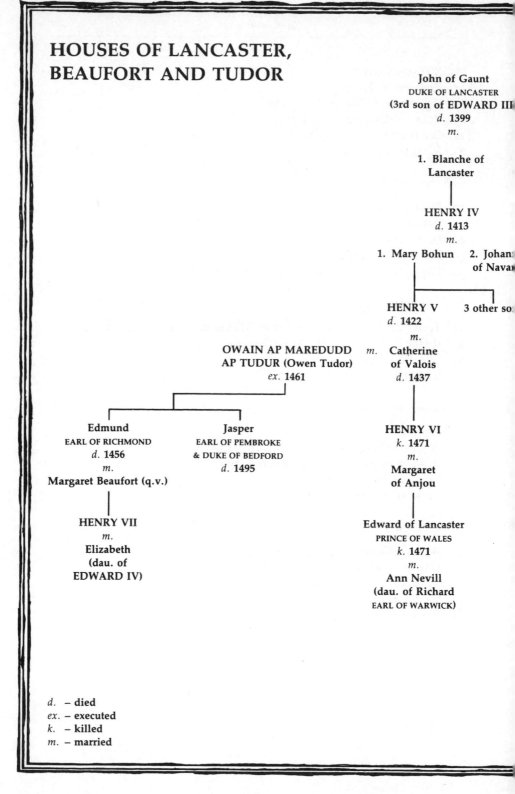

John of Gaunt
DUKE OF LANCASTER
(3rd son of EDWARD III)
d. 1399
m.

1. Blanche of
Lancaster

HENRY IV
d. 1413
m.

1. Mary Bohun   2. Johan
of Nava

HENRY V   3 other so
d. 1422
m.

OWAIN AP MAREDUDD   *m.*   Catherine
AP TUDUR (Owen Tudor)   of Valois
ex. 1461   *d.* 1437

Edmund   Jasper   HENRY VI
EARL OF RICHMOND   EARL OF PEMBROKE   *k.* 1471
d. 1456   & DUKE OF BEDFORD   *m.*
m.   *d.* 1495   Margaret
Margaret Beaufort (q.v.)   of Anjou

HENRY VII   Edward of Lancaster
m.   PRINCE OF WALES
Elizabeth   *k.* 1471
(dau. of   *m.*
EDWARD IV)   Ann Nevill
                                        (dau. of Richard
                                        EARL OF WARWICK)

d. – died
ex. – executed
k. – killed
m. – married

8

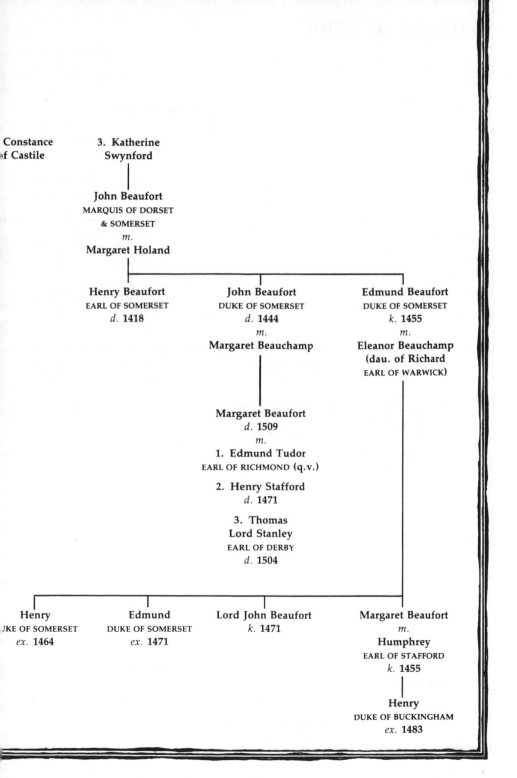

Constance
f Castile

3. Katherine
Swynford

John Beaufort
MARQUIS OF DORSET
& SOMERSET
m.
Margaret Holand

Henry Beaufort
EARL OF SOMERSET
d. **1418**

John Beaufort
DUKE OF SOMERSET
d. **1444**
m.
Margaret Beauchamp

Edmund Beaufort
DUKE OF SOMERSET
k. **1455**
m.
Eleanor Beauchamp
(dau. of Richard
EARL OF WARWICK)

Margaret Beaufort
d. **1509**
m.
1. Edmund Tudor
EARL OF RICHMOND (q.v.)

2. Henry Stafford
d. **1471**

3. Thomas
Lord Stanley
EARL OF DERBY
d. **1504**

Henry
JKE OF SOMERSET
ex. **1464**

Edmund
DUKE OF SOMERSET
ex. **1471**

Lord John Beaufort
k. **1471**

Margaret Beaufort
m.
Humphrey
EARL OF STAFFORD
k. **1455**

Henry
DUKE OF BUCKINGHAM
ex. **1483**

HOUSE OF YORK

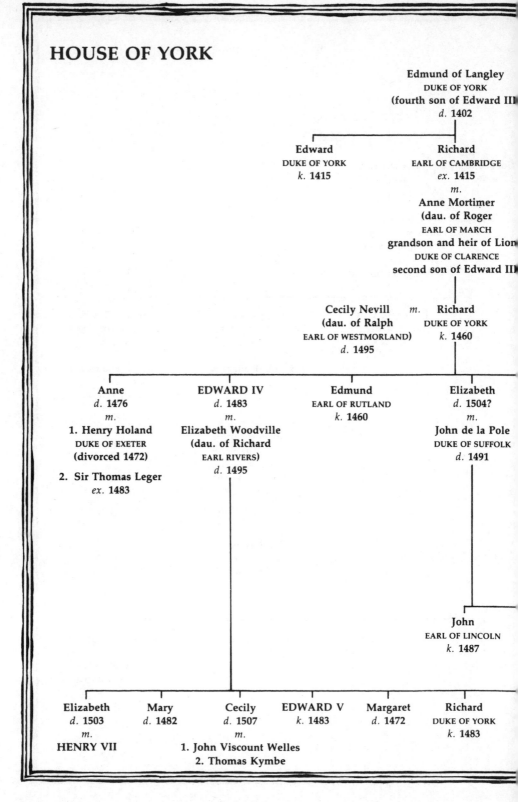

Edmund of Langley
DUKE OF YORK
(fourth son of Edward III)
d. **1402**

Edward
DUKE OF YORK
k. **1415**

Richard
EARL OF CAMBRIDGE
ex. **1415**
m.
Anne Mortimer
(dau. of Roger
EARL OF MARCH
grandson and heir of Lion
DUKE OF CLARENCE
second son of Edward III)

Cecily Nevill   *m.*   **Richard**
(dau. of Ralph   DUKE OF YORK
EARL OF WESTMORLAND)   *k.* **1460**
d. **1495**

Anne
d. **1476**
m.
1. Henry Holand
DUKE OF EXETER
(divorced 1472)
2. Sir Thomas Leger
ex. **1483**

EDWARD IV
d. **1483**
m.
Elizabeth Woodville
(dau. of Richard
EARL RIVERS)
d. **1495**

Edmund
EARL OF RUTLAND
k. **1460**

Elizabeth
d. **1504?**
m.
John de la Pole
DUKE OF SUFFOLK
d. **1491**

John
EARL OF LINCOLN
k. **1487**

Elizabeth
d. **1503**
m.
HENRY VII

Mary
d. **1482**

Cecily
d. **1507**
m.
1. John Viscount Welles
2. Thomas Kymbe

EDWARD V
k. **1483**

Margaret
d. **1472**

Richard
DUKE OF YORK
k. **1483**

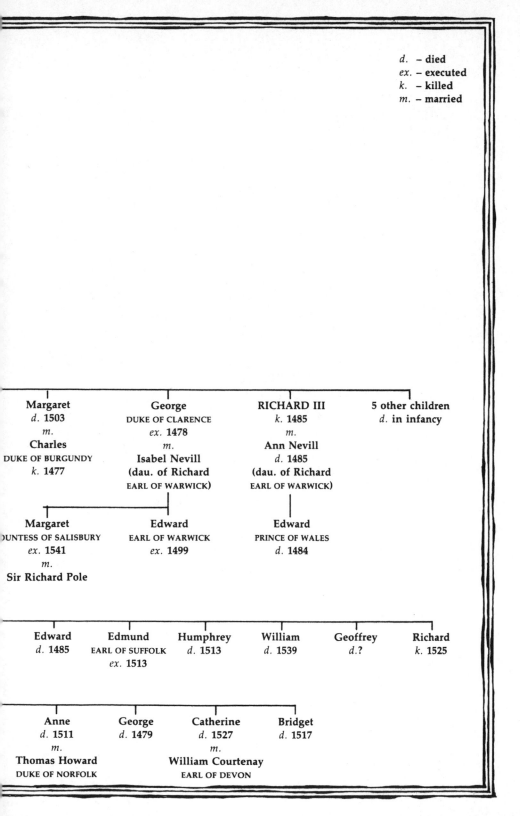

Margaret	George	RICHARD III	5 other children
d. 1503	DUKE OF CLARENCE	k. 1485	d. in infancy
m.	ex. 1478	m.	
Charles	m.	Ann Nevill	
DUKE OF BURGUNDY	Isabel Nevill	d. 1485	
k. 1477	(dau. of Richard	(dau. of Richard	
	EARL OF WARWICK)	EARL OF WARWICK)	

Margaret	Edward	Edward
)UNTESS OF SALISBURY	EARL OF WARWICK	PRINCE OF WALES
ex. 1541	ex. 1499	d. 1484
m.		
Sir Richard Pole		

Edward	Edmund	Humphrey	William	Geoffrey	Richard
d. 1485	EARL OF SUFFOLK	d. 1513	d. 1539	d.?	k. 1525
	ex. 1513				

Anne	George	Catherine	Bridget
d. 1511	d. 1479	d. 1527	d. 1517
m.		m.	
Thomas Howard		William Courtenay	
DUKE OF NORFOLK		EARL OF DEVON	

FOREWORD

This is a very personal interpretation of Richard III. No book on the Heathcliff of English Kings can be anything else. It is difficult to avoid having strong views on a man who committed the nastiest state murders in English history.

I have been enthralled by him since I was eleven years old. For a long time I believed passionately in his innocence (so well and persuasively argued in Josephine Tey's charming novel, *The Daughter of Time*). As I grew older and learnt to appreciate Thomas More, I began to wonder how someone of such integrity could stoop to character assassination—even though posthumous—as he appeared to, in his history of Richard. Then, having read Paul Murray Kendall, I was inclined to think that the Duke of Buckingham had killed Edward V and his brother (although this was not Kendall's view). Yet More, not a man to tell lies, still made me uneasy. My final position as a believer in Richard's innocence was a despairing compromise. Something 'must have gone wrong'—he had been misunderstood by his henchmen, who perhaps killed the boys during a crisis.

At last I read the actual sources, the testimony of men who had been observers in London when he seized power in 1483. Reluctantly, I became convinced of his guilt. Once the conversion started I found myself suspecting that the seizure and the murders were both part of a contingency plan—in case his brother Edward IV should die prematurely—which he had laid well in advance.

As others have discovered before me, the evil Richard is even more interesting than the good Richard. Instead of being the victim of a lost cause, he becomes one of the most alarming figures in European history. But to accept his guilt it is indispensable to read at least a summary of the sources. Hence my regrettably complex Introduction to the book.

This is the most hostile life of Richard III to appear for over a century. I must apologise for any affront to the feelings of so many people who are—and who always will be—convinced of his innocence. I once shared their conviction and know how sincerely it is held.

I would like to thank Mr Reresby Sitwell, Elisabeth, Viscountess Pollington, Mr Jonathan Martin and Mr Steven Lyle-Smythe for reading the typescript. I am also indebted to Miss K. M. Longley, Archivist to the Dean and Chapter of York Minster, to Dom Sylvester Houédard of Prinknash Abbey, to the Hon. Nicholas Assheton—the latter helped me with details of the career of his ancestor, Sir Ralph Assheton, Vice-Constable of England during Richard's reign—and to Peter Drummond-Murray of Mastrick, Slains Pursuivant-of-Arms, who explained the heraldic significance of the white boar. Mr and Mrs Steven Bingham, who took me over Bosworth Field and showed me Fotheringay where Richard was born, gave me enormous encouragement. I am grateful to Miss Susan Butterworth, Miss Anne Siddall and Mrs Patricia Pierce for their constructive editorial criticisms, and to Miss Charlotte Deane who found the pictures. As so often before, I owe a very great deal to the staffs of the British Library and the London Library for their invaluable assistance.

THE BLACK LEGEND

*'it is therefore convenient somewhat to show you ere we further go,
what manner of man this was that could find in his heart so much
mischief to conceive.'*
Sir Thomas More, The History of King Richard the Third

*'There is a kind of literary superstition, which men are apt to contract
from habit, and which makes them look on any attempt towards
shaking their belief in any established characters, no matter whether
good or bad, as a sort of profanation.'*
Horace Walpole, Historic Doubts on the Life
and Reign of King Richard III

Richard III casts a strange spell. To fascinate Shakespeare, Sir Thomas
More, and Horace Walpole is no mean feat. *The Tragedy of King
Richard the Third* is arguably its author's greatest historical play, while
More's history of the King was admitted to be 'a very beautiful one'
even by Walpole; the latter's elegant *Historic Doubts* about Richard's
villainy were admired by Edmund Gibbon. In modern times the King
has attracted a remarkable assortment of writers. He is the focus of
a romantic cult.[1]

Last of the old Plantagenet dynasty, Richard was not just the last
Englishman but the sole Northcountryman—if by adoption—to reign
over England. We have had English Kings, French Kings, Welsh
Kings, Scots Kings, and German Kings but only once a Northcountry
King. His reign was the one reign when the Southern English had
cause to resent an influx of Northerners into positions of power and
influence. At the same time he possessed the qualities of an Italian
tyrant. He was the most terrifying man ever to occupy the English
throne, not excepting his great nephew Henry VIII. His short life
was filled by intrigue and slaughter, and he was the only King of
England—other than Harold—to be defeated and killed in battle.[2]
Above all, he still remains a mystery.

Richard has left two popular legends. The earlier is Shakespeare's
crookback, whose element of caricature has been heightened by a
theatrical tradition stretching from Colly Cibber to Laurence Olivier
(though Shakespeare was nearer the truth than some of the King's
latter-day defenders). The second, later, legend is of a folk hero
manqué, a gallant young ruler, the supreme victim of political vilifi-
cation in English history. Supporters of this 'white' legend have
produced some very entertaining literature in portraying Richard as
a martyr to Tudor propaganda. Horace Walpole is at his most polished in questioning the 'black' legend while Sir Clements Markham
shows inspired ingenuity in attributing the murder of the 'Princes in
the Tower' to Henry VII, but the writings of Walpole and Markham

belong no less to fiction than does Josephine Tey's delightful novel, in which she too questions the case against Richard.

On the whole modern historians take the view that he was more like the white legend, though admitting he was responsible for the deaths of Edward V and his brother. They acquit him of other crimes and have developed a 'grey' legend. They cannot accept that any Englishman could have been so much of a Renaissance tyrant. The case for the black legend is in danger of being lost by default— because nowadays it is so seldom heard. Yet, amended in the light of modern research, it offers much the most convincing portrait of Richard.

There are two short contemporary accounts of his reign—the résumé in the Crowland Chronicle (the chronicle of the monks of Crowland Abbey) and Mancini's eyewitness description of the usurpation of 1483. Polydore Vergil's *Anglica Historia*, which deals comparatively briefly with Richard, was finished by 1513. Vergil (who came to England in 1502) had spoken to many survivors from the King's time. Probably he also had access to material unknown to Thomas More though the latter, a personal friend, may have read his work in draft. More is unquestionably the most influential of Richard's early historians; but for him the King would be a shadowy figure. Clearly he was writing an epic as well as history and strove for dramatic effects, yet as a man famous for plain dealing and love of truth—he paid for it with his life—it is impossible to dismiss his account. When his *History of King Richard the Third* first appeared in the 1540s, incorporated into popular chronicles, it is surely significant that it was at once accepted at face value. Further, a meticulous analysis of the evidence together with skilful textual criticism have established beyond question that during the King's short reign many people believed that he had murdered his nephews and others too. (By September 1483 at latest, it was certainly obvious to the highest in the land—including the boys' mother—that the 'Princes in the Tower' were dead.) Early in 1485 he actually had to assure publicly a specially summoned assembly of London citizens that he had not poisoned his wife.

Admittedly some distinguished scholars reject the black legend. The late E. F. Jacob in *The Fifteenth Century* (1961) considers Richard 'very far from being the active monster of tradition', while Professor Myers quotes in 'The Character of Richard III' (1954) with approval a Tudor opinion—'Although he did evill, yet in his tyme wer many good actes made.'[3] Perhaps, though when he reigned the evil outweighted any good he might have done in the eyes of most Englishmen. And Myers omits to point out that 'actes' refers to Acts of Parliament.

Remarkable ingenuity is shown in trying to explain away More's testimony in particular. The late Professor Kendall, the author of *Richard the Third* (1955), which has been for many years the most detailed and popular modern life of the King (even if Dr Alison Hanham in her *Richard III and his Early Historians* [1975] dismisses it to 'the realm of fiction') suggests that More wanted 'not primarily to blacken Richard's character for the gratification of the Tudors, but to make the malign figure given him even more malign in the good cause of humanist education', and that the book was meant 'in part at least, as an attack, by horrible example, on the *realpolitik*, the new power politics of the age'.[4]

Professor Charles Ross expresses this argument more subtly in *The Wars of the Roses* (1976), by stating simply that Sir Thomas's book is 'very much a treatise on tyranny', which does not alter the fact that Richard was very much a tyrant. Myers is of the same opinion as Kendall and Ross, considering it 'questionable whether More regarded himself as writing history; his story is much more like a drama, unfolded in magnificent prose, for which fidelity to historical fact is scarcely relevant.' Even Dr Hanham accepts this view, carrying it to extremes. She believes that Sir Thomas was determined to shape his story into a satisfyingly epic form, that he used models from Roman history as to how wicked men should behave, that he treated his sources with scant respect, altering and embroidering the historical record, and that his imagination was excessively dramatic. Above all, she dismisses the *History* as a 'satirical drama' and 'a joke against historians'.[5]

But More is not our only source of information about Richard III. Kendall is hardly convincing in his attempts to justify the grey legend. He cites 'general agreement' among modern scholars. 'Discarding once and for all the Tudor tradition, and basing their researches on fifteenth-century sources, they [the scholars] have worked to illuminate the complex character and the strangely flawed career of the man who was successively a loyal brother, usurping uncle and able King.' The truth is that nothing of importance in Richard's defence has been found for a century. Even by 1878 the hostile Gairdner was already aware of the King's popularity with the citizens of York. The few discoveries in recent times have all confirmed that he was violent and ruthless.[6] Moreover a surprising amount of evidence cited by proponents of the grey legend to acquit Richard of such lesser crimes as murdering Henry VI—or even Edward of Lancaster—will bear a precisely opposite interpretation.

There are, however, signs that academic opinion is at last turning from the grey to the black legend. In *Government and Community; England 1450–1509* (1980) Professor Lander concedes that 'Richard's reputation had fallen extremely low in his own lifetime. There was not really much scope for it to be posthumously blackened by Tudor propaganda.'

The King's first modern biographer was James Gairdner, who published his *History of the Life and Reign of Richard III* in 1878. Gairdner was an extremely professional and knowledgeable nineteenth-century historian, the editor of the *Paston Letters* and of the *Letters and Papers of the Reigns of Richard III and Henry VII*. He had no hesitation in accepting the black legend. He confesses to have been momentarily shaken in his youth by Walpole's *Doubts*, but since then 'a minute study of the facts of Richard's life has tended more and more to convince me of the general fidelity of the portrait with which we have been made familiar by Shakespeare and Sir Thomas More.' Admittedly Gairdner is old fashioned, occasionally naive, and much too unquestioning in his acceptance of Tudor tradition. Nevertheless, he had an almost encyclopaedic knowledge of most of the sources and his instinct was often a sure one.

While Kendall may claim 'general agreement' among scholars, there have been some very distinguished historians in recent times who largely accept the black legend and much of More. They include the late Professor Pollard and Dr A L Rowse. In 1933 Pollard, in 'The Making of Sir Thomas More's Richard III', demolished the argument that the material for More's history was given to him as a credulous young man by Cardinal Morton, an enemy of Richard. Sir Thomas is unlikely to have begun the book before 1513 when he was thirty-five. (Dr Hanham has suggested that he may not have started it until 1519 and may still have been working on it in the 1530s.) Pollard shows that More—old enough to have seen King Richard, being seven at the time of Bosworth—was acquainted with many others besides Morton who remembered his reign. Sir John Cutts, Richard's Receiver of Crown Lands and the King's cousin by marriage, was More's predecessor as Under-Treasurer while his kinsman William Roper was Richard's Commissioner of Array for Kent. He also knew such influential and informed prelates as Archbishop Warham and Bishops Fox and Fitzjames—the latter had been Treasurer of St Paul's during Richard's reign. And as a successful London lawyer, even More's father must have known the City gossip of the day.

In Dr Rowse's view, in *Bosworth Field and the Wars of the Roses* (1966), 'The traditional story, as it has come down to us is perfectly plain and clear . . . everything that has come to light in our own time is completely consistent with it, bears it out, confirms it.' As for Sir Thomas, 'More has so much to tell us that comes from people concerned in those happenings.' Like Pollard, Rowse considers 'There was no lack of people who knew what had happened; but it was too appalling and too dangerous to write it down.' Rowse also agrees with Pollard in attributing much of More's errors to reliance on oral tradition, though emphasising how he is borne out again and again by contemporary writers of whose existence he was unaware.

Dr Hanham is another distinguished scholar who inclines to the black rather than the grey or white legends. Her study of Richard and his early historians is deeply impressive. Yet one questions her judgement that More was writing 'primarily as a literary craftsman, not as the investigator of historical evidence'—his instincts as a lawyer cannot be dismissed so cavalierly. There is no sign of contemporaries regarding his book as satirical, though they appreciated its irony and humour; Roger Ascham, Queen Elizabeth's tutor, considered it a model of historical writing. On the other hand Dr Hanham stresses that 'In some ways, indeed, Richard's contemporaries were severer critics than their sixteenth-century successors. Mancini's informants were at pains to explain to him how rudely everyone had been deceived by the usurper; the Crowland chronicler (and whoever he was, he was not John Morton or any other of Henry's fellow exiles of 1483–5) fails even to credit Richard with the remorse allowed him by Vergil and More.'

Professor Ross, the author of the latest academic study of the King, *Richard III* (1981), admits that his contemporaries believed that he had murdered his nephews, that the black legend is of pre-Tudor origin and dates from Richard's lifetime. He too regards the Crowland Chronicle as the most important source of all. But even Ross cannot quite bring himself to accept the logical implications of his own magisterial scholarship.

The whole controversy about Richard III hinges on the interpretation of a very brief part of his life, known from a very small corpus of material. The usurpation of April to July 1483 is the one time when we are reasonably well informed about him, the single period dealt with fully by Mancini and More, who are substantiated by the Crowland writer and Polydore Vergil. Almost every aspect of the King's personality known to us derives from what they say of his behaviour during these vital days. Apart from certain incidents of his reign, described tersely by the Crowland chronicler and Vergil, the descriptions of his *coup d'état* provide almost the sole means of interpreting his career and his character.

Dominic Mancini's account was written in December 1483, in France, and remained forgotten until the present century. Although this scholarly Roman visitor to London gives us no description of Richard—no doubt simply because he had not seen him—he is plainly convinced that the King is a very bad man indeed. As a foreigner it would have been hard to find a more unbiased observer.

Another foreign contemporary, to whose evidence perhaps insufficient importance has been attached, was the very well informed Philippe de Commynes, that shrewdest, most objective and most modern of fiteenth-century observers. He had actually seen Richard. In his memoirs he claims that he was 'more filled with pride than any King of England these last hundred years.'[7] He also tells us that Louis XI of France, who was not exactly squeamish, thought Richard 'extremely cruel and evil', and states categorically that he killed Henry VI—'or at least had him killed in his presence'—as well as his nephews. Like Mancini, Commynes (who probably wrote between 1489 and 1491) had no particular reason to blacken the name of a foreign monarch.

The best informed of those severely critical contemporaries of whom Dr Hanham speaks was of course the author of the original source of the Second Continuation to the Crowland Chronicle.[8] It is now virtually established that the continuation incorporates a lost text written by Richard's Lord Chancellor—far from being the production of Markham's 'credulous old Croyland monks'. This was John Russell, Bishop of Lincoln, who must have been present at most meetings of the King's Council. Unfortunately, in keeping with his training as a professional bureaucrat, the 'Crowland chronicler' is often infuriatingly discreet. Even so he had plainly been horrified by Richard.

Polydore Vergil, a professional Italian historian, came to England in 1502. If naturally disinclined to displease his patron Henry VII, and prone to poetic licence in wishing to write good literature, he was nonetheless objective and methodical. He tells us that when unable to find written records 'I went to every elderly man pointed out to me as having once held an important position in public life and obtained from them information about events before 1500.' (We know that he questioned survivors from Edward IV's court about the death of the Duke of Clarence.) Moreover textual criticism has shown that he may well have had access to the text behind the Crowland Continuation, although Russell had died in 1494. Vergil makes slips in details and is ignorant of much which we now know about Richard, but on the whole he gives the impression that he is telling the truth as he sees it.

When all is said, however unreliable, Sir Thomas More remains the fullest source of information about Richard III. The white and grey schools both quote whole passages from him in support of their cases, rejecting only those which contradict them—just as they do with the Tudor chroniclers. Undeniably his history has many faults. There is no question that it dramatises the principal characters' speeches and much else besides. It is wrong about Edward IV's age and Lord Hastings's Christian name, it confuses Eleanor Butler with Elizabeth Lucy, and it portrays Queen Elizabeth Woodville as a spotless figure when in reality she was a grasping intriguer. But a good deal of this was due to absence of proper records, and to the fact that the historical methods of the early 1500s were not those of today. In any case the book was never finished and is only a draft. (I have modernised quotations from More to make them read more easily. However in general I have used the Yale edition of his works [ed. R. S. Sylvester].)

Certainly Sir Thomas had strong moral convictions about public life, and certainly wanted to tell a good story. Yet it should never be forgotten that he was a brilliant and a very experienced lawyer—Erasmus thought he had the finest legal brain in Europe. No one could have been more sceptical of allegation or rumour, fairer in weighing evidence. Describing the murder of the Princes, he says he

1. *Richard III, possibly when still Duke of Gloucester. Copy of c. 1520 of a lost original. The Society of Antiquaries of London.*

2.   *Edward IV, from a stained glass window at Canterbury Cathedral.*

ELIZABETH VXOR
EDWARDVS IIII

3. *Richard's sister-in-law and enemy, Queen Elizabeth Woodville. Queens'*
College, Cambridge.

4. *Model of Baynards Castle, the London house of Richard's mother, Cecily, Duchess of York. Museum of London.*

5. *Middleham Castle, where Richard spent part of his youth. It later became one of his favourite residences.*

does so 'not after every way that I have heard, but after that way that I have so heard, by such men and by such means as me thinketh it were hard but it should be true.' Indeed his book can be seen as a remarkable piece of detective work.

The argument that More was writing 'propaganda' to curry favour with a new dynasty is sufficiently refuted by the circumstances of his death.[9] If anything, he was incredibly tactless. He says that the father of his powerful friend, the Duke of Norfolk, had lured Lord Hastings to his death besides plundering Mistress Shore of all she had and reducing her to beggary, that his friend's grandfather—the first Duke—had been one of those most closely involved in plotting and carrying out Richard's usurpation. Nor did he have any need to blacken Richard, whose reputation was already quite black enough. For all his literary and moral conceits and his mistakes, Sir Thomas's *History* contains valuable information. Probably some of it has not been properly assessed even now.

Kendall considers that More's Richard cannot be 'in any way the portrait of a human being'. On the contrary, Sir Thomas's King Richard is all too human, far more of a real person than he is in most modern biographies. He was, as Gairdner says, 'the natural outgrowth of monstrous and horrible times' and a practitioner of the new Renaissance statecraft. When Shakespeare makes him claim to 'set the murderous Machiavel to school', there is a substantial element of truth. Richard was by no means an isolated phenomenon, let alone a freak. He belongs to the same ferociously ruthless company as Louis XI, Ferdinand of Aragon, and Cesare Borgia—and Edward IV and Henry VII.

This book is an attempt to produce a new and truer likeness of Richard III. It tries to see him through the eyes of his contemporaries, while taking modern research into account. Among these contemporaries it numbers not only Mancini and the Crowland chronicler, but Polydore Vergil and Sir Thomas More—discounting his dramatic effects and didactic intentions—and also the earliest Tudor chroniclers. A new, yet entirely credible, Richard emerges; certainly not a monster; but a peculiarly grim young English precursor of Machiavelli's Prince.

CHAPTER ONE

THE DIFFICULT BIRTH

*'For I have often heard my mother say
I came into the world with my legs forward.'*
Shakespeare, King Henry VI, Part III

*'He left such a reputation behind him that even his birth was said to
have proclaimed him a monster.'*
James Gairdner, History of the Life and Reign
of Richard the Third

Richard III was born on 2 October 1452 at Fotheringay in North-amptonshire, sixth and youngest son of the Duke and Duchess of York. The castle, one day to see the imprisonment and execution of Mary, Queen of Scots, was where he would spend his earliest years. It was a principal house, though only an occasional residence, of his parents.

It is likely that he had a difficult birth. John Rous was plainly anxious to vilify the dead King when he wrote his *Historia Regum Angliae*—dedicated to Henry VII—between 1485 and 1491. Yet there may be a grain of truth in his fanciful account of Richard being 'retained within his mother's womb for two years and emerging with teeth and hair to his shoulders'. If clearly nonsense, it could none-theless recall a long and worrying pregnancy. By mediaeval stan-dards, even modern, his mother at thirty-seven was old for childbearing. (She had only one more baby after him, a girl three years later who does not appear to have survived infancy.) More tells us he had heard similar tales about the King's birth, which he is inclined to attribute to popular hatred, but he adds significant details. 'It is . . . reported that the Duchess his mother had so much ado in her travail that she could not be delivered of him uncut, and that he came into the world with the feet forward.' It sounds like a breech birth—children are not infrequently born upside down. There was no such instrument as forceps in the Middle Ages so the baby may have been damaged by the midwife's efforts to pull him out. Perhaps that is why Richard's right shoulder was slightly higher than his left—not the left higher than the right, as Sir Thomas says.[1] More also informs us that he had a withered left arm (the same affliction as that of Wilhelm II in our own century). 'Like a blasted sapling', as Shakespeare puts it. This too could have been caused by a clumsy delivery.

His father Richard, Duke of York, was a small, hard-featured man. It was later said that King Richard bore a remarkable facial likeness to him. Very haughty and arrogant in manner, the Duke was always conscious that since 1447 he had been the only living Prince of the Blood Royal apart from his own sons and was therefore heir presumptive to the throne. In the male line he was the grandson of Edmund of Langley, first Duke of York and Edward III's youngest son, while in the female line, through his mother, Anne Mortimer, he was also great great grandson and ultimate heir of Lionel, Duke of Clarence who had been Edward III's third son. The reigning sovereign Henry VI was only the great grandson of Edward's fifth son. As befitted such a descent, he was the richest man in England. Although his father, the Earl of Cambridge, had been beheaded for treason in 1415 (the year he was born) Richard inherited not only the patrimony of the Dukes of York—after his uncle was killed at Agincourt—but that of his mother's family, the Earls of March. He possessed estates and palaces throughout England and Wales, and also Ireland where he had wide lands in the Pale. The headquarters of his vast territories in Wales and on the Welsh Borders was in Shropshire at his great castle of Ludlow, on the River Teme, where his elder sons Edward and Edmund were brought up.

York had seen some fierce campaigning in the Hundred Years War, having been Lieutenant-General (Viceroy) of 'France'—the English occupied areas of the Ile de France and Normandy. A mixture of pugnacity and indecision, he was not a good soldier but he had with him that legendary warrior 'Old Talbot', so that despite the French revival he was surprisingly successful. His wife accompanied him, their eldest surviving son Edward being born at Rouen. A contemporary chronicler, Thomas Basin, describes what claustrophobic and altogether terrifying lives were led by the English in France at this time—'shut up for years behind town walls or in castles as though condemned to life imprisonment, living in fear and danger.' Duke Richard and his Duchess must have experienced such an existence. However at home the court party were alarmed by York's growing popularity and replaced him by the incompetent Duke of Somerset. Since 1448 York had been Lord-Lieutenant of Ireland where, notwithstanding his haughtiness and though he spent barely a year there, he won the lasting friendship of the Anglo-Irish lords by his lavish generosity. Even the Celtic chieftains—including the greatest, O'Neill himself—paid him homage and swore to be his liegemen.

In 1424, when he was nine, Richard of York had married Cicely Nevill, daughter of Ralph Nevill, Earl of Westmorland in whose household he was spending his boyhood. She was the twenty-second of the Earl's twenty-three children, the thirteenth by his second wife Joan Beaufort. Cicely was herself descended from Edward III since her mother's father had been John of Gaunt. Ralph was the head of the Nevills, an ambitious and already powerful Northern family which, largely by carefully calculated marriages, was fast becoming one of the richest and most influential clans in England. Ralph's second son was the Earl of Salisbury, whose own son acquired in addition the magnificent Earldom of Warwick—which made him the wealthiest man in the realm after York—while three other of Ralph's younger sons also obtained peerages for themselves, Lords Fauconberg, Latimer and Abergavenny.[2] Yet another was Prince Bishop of Durham, the greatest prelate in England after Canterbury and York, and ruling his immensely rich palatinate almost as an independent state.

Born in 1415 like her husband, Cicely had spent her childhood at her father's bleak stronghold of Raby in Co. Durham where she became famed for her beauty, acquiring the name of 'The Rose of Raby'—later she was given another name, 'Proud Cis'. She appears to have begun to live with York as his wife about 1438, bearing him at least ten children though several of these died in infancy. So many brothers and sisters together with such a vast kindred were to mean that few English Kings have ever been so widely and so closely related to their aristocracy as was Richard III.

His early life is unknown, but was no doubt uneventful. Yet these years saw the outbreak of the longest period of civil war in English history. To understand Richard and why the Wars of the Roses began, one has to know something of the 1450s. England was in a thoroughly unhappy condition. The government was almost bankrupt under a weak King, Henry VI, whose personal reign has been described as the most calamitous of any of our monarchs and who went mad within a year of the birth of the cousin who would one day murder him. The Lancastrian monarchy—so called because of its descent from John of Gaunt, Duke of Lancaster—was collapsing. Already unpopular, ostensibly because of venal and mediocre ministers, it was discredited even more by the loss of English France. Normandy went in 1450 and Guyenne, English for three centuries, in 1451—Talbot managed to re-occupy Bordeaux the same October that Richard was born, only to perish with his entire army the following year. At home Kent had risen under Jack Cade in 1450 in an especially vicious revolt.

Oddly enough, it was an age of prosperity for most people. Ninety per cent of a diminishing population of perhaps as low as three million earned their living on the land—even if they were always pitifully vulnerable to a bad harvest—and for the majority wages had never been higher nor food cheaper, despite the agricultural depression of 1430–60. The mortality caused by the Black Death and recurring visitations of plague had ruined the traditional manorial economy dependent on serf labour; lords of manors switched over to tenant farming, leasing out their land on competitive rents or, where they still farmed themselves, tried to attract labourers by good wages. At the same time, however, arable land was being turned into sheep runs or going back to forest; there were vast tracts of uncultivated land and huge woods, while many hamlets simply disappeared, their inhabitants moving into the towns. All this made country folk uneasy. In addition the roads were full of refugees from France who had become either beggars or brigands. Life in the towns was noticeably affected by the troubles of the cloth and wool trade; it was seriously interrupted by hostilities with France and Burgundy and with the Hanseatic League. Nevertheless, though there was considerable urban unemployment, the larger English cities remained wealthy enough. Besides cloth and wool, they exported hides, tin, lead and carved alabaster; in return the French brought wine, the Genoese and Venetians silks, velvets, spices, sugar, gems, precious metals, armour and drugs, and the Germans timber, corn, amber and furs. For all their narrow streets and wooden houses, English merchants were busily building glorious guildhalls and soaring churches in the new Perpendicular style. The clergy too were prospering. Abbeys were richer than ever—'more like baronial palaces than religious houses' wrote a Venetian at the end of the century— even if there were fewer monks. Secular priests made an excellent living while the Bishops were mighty lords. Indeed there was much envy of the clergy, often expressed in a sometimes ferocious anticlericalism.

The class who suffered most were the landowners, especially the great. Although by continental standards the English aristocracy were not really a nobility but simply rich gentlemen, they nonetheless constituted a warlike élite who dominated the country. The combination of declining revenues among them and of exceptionally inept central government produced anarchy. The sixty or so English peers degenerated into something halfway between war lords and gang bosses, in the phenomenon known as bastard feudalism; they built up personal armies, 'retaining' local gentry with annuities. Any country gentleman who wished to save his estate and his goods—occasionally his life—had to be retained and have a protector. Finding themselves increasingly short of money, most magnates saw good reason to quarrel with each other over lands and local influence, even fighting private wars—sometimes there were full-scale pitched battles. More usually, in the struggle to preserve their wealth and authority, they simply terrorised the country round about; they beat up or murdered their weaker neighbours, or else forced them to submit by law cases during which juries were bullied into finding against them. Law and order broke down and there was widespread banditry. In consequence there was no security for property, whether houses, moveables, farmland or livestock. In the Act of 1461 which deposed King Henry, Parliament stated that under his rule 'not plenty, peace, justice, good governance, policy and virtuous conversation, but unrest, inward war and trouble, unrightwiseness, shedding and effusion of innocent blood, abusion of the laws, partiality, riot, extortion, murder, rape and vicious living, have been the guiders and leaders of the noble realm of England.'

It was only too easy, as lesser lords allied with greater, for private gang battles to escalate into civil war on a national scale. For the greatest lords, the 'overmighty subjects'—as a contemporary, Chief Justice Fortescue, termed them—had the military strength to pursue their political aims by other means. An unusually strong King like Henry V might have held them in check, but not his son.

The traditional view of Henry VI is that he was too holy and too simple to rule, and that his Council of greedy favourites were responsible for the country's miserable condition. Recently, however, it has been argued that the King himself must take much of the blame and was as perversely wilful as he was incompetent.[3] Yet his subjects were reluctant to blame him. In 1450 the men of Kent complained that his 'false Council has lost his law, his merchandise is lost, his common people is lost, the sea is lost, France is lost, the King himself is so beset that he may not pay for his meat and drink.' Not until the end of the 1450s could the English conceive of replacing Henry by another King. Most magnates supported the court party in any case, if only because it was the King's party. As leader of the anti-court faction, the Duke of York would at first find little support among the lords, save from this Nevill kinsmen. Nonetheless Henry and his Council were very conscious of their unpopularity and extremely nervous about an heir presumptive to the throne who was quite so rich, so powerful and so popular, as York.

Duke Richard returned from Ireland in 1450 to begin his long campaign to obtain power. He was alarmed by his exclusion from the King's Council. Despite his enormous wealth he was heavily in debt as a result of his expenses in France, and there was every sign he would never be repaid the £10,000 he was owed while Somerset controlled affairs.

Edmund Beaufort, Duke of Somerset, the leader of the court party, was John of Gaunt's only surviving grandson and therefore York's second cousin. Even had he wished, Somerset dared not relinquish power—it would have meant his ruin. In any case he was greedy, determined to be the first prince in the land. He had an alternative candidate to block Duke Richard's succession to the throne: his elder brother's daughter, Margaret Beaufort, whose son would one day prove indeed to be the ruin of the House of York.

Moreover, Somerset was supported by the Queen, Margaret of Anjou. A scion of a younger branch of the French royal house, she had dominated her husband from the very moment of her arrival in England at the age of fifteen, besides allying herself with the third-rate ministers who had given her a crown and wanted peace with her fellow countrymen. Beautiful, in a dark-haired foreign way, she was proud, hard and meddlesome, excessively ambitious but with poor political judgement, and strong willed to the point of ferocity.

She was incapable of compromise. A correspondent of the Pastons—that rising East Anglian family who so diligently preserved their letters—comments 'The queen is a great and strong laboured woman, for she spareth no pain to an intent and conclusion to her power.'

Just what York had to fear may be seen from the destruction of the Duke of Gloucester during the previous decade. In 1441 the court party had ruthlessly exploited the scandal when his silly Duchess, Eleanor Cobham, was found guilty of dabbling in sorcery—to find out if she would ever be Queen—and was made to walk barefoot through London for three days carrying a lighted taper before being imprisoned for life. Her husband was totally discredited. When the government finally arrested him in 1447 he quickly expired from a stroke, probably brought on by rage—fifty-seven, a ripe old age for the time, he had already suffered attacks of 'palsy'. Nevertheless public opinion believed that 'the good Duke Humphrey' had been murdered.

When Duke Richard came to London he demanded that the King should put on trial the ministers responsible for the disasters afflicting the realm. Henry made vague promises, summoning a Parliament. When it met in October 1450 the Commons was strong in support of York, but very few of the Lords. None of his wishes was met. By the end of 1451 he was gathering an army and preparing to march on London. In the event he was arrested the following year and by 1453, although set at liberty, had been humiliated and isolated—he lost his Lord Lieutenancy of Ireland and his allies deserted him.

Then in August 1453 Henry VI went mad from a 'sudden fright', unable to speak or move. (Catatonic schizophrenia has been suggested.)[4] But two months later Margaret of Anjou bore a son, Edward of Lancaster, and demanded the regency. However a number of peers had begun to support Duke Richard, notably his Nevill in-laws—Salisbury and his son Warwick—largely because they were waging a private war on the Percy family in the North. In March 1454 York was made Protector. He ruled with surprising moderation. Most unfortunately, King Henry recovered his wits at the end of 1454, and with the Queen's assistance Somerset and the court party had regained control of the government by the following spring. Given their refusal to compromise and the availability of private armies and of veteran commanders from the Hundred Years War, bloodshed was inevitable. Admittedly there can have been no more than 5,000 front-line troops in England who had served in the French campaigns; yet even so, most leaders in the first battles of the Wars of the Roses had fought in France and all of them must have possessed a nucleus of experienced men-at-arms.

Somerset and the Queen soon overplayed their hand. York, Salisbury and Warwick were summoned to appear at a council at Leicester on 21 May 1455. Plainly they were to be destroyed. They gathered an army and marched South. Somerset also assembled troops and, taking the King with him, went to meet them at St Albans on 22 May. In what was scarcely more than an armed affray Henry was wounded in the neck by an arrow; there were only a few hundred casualties—but among these was Somerset. However there would be no more fighting for another four years. The court party had lost its leader and was not yet ready to accept Margaret in his place.

It is unlikely that little Richard ever saw much of his father. We may guess that his childhood was as painful as his birth; towards the end of the 1450s a doggerel poem about the Duke of York's family comments, with apparent surprise, 'Richard liveth yit'—he must have had difficulty even to survive. We know that he spent a good part of his early years at Fotheringay with his sister Margaret, who had been born in 1446, and his brother George, who had been born in 1449 (in Dublin). It has been fancifully suggested that Margaret 'played mother to him' but it is more likely that nurses performed this role.

The Tudor antiquary John Leland, who visited it about 1538, informs us that the town of Fotheringay was 'but one street, all of stone building'. The castle was demolished long ago and only a grassy mound now remains, on a pleasant site amid lush meadows and rich cornfields by the banks of the beautiful River Nene. To the East it is not far from fenland, to the West from the Forest of Rockingham. We know that it was then very splendid and imposing, a double-moated castle with an unusally tall gatehouse. It had been largely rebuilt in the late fourteenth century in the shape of a fetter-lock (a closed, semi-oblong), an instrument for tethering horses which formed part of one of the badges of the House of York—the 'Falcon and Fetterlock'. Leland, who saw it when it was still standing, says that it was 'strong with double dykes and hath a keep very ancient and strong' and that 'there be very fair lodgings'.[5]

However Leland also tells us that 'the glory' of Fotheringay 'standeth by the parish church'. This was the mighty Perpendicular church of St Mary the Virgin and All Saints, built by the Dukes of York and only completed just before Richard's birth. In those days it was a college of priests and choristers and as big as a cathedral— half pulled down at the Reformation—its walls a mass of eighty-eight stained glass windows and its soaring, fan-vaulted tower crowned by a striking octagon lantern. To the north of the church were the conventual buildings, which housed a community of some thirty clerks—a cloister with a library and carrels, dormitories, a dining hall and a kitchen, a chapter house, and the Master's lodging.[6] No doubt the children attended many imposing and gloriously sung services in St Mary's. (Alas, today the tower is in a condition which makes it impossible to ring the bells.)

By 1456 the Queen and the court party had again regained control—causing Duke Richard 'to stink in the King's nostrils even unto death, as they insisted that he was trying to take the Kingdom into his own hands' says the Crowland Chronicle. There was an attempt at reconciliation, the 'Loveday' of 24 March 1458 when the Yorkist lords and the sons of those killed at St Albans walked arm-in-arm to St Paul's. But despite efforts by prelates, the political climate grew steadily more poisoned and more menacing. Margaret of Anjou took the court to the Midlands and began to build a power base on the estates of the Duchy of Lancaster, centred on such strongholds as Kenilworth. She was preparing for civil war.

By 1459 she was ready to strike. A council of the realm was summoned to Coventry in June—York and his supporters were ostentatiously un-invited. Anxiously they assembled at Ludlow, collecting an army with which they hoped to force their way through to King Henry to justify themselves. Duchess Cicely joined her husband, bringing Margaret, George and Richard with her. Everything went wrong for the Yorkists. On the way to Ludlow Salisbury fought an indecisive battle at Bloreheath and had two of his sons taken prisoner. Then most of Warwick's troops deserted when the royal army finally marched on Ludlow in October. York lost his nerve and fled to Ireland. Salisbury and Warwick took refuge in Calais where the latter was captain, taking with them the Duke's eldest son Edward, Earl of March. The younger children stayed behind at Ludlow with their mother, where they were captured in the town on 13 October.

Cicely and her children were escorted to Coventry, where Parliament was in session. It attainted York and confiscated all his lands, the Duchess being left with a pittance for her support. She and her children were confined at a manor house belonging to her brother-in-law, the Duke of Buckingham, which has not been identified. This may well have been when Richard first began to know his mother.

Meanwhile York and his kinsmen were not idle. The Duke was welcomed ecstatically in Ireland by both Anglo-Irish lords and 'wild Irish' chieftains. An emissary from Somerset's son and successor who tried to serve a writ on him was hanged, drawn and quartered. The Duke was visited early in 1460 by Warwick, who planned a joint invasion with him before sailing back to Calais, which he had made a centre of Yorkist intrigue. From there the exiled Earls waged a pirate war on royal ships, besides sending a stream of propaganda into England where they were already regarded with considerable sympathy. The court party's administration was as venal and unsatisfactory as ever. At last in June Salisbury, Warwick, and March landed in Kent and advanced on London, gathering support all the way. The following month they defeated the royal army near Northampton—one of the few casualties was little Richard's gaoler, Buckingham—and captured Henry VI. Parliament was summoned to meet at Westminster in October, to reverse the attainders against York and the Earls. But even the latter had no intention of deposing King Henry.

John Paston's man in London wrote that on the Monday after Lady Day (15 September) 'my master Bowser, Sir Harry Ratford, John Clay and the harbinger of my Lord of March' had come 'desiring that my Lady of York might lie here until the coming of my Lord of York, and her two sons, my Lord George and my Lord Richard and my Lady Margaret her daughter, which I granted them in your name.' This was at Fastolf Place, Sir John Fastolf's mansion inherited by Paston; it was in Southwark, near Tooley Street, on the South bank of the Thames opposite the Tower, a great moated and walled house with a large tree-filled garden and its own wharf.[7] However, the Duchess 'had not lain here two days but she had tidings of the landing of my lord at Chester. The Tuesday next after, my Lord sent for her, that she would come to him to Hereford and thither she is gone. And she hath left here both the sons and the daughter, and my Lord of March cometh here every day to see them.' Cicely travelled in a wagon roofed with blue velvet and drawn by eight horses—one wonders if Richard saw her set off. Soon the Duke and Duchess were marching to London with 500 troops, who bore banners with the Royal Arms of England.

When they reached London Duke Richard went to Westminster Hall. He walked arrogantly through the assembled House of Lords, with a sword of state borne before him as though he were King, and going up to the throne clapped his hand on it. There was a long, embarrassed silence. Then his kinsman Thomas Bourchier, Archbishop of Canterbury (and his wife's brother-in-law) asked York if he wished to have an audience of King Henry. The Duke replied 'I know of no person in this realm which oweth not to wait on me, rather than I on him.' Even Salisbury and Warwick were taken aback. York moved into the royal apartments, sword in hand, ordering his men to break open the doors. A week later he formally claimed the throne as senior descendant of Edward III. (For the first time he took the surname Plantagenet—there is no evidence that it was ever used by his son Richard.) Asked why he had not made his claim before, he replied proudly 'Though right for a time rest and be put to silence, yet it rotteth not nor shall it perish.' The Lords insisted on a compromise. Henry VI would keep the crown so long as he lived but Duke Richard was to be Protector, receiving the Principality of Wales and Earldom of Chester and the Duchy of Cornwall; on Henry's death he would become King and the succession would pass to his children. The helpless Henry gave his assent, disinheriting his own son.

Unfortunately for York the Lancastrians quickly recovered their strength, mustering troops in the North. They began to lay waste his own estates in Yorkshire, so in December he went up to deal with them. He did not realise that he would face a great army and when he and Salisbury decided to spend Christmas at Sandal Castle near Wakefield they found themselves cut off. Duke Richard sent a message to Edward of March to come and relieve him—strongly fortified, the castle could have held out for months. But York was too impatient. Commanded by the young Duke of Somerset—his old enemy's son—the Earl of Northumberland and Lord Clifford, the Lancastrians challenged him to give battle. Although his force was hopelessly inferior, on 30 December 1460 Duke Richard galloped out to charge his enemies. He was taken in flank by a shattering countercharge and killed, while his army was routed. (A quarter of a century later his youngest boy would behave in a very similar way at Bosworth.) His seventeen-year-old son, Edmund of Rutland, was caught on Wakefield bridge by Lord Clifford, who shouted 'By God's blood thy father slew mine and so will I do thee' and stabbed him to death despite his begging for mercy. Salisbury was captured and speedily beheaded. His head, together with those of Rutland and York were stuck over the main gate into York, the Duke's being crowned in derision with a paper coronet.

Margaret of Anjou and her army now marched south, while the Tudor family raised Wales for her. Warwick waited for her in London, Edward of March setting off to stop the Welsh, whom he soon broke at Mortimer's Cross near Wigmore—heartened by the uncanny spectacle of three suns in the sky which became one (a parhelion). The Queen's northern troops advanced plundering, burning, and raping, like 'pagans or Saracens' says the Crowland Chronicle. Although they won a considerable victory at the bloody second battle of St Albans, London refused to admit the Queen, instead letting in Warwick and Edward of March who had joined forces. When the latter proclaimed himself King Edward IV in March 1461, Londoners cheered him rapturously.

After the fresh disaster on St Albans, the mourning Duchess of York—still presumably lodged at Fastolf Place—hastily sent George and Richard across the sea to the Low Countries with a few trusted servants, to find refuge with the Duke of Burgundy. The Burgundian lands—modern Holland and Belgium together with a large block of eastern France—were almost an independent Kingdom under Duke Philip the Good, who was England's natural if faithless ally against the French (just as the King of Scots was the latter's traditional ally against the English). At first he took ostentatiously small notice of these embarrassing refugees, who were sent to obscure lodgings at Utrecht. But on 12 April news reached the Duke that Edward had won a decisive victory and must henceforward be regarded as undoubted King of England. Philip at once gave orders for the two boys to be treated as royal princes and brought to his glittering court at Bruges. When they arrived he was flatteringly attentive—the Milanese envoy reported that 'The Duke, who is kind in every way, has visited them at their lodgings where he showed the utmost respect.'

On the bitterly cold Palm Sunday (29 March) of 1461 Edward—recently acclaimed in London as King—had engaged the Lancastrian army at Towton, about eight miles from York. He had taken a fortnight to march up from the capital, gathering recruits as he came. Twenty-eight lords (nearly half the peerage) and possibly as many as 50,000 troops took part in the battle. It snowed all day, the flakes blowing uphill with Yorkist arrows into the Lancastrians' faces. The latter's arrows fell short, but they charged downhill blindly and, after several hours of hacking and stabbing, their superior numbers had nearly broken Edward's army. Then his ally the Duke of Norfolk arrived with fresh troops and the Lancastrians ran. Terrible slaughter ensued. The River Wharfe ran with blood while the snow on the ground was crimson over an area six miles long and half a mile wide. Later the heralds claimed to have counted 28,000 corpses. Among them was that of Rutland's butcher, Lord Clifford. Every captured nobleman and gentleman was beheaded, including forty-two Knights. Margaret escaped to Scotland, taking Henry VI and their son with her.

Not only had the Lancastrian North perished but, for the time being, the Lancastrian cause. Its surviving magnates hastened to transfer their allegiance to the triumphant House of York, if they were not dispossessed. Richard's brother-in-law, the Duke of Exeter, one of the richest and haughtiest noblemen in England, was reduced to begging his bread in Flanders—barefoot, and from door to door. (Eventually he was recognised and given a small pension by the Duke of Burgundy.)

On 28 June Edward IV was finally crowned King of England at Westminster Abbey, with the utmost splendour. That night his nine-year-old brother, together with twenty-seven other young men and boys including George, was created a Knight of the Bath. Having been ritually bathed, they made a vigil in the chapel of St John at the Tower of London which lasted until Matins and Mass at dawn, after which they received the accolade from the King.

On All Saints Day (1 November) Richard was created Duke of Gloucester, Edward IV girding him with a sword of state and placing a cap of maintenance on his head. It was an ill-omened title—of the only two previous Dukes of Gloucester, the first had been murdered and the second had died in suspicious circumstances. Nevertheless he had become a mighty prince, brother of an annointed King and second in succession to the throne—George, now Duke of Clarence, being heir presumptive. Was this the beginning of Richard's 'execrable desire of sovereignty'?

CHAPTER TWO

'OUR BROTHER OF GLOUCESTER'

'this name of Gloucester is taken for an unhappy and unfortunate style, as the proverb speaks of Sejanus's horse, whose rider was ever unhorsed and whose possessor was ever brought to misery.'

Anon., 16th century

'For Gloster's Dukedom is too ominous.'

Shakespeare, King Henry VI, Part III

No doubt the young Duke was treated with the utmost respect, both at Fastolf Place and at his mother's London house—it had been his father's too—Baynard's Castle, beside the Thames and not far from the Tower. Although he was only a small boy, his brother the King heaped honours on him. He was made Admiral of the Sea and Commissioner of Array for the North Parts (Northumberland, Yorkshire, Cumberland and Westmorland). With George and Margaret he moved to more royal accommodation at Greenwich Palace. Little is known of him during these early, prosperous years of his brother's reign.

Richard Gloucester—as he signed himself, not 'of Gloucester'—in his capacity as a Commissioner of Array, with power to recruit troops took a contingent to join Edward IV's army at Leicester early in 1464. The reason was a potentially very serious Lancastrian rising in Northumberland under the Duke of Somerset, but it was speedily crushed before Richard was able to see any fighting. Despite his extreme youth he was already a power in the land, if obviously something of a figurehead. His Commissions of Array in 1464 extended to nine counties. For some time King Edward had been bestowing important offices on him. In 1462 he had received the Honour and Lordship of Richmond and the Honour and Lordship of Pembroke, besides being made Admiral of England, Ireland and Aquitaine and Constable of Corfe Castle. Every year he was given more confiscated Lancastrian estates, including the entire lands of the Duke of Somerset in 1463. The King's purpose seems to have been to stop his brother Clarence from becoming over-mighty by providing a makeweight. Certainly George was undoubtedly jealous, protesting so much about the Honour of Richmond being given to Richard that Edward took it back and bestowed it on Clarence. In the light of future events, of George's treachery and of Richard's loyalty, one may well wonder if the King already distrusted the former brother and preferred the younger.

33

Some time in 1465, he found himself a 'henchman' in the household of his first cousin the Earl of Warwick, where he was to be brought up—just as his father had been a henchman of their mutual grandfather, Lord Westmorland.[1] One surmises that the three years which Richard spent at Warwick's castle of Middleham in Yorkshire were the most formative of his childhood. Here he acquired his abiding love of Northern England, together with that understanding of its inhabitants which one day enabled him to make them his most formidable tools. He may even have learnt to speak with their own harsh accent which Southerners found so difficult.

Middleham was in Wensleydale, a twenty-mile stretch in the upper valley of the fast running River Ure, in the heart of the North Riding moors but only a short distance from the Pennines. Leland, speaking of it in 1538, says it 'is a pretty market town and standeth on a rocky hill, on the top whereof is the castle . . . The town itself is small.' The inhabitants spoke the dalesmen's dialect, full of Norse words inherited from Viking settlers, though on the moors some shepherds still counted their sheep in a Celtic jargon. Yorkshire has a curiously hard quality and has always been famous for producing hard men. The winters can be surprisingly severe—no doubt Richard had the experience of being snowed up.

As Scottish raids were a constant danger, the castle was strongly fortified, with a vast Norman keep whose walls were ten-foot thick and fifty-five high (from the top of which there was a wonderful view of the surrounding countryside). It was separated by a great guard tower and drawbridge from a wide outer court to the east and ringed by a deep moat and massive curtain walls. It nevertheless seems to have been surprisingly comfortable, possessing more lavatories than almost any other English mediaeval house which has survived, and having three large parks next to it.[2] Leland thought it 'the fairest castle of Richmondshire next Bolton'.

Neighbouring magnates included Lord Scrope of Bolton, whose castle was even more impressive than Middleham, and Metcalfe of Nappa Hall, who was the head of an innumerable clan of warlike Borderers.[3] Then there was the Cistercian Abbot of Jervaulx two miles away, whose monks were as famous for their horses as for their sheep. There was also the Abbot of the White Canons of Coverham, again only two miles away but on the other sides of the river— Premonstratensian Abbots were splendidly decorative figures who wore white fur capes. (The canons took their name from their mother house of Prémontré in France.) However the neighbours who probably loomed largest were the Mayor and Corporation of York, who frequently entertained Warwick and his family.

The Earl himself was undoubtedly the most imposing personality whom Richard encountered in his early years, commanding almost as enormous authority as King Edward. Sadly, we know nothing about Warwick's relations with the boy, though he must have met him often during his visits to Middleham and afterwards at court. Born in 1428 Richard Nevill had, as has been seen, acquired two of the richest Earldoms in the realm and possessed vast estates all over England, amounting to more than a hundred manors, and also the Lordship of the Channel Islands. Commynes, a Burgundian contemporary, estimated that in addition he drew an income from his offices which was worth at least 80,000 Flemish gold crowns. No other English magnate commanded so huge an army of retainers and dependants, all of whom were proud to wear his livery of a red jacket with a white bear and ragged staff, while no other was head of such a powerful clan as the Nevills—a large proportion of members of the House of Lords were his kinsmen.

Warwick was immensely popular, not just in the North Country but in London as well. At his house, The Harbour—it was on the site of today's Cannon Street Station—in Warwick Lane on Dowgate Hill which overlooked the Pool of London, six oxen were roasted and boiled for breakfast every day; the surrounding taverns were full of people eating his meat since any friend of his servants might take away as much as they could carry on a long dagger—there must have been a whole host of them since he never travelled without a retinue of 600 men. He was deeply admired for his dashing exploits at sea in his capacity as Captain of Calais; he had destroyed an entire Spanish fleet besides terrorising Flemish and Italian merchantmen, and he had swept the English coastal waters free of privateers—he was literally worshipped in the South Coast ports. And everyone knew that to a very large extent the King owed his throne to him. (Though the title of 'King-maker' was not bestowed on him until the next century.) Commynes thought that 'he might also be called the King's father as a result of the services and education he had given him.' Indeed it is not too much to suggest that he was something of a father-figure to all three brothers.

Edward gave the Earl unparalleled powers, which made him a sort of mayor of the palace. He was allowed to manage most of the highest affairs of state, including defence and foreign diplomacy— for a long time the French and the Scots believed that he was omnipotent. As Captain of Calais he had an unrivalled power base across the Channel, yet he was even stronger in the North of England. The once supreme Percys were deprived of their lands, as Lancastrians, and these were given to Warwick's brother, Lord Montagu, who was also made Earl of Northumberland and Chamberlain of the Royal Household. His youngest brother, George Nevill, was promoted to Archbishop of York and appointed Lord Chancellor.

In person the Earl of Warwick must have appeared quite as splendid as his rank and possessions. He was noted not only for a magnificent bearing, but also for his charm, his condescension and his generosity. Unfortunately he was also a man of diabolical pride and vanity, overwhelmingly ambitious, though these traits were carefully concealed. If he had had any sort of plausible claim to the throne he would certainly have seized it for himself. Moreover he seems to have been blind to any of his short-comings—in particular to his ultimately ruinous incapacity as a soldier. Merciless as he was in victory, he had a streak of timidity and a tendency to panic when in battle which verged on cowardice. In the early years of the new reign, however, his flaws and inadequacies went unrecognised, and he was the natural and greatest friend of his first cousins, the young princes of the House of York.[4]

The sort of education which Richard received would have been like that known to have been given to his brother Edward. He was taught how to write the crabbed 'bastard secretary' hand of the age, which he did with a neat elegance, and enough mathematics for simple accounts. He learnt to speak and read French, notably chivalric romances and moralising chronicles, though if he could understand some Latin it was not enough to enable him to read the scriptures. No doubt he acquired a smattering of law, and also some knowledge of heraldry in which he later showed a distinct interest.

One may guess that his mother insisted on strict religious instruction by the chaplains. She was noted for piety, something of a mystic who read the works of Walter Hilton, St Catherine of Siena and St Bridget of Sweden.[5] Directly or indirectly, Richard must have derived much of his own brand of religion from her.

His tutors would have attached immense importance to physical disciplines. Every great lord had to be a soldier and had to learn combat skills as early as possible; as Machiavelli observes, 'A prince should have no other object or interest, nor study anything, but war and its science and conduct, because it is the one skill above all which is necessary to a ruler.' For boys of family in any noble household there was constant daily practice, wearing specially heavy armour, with all types of weapon from swords and pole-axes to maces and battle-hammers. There was also training for the tournament, both on foot and on horseback. Sinews and endurance were toughened by hunting, which was regarded as a semi-military exercise. There were still forests in Yorkshire harbouring stag and boar—according to Leland one stretched all the way from Middleham to Ripon—while deer parks next to the castle contained fallow buck. Yorkshiremen often made do with martens or otters (in summer) or even the big, sandy moorland hares, all of which gave excellent sport before hounds. Falconry—peregrines and merlins were obtainable locally—took the place of modern shooting.

Such activities must have been a terrible challenge to a boy with so weak and frail a body as the young Richard. He conquered, but presumably at a cost. Shakespeare may not be so very far from the mark in making Duchess Cecily say that her youngest son's schooldays were 'frightful, desperate, wild and furious'. If the Duke's desperate efforts gave him self-control, they were no doubt also responsible for his nervousness and anxious nature, even his secretiveness. Furthermore (though this is only surmise) excessive use of one arm, since the other was inadequate, produced a muscular development which exaggerated the slight unevenness of his shoulders and the curvature of his spine and gave him an imperceptible crookback. As it was, he grew up to be noticeably small and thin.

It has been suggested that during his time at Middleham the young Duke acquired friends of his own age. Among these may have been some of the younger Metcalfes from Nappa, and it is very likely that a certain Francis Lovell from Oxfordshire was a fellow 'henchman' in the castle—later Lovell would be one of Richard's right-hand men.[6] Another companion at Middleham seems to have been Robert Percy, a kinsman of the Earl of Northumberland, who would also become one of his most faithful and committed supporters.

It is probable that some time during his stay there, he also first met his future wife, Warwick's daughter Anne Nevill. Her mother— the great Beauchamp heiress, who had brought Warwick his Earldom and the best part of his wealth—is known to have been at Middleham often, since the castle was a favourite residence of her husband's, and that she brought her daughters with her. Anne's elder sister Isabel, who would one day marry Clarence, was Richard's contemporary, but Anne was at least four years younger. No doubt, like most boys, he would have taken little notice of anyone quite so insignificant.

In 1466 the young Duke of Gloucester attended the Nevills' lavishly ostentatious celebrations at Cawood Castle after the enthronement of his cousin George Nevill as Archbishop of York and Primate of England. Incredible quantities of food were served. Over a hundred oxen, 500 stags and more than 4,000 sheep were eaten, together with 13,000 puddings, while a hundred casks of wine, 300 casks of ale and 105 gallons of hypocras (spiced wine cup) were drunk. All this profusion, intended to display the Nevill wealth and magnificence, was presided over by Warwick, the new Archbishop's brother, as 'steward of the feast'. Interestingly, Gloucester was the only male member of the Royal Family present. He sat at the same table as his cousin, Warwick's small daughter Anne.[7] In 1467 he and the Earl sat together on a commission to investigate some disturbances at York. In 1468 he and Warwick, this time accompanied by Clarence, rode to escort Margaret of York on her way to Margate, where she took ship for Burgundy and her ducal husband. Even before she arrived in the Low Countries the Burgundians were singing songs about her whoring—she seems to have shared her brother the King's promiscuity.

Richard finally ceased to be his cousin Warwick's 'henchman' some time during 1468, the Earl being granted, in the autumn of that year, £1,000 for expenses incurred by his maintenance. There was good reason for the young Duke to say goodbye to Warwick and to go to court. Although no one realised it at the time, something had happened four years before which would lead to a mortal quarrel between the Earl and the House of York, and which would eventually contribute to the total destruction of the dynasty. By 1468 the crisis was already on the horizon.

In September 1464 the great council of the realm had met at Reading Abbey. It was expected that matters of some importance would be discussed, and indeed the King announced the introduction of an entirely new gold coinage (including the famous angel of six shillings and eightpence, the most beautiful of all English coins). It was expected that the topic of Edward's marriage would be raised; Warwick was already negotiating for the hand of Louis XI's sister-in-law, Bona of Savoy—immortalised as 'Lady Bone' by English chroniclers. To the assembly's amazement, the King suddenly announced that he was already married, to 'Dame Elizabeth Grey', the young widow of a Lancastrian knight.

In fact Edward had married her five months earlier, on May Day, in secret at her mother's manor house of Grafton in Northamptonshire. A compulsive womaniser, the King had been pursuing her for some months, but according to Mancini she had held out for marriage even when he held a dagger at her throat.[8] Another popular tale says that she had lain in wait for him when he was hunting in the forest near Grafton, to solicit the return of her husband's confiscated estates. She was twenty-seven, five years older than Edward, and clearly most attractive.

We have a better idea of what she looked like than of any other mediaeval English Queen—from a portrait at Queens' College, Cambridge and from a picture of her with her husband and children in a stained glass window at Canterbury Cathedral. The portrait shows a face of delicacy and elegance, while the window depicts long, flowing golden hair and heavy, hooded eyes. The Tudor chronicler Hall probably reports an accurate tradition when he speaks of 'her lovely looking and feminine smiling (neither too wanton nor too humble)'.

Unfortunately her social and political background were not so enamouring. Admittedly her mother, Jacquetta of Luxembourg, was sister to the Burgundian Count of Saint-Pol and the widow of the Duke of Bedford, Henry V's brother. But Jacquetta had married a second husband beneath her. Elizabeth's father, Richard Woodville—one of the handsomest men of his day—had been made Lord Rivers in 1448, but was always despised as an upstart by his peers. Salisbury once called him 'a knave's son' while Warwick told him his 'father was but a little squire' and that he had 'made himself by marriage'. Old Rivers and his sons were Lancastrians. So was Elizabeth's late spouse, Lord Ferrers of Groby, who had been killed at the second battle of St Albans. She herself had been woman of the bedchamber to Margaret of Anjou—'in service with Queen Margaret' as More puts it.

When she heard of the marriage the Duchess of York threatened to denounce the King as a bastard. (Richard always remembered the threat.) She told him that a monarch must be all but priestlike and could not be 'defiled with bigamy'. Edward answered that being a widow was an advantage since she 'hath many children. By God's Blessed Lady, I am a bachelor and have some too. And so each of us has a proof that neither of us is like to be barren.'

The King compensated for Elizabeth's unsuitable origins by giving her a truly regal Coronation on Whit Sunday 1465. When she processed into Westminster Abbey under a canopy of cloth of gold, with a sceptre in each hand, she was preceded by Clarence and followed by her royal sisters-in-law. Her mother was with her, supporting the crown with her hands when it proved too heavy for her daughter. Jacquetta was amply recompensed for many humiliations. Writing twenty years afterwards, Mancini says both Richard and Clarence were 'sorely displeased' by the marriage and that the latter's anger was publicised by 'his bitter denunciation of the Queen's obscure family'. Yet George was forced to play a prominent part in the Coronation, even having to hold her wash basin.

The new Queen was not a woman to worry about upsetting the King's brothers, let alone his friends. Thrusting and grasping, she had inherited her father's avarice with her mother's determination not to be slighted. Elizabeth was insatiably greedy for herself and her vast kindred—two sons by her first marriage and a whole tribe of needy brothers and sisters. She also behaved with repellent haughtiness, insisting on being treated with more respect than Margaret of Anjou.

Edward made things worse by heaping favours on the entire Woodville clan. Old Rivers, now an Earl, was made Lord Treasurer of England, enabling him to divert large sums of money into his own pocket. Her eldest brother Anthony, who in the family tradition had already married his heiress to become Lord Scales, received the Governorship of the Isle of Wight. A younger brother John, only twenty, was also provided with a rich heiress—the dowager Duchess of Norfolk, who was nearer eighty than seventy. The Queen even tried—unsuccessfully—to have her youngest brother Richard made Grand Prior of the English Knights of Rhodes, although he was still a boy and not even a member of their Order. Her penniless sisters were married to the heirs of the Earls of Arundel, Essex and Kent and of the Lords Herbert and Strange of Knockyn and, greatest catch of all, to the eleven-year-old Duke of Buckingham. Her eldest son, Thomas Grey, obtained the hand of the heiress of the banished Lancastrian Duke of Exeter. All this was done before the end of 1467.

She caused much popular indignation and made her husband some very dangerous enemies. A contemporary chronicler describes the marriage of the aged Duchess of Norfolk as 'diabolical'. Moreover the old lady was a Nevill by birth and Warwick's aunt. The Earl was also angered by Thomas Grey's marriage since the Duke of Exeter's daughter had been betrothed to his nephew. The boy Duke of Buckingham hated his Woodville bride and never forgave her or her family—one day Queen Elizabeth would have to pay a dreadful reckoning to her unwilling brother-in-law.

If Edward IV's rashness in marrying her may be attributed to the lust of an exceptionally self-indulgent man, it is nonetheless difficult to understand why he apparently did not realize that he had mortally offended Warwick. He made no effort to placate the Earl. Perhaps his resentment of Warwick's domination had reached the point where he could no longer control it. By his marriage he had humiliated him, especially abroad and in particular in France. It demonstrated all too clearly that the Earl was not all powerful in England, as he pretended, and that he certainly did not enjoy the full confidence of the King.

Furious though Warwick must have been at the advancement of such upstarts as the Woodvilles, he was far more angry at the implications for his foreign policy. It seems that he had been ensnared by the spidery wiles of Louis XI of France, who addressed him flatteringly as 'cousin' in his letters and who promised rich rewards for his help. At the end of 1465 the Earl was still pretending to Louis that he was in complete control of English foreign policy and promising that Edward would not support the French king's rebellious brother. In June the following year he sailed from his stronghold at Calais and up the Seine to meet Louis, who enchanted him by his attentions and expensive presents.

However, in July 1468 Edward's sister Margaret married Charles of Charolais, the eldest son of Philip, Duke of Burgundy. This was the one match which Louis XI was most anxious to prevent, since he dreaded a revival of the Anglo-Burgundian axis, which had once ruled half France and all but destroyed the Valois monarchy. In any case Charolais and Warwick had disliked each other on sight on the only occasion when they met. The Crowland chronicler, a contemporary and a professional diplomatist, believed that the marriage of Margaret of York rather than the King's marriage to Elizabeth Woodville was the real reason for the conflict which now broke out between Warwick and Edward IV. Soon England was allying with Burgundy and Brittany against Louis XI, and Parliament voted a substantial sum for an invasion of France. The frantic Louis stepped up his efforts to set Warwick against Edward, even offering him a principality to be created out of the provinces of Holland and Zeeland.

As he was still only a boy Richard could not hope to have much influence on events. Nevertheless, he was at court and sometimes an obviously angry spectator. Mancini heard that like Clarence he had been very displeased by the Woodville marriage, but that unlike his brother he tried to conceal his resentment. He accompanied the court to Greenwich—now a manor of the Queen—so presumably he was at her Coronation, even if he does not seem to have been made to play a prominent part in that distasteful ceremony. He cannot have relished watching his mother and sisters kneel in front of Elizabeth Woodville, according to the etiquette of the period, when she ate in public. There was further irritating pomp at the birth of the Queen's first child by Edward in February 1466, a daughter who was named Elizabeth like her mother.

Warwick had lost the King, but he still hoped to control the two Princes of the Blood. In the autumn of 1464, after Edward's announcement of his marriage, he had lured them to Cambridge where he suggested that Clarence should marry his elder daughter and become heir to half his vast possessions. It is likely that he offered the younger girl to Gloucester on the same terms. The King heard what had taken place and at once summoned the boys to his presence.[9]

Edward IV was perhaps the most impressive monarch England has ever known. Golden headed and strikingly handsome, he was six foot three-and-a-half inches tall and broad in proportion, though in these early days he was lean and without an ounce of surplus fat on his soldier's body. 'Very princely to behold' comments More, 'of visage lovely, of body mighty, strong and clean made.'[10] A very young man, who was still only twenty-two in 1464 and who lived life to excess, devoted to pageantry and feasting and—despite his marriage—to hunting and whoring, normally he was unfailingly cheerful and amiable in manner. But, Mancini tells us 'should he assume an angry face he could appear very terrible', as no doubt he did on this occasion. Wavrin reports that he gave his brothers a ferocious reprimand and then had them arrested.

Even at fifteen George felt himself as good a man as the King. After all he was still heir presumptive and for some years to come remained the next senior male of the House of York. Unimpressed by the outburst, he ignored the order to stay away from Warwick's daughters.

But puny little Richard, only twelve, took the warning to heart. It is significant that Edward had no qualms about making him Warwick's henchman. At his tallest, when full grown, Gloucester was probably almost ten inches shorter than his royal brother; in 1464 the King must have seemed a giant, as would Clarence later, both of them big, blond men. (There is some indication that Richard took great pride in the fact that he alone of the brothers bore some resemblance to their father the Duke of York, who like him was small and dark and whom he resembled facially.) This terrifying interview was surely vital to his development. He never grew out of his awe, very likely resentment, of Edward IV, never overcame his fear of him. Which does not necessarily mean that he held him in deep affection.

CHAPTER THREE

WARWICK TRIES TO UNMAKE A KING

*'But when the Earl of Warwick understood of this marriage, he took it
so highly that . . . thereof ensued much trouble and great bloodshed.'*
Sir Thomas More, The History of King Richard the Third

*'Confess who set thee up and plucked thee down? Call Warwick
patron, and be penitent.'*
Shakespeare, King Henry VI, Part III

By the end of 1468 Warwick was able to inform the King of France
that he had 'drawn over' Clarence. Indeed he had achieved an extraordinary influence over the Duke, having all but bewitched him, so
seductive were his arguments.[1] For the Earl was maturing a plan to
depose Edward and replace him by his more amenable brother,
whom he intended to secure by making him his son-in-law. However, he was not yet quite ready, still uneasy about taking such a
desperate step. Nor did the King suspect him. That summer a Lancastrian agent had been captured and, after being 'burnt in the feet',
had accused several people of corresponding with Margaret of Anjou.
Among them was Lord Wenlock, well known to be a firm friend of
Warwick. Still confident of the Earl, Edward commissioned him to
investigate the matter.

The business dwindled into insignificance in the light of the latest
piece of scandalous Woodville greed. A distinguished City merchant
and former Lord Mayor of London, Sir Thomas Cook, had been
implicated with Wenlock. The Queen's father persuaded Edward to
arrest Sir Thomas and then plundered his house, stealing all his plate
and moveables—including some gold-thread tapestries which the
Queen's mother was well known to have tried to buy in vain. When
the Lord Chief Justice acquitted Cook, old Rivers still contrived to
have him fined in such a way that his daughter got £800 of 'Queen's
Gold' out of it. Soon afterwards the Lord Chief Justice was dismissed.

The Woodvilles were almost certainly responsible for an even more
vicious crime in Ireland. In 1465 the Lord Deputy, Thomas Fitz-
Gerald, seventh Earl of Desmond, had visited England and during
his stay had told the King that he would have done better to marry
a princess of some great foreign house. Two years later, on being
replaced as Deputy by the Earl of Worcester, Lord Desmond was
promptly arrested, arraigned on frivolous charges and beheaded,
while two of his young children were murdered in prison. Nearly
two decades after, when he was King, Richard wrote to the then Earl

of Desmond to say that his father and brothers had been killed by the same people who had destroyed his own brother Clarence—the Woodvilles.[2]

What with Woodville crimes and Warwick's intrigues, 'many murmerous tales ran in the City [of London]' and indeed throughout the country. The atmosphere was explosive. The crisis burst early the following year, 1469, in the North. A certain 'Robin of Redesdale'— in reality Sir John Conyers, a kinsman of Warwick—rose in revolt, together with 'Robin of Holderness' and 'John Amend-all'. In their manifestos they complained of pointed grievances, and in particular of Lord Rivers and all the Queen's kindred. Still more suspiciously, a rumour began to circulate, and to circulate very widely, that Edward IV was a bastard and that the rightful King was the Duke of Clarence. One rising was promptly and apparently zealously repressed by Warwick's brother, the Nevill Earl of Northumberland, yet almost immediately another broke out in Lancashire.

King Edward did not appreciate the seriousness of the situation, nor did he detect the sophisticated organisation behind the risings. Above all, he did not understand that he had failed to give England the peace and prosperity which it had expected from him when he replaced Henry VI. Nevertheless, he was sufficiently worried to go North himself with a small army. Richard accompanied him. Not realizing how grave was his danger, Edward moved slowly enough. En route he passed through Norwich, where the Paston family presented themselves to the royal brothers and complained of the depredations of the Duke of Suffolk, their brother-in-law.

While Richard was in Norfolk he found himself so short of money that he wrote—or rather dictated—an anxious letter to one of his retainers to borrow 'an hundred pound of money until Easter next coming' because 'I am so suddenly called.' The letter, from Castle Rising, is dated 24 June. He and his brother spent the night of 26 June at Crowland Abbey, for whose monks Bishop Russell would write a damning account of Richard's reign nearly twenty years later. They continued by boat up the River Nene to his childhood home of Fotheringay to stay with their mother, who was in residence.

Duchess Cicely no doubt gave them disturbing news of their brother George. She had recently seen him at Warwick's castle of Sandwich in Kent, where a threateningly large contingent of Nevills were gathering, including the Archbishop of York. Clarence had gone there on 7 June. He must have been painfully embarrassed by the unexpected arrival of his mother a week later—clearly she had learnt of a plot and hoped to dissuade him from taking part in it. Probably she guessed that she had been unsuccessful and hastened to the Midlands to warn Edward.

In the event Clarence and Warwick crossed to Calais shortly after her departure. On 11 July George married the Earl's sixteen-year-old daughter, Isabel, the service being performed by the bride's uncle, the Archbishop. Within another week Clarence and Warwick were on their way back to England with fresh troops from the Calais garrison. They landed on 20 July and marched north.

Meanwhile Edward had suddenly realized that he was in grave danger. Not only was he outnumbered by 'Robin of Redesdale' but he now knew that Warwick was behind the rising. The King and Richard took refuge in Nottingham Castle, waiting to be relieved by the Earl of Pembroke and his Welshmen. Then Robin and Warwick joined forces and routed Pembroke at Edgecote near Banbury, capturing and beheading him together with other leading supporters of the King.

Edward IV, as strong-nerved as he was cunning, now adopted a policy of totally passive resistance. He disbanded his outnumbered troops and then waited for Warwick to take him prisoner. It was a calculated gamble—everyone remembered how Richard II had been dethroned and murdered in similar circumstances. Certainly the rebels were in no very merciful mood. Old Rivers and his son John—the aged Duchess of Norfolk's youthful husband—were quickly caught and executed. There was a general massacre of Woodville supporters. The Queen's mother was accused of trying to bewitch Edward by means of 'an image of lead made like a man-at-arms, being the length of a man's finger and broken in the middle and made fast with wire'. However Warwick was not quite brave enough to take the only step which might have ensured victory—to kill the King, as had been done with Richard II. Edward was placed in honourable confinement, first at Warwick Castle, then at Middleham, then at Pontefract. He showed the utmost amiability, graciously co-operating with his captors and signing documents drafted by them without demur. Warwick appointed a new Lord Treasurer and appeared to be in complete control of the realm. In reality all he had achieved was to plunge it into anarchy without eliminating the captive King's supporters.

It seems that the young Duke of Gloucester had not been arrested with his brother. We know that Edward's chamberlain, his cousin and friend Lord Hastings, was busy raising troops in Lancashire while the King was being held, and it is likely that Richard was doing the same somewhere else in the North Country. It is also known that when Edward suddenly summoned his lords to come to him at Pontefract at the end of September, Gloucester and Hastings rode there together at the head of a very strong force. The King's unofficial gaoler, the Archbishop of York, could do nothing when in October Edward announced he was going to London. In the capital he was welcomed with unfeigned relief. Warwick watched helplessly from the North as the King reasserted his authority. The Earl and Clarence finally dared to go down to London in December, where they were received with apparent forgiveness.

The Duke of Clarence had gained less than nothing from his treachery. By contrast Richard was magnificently rewarded, being made Constable of England and receiving many other great honours and estates, among them the beautiful castle of Sudeley in Gloucestershire. He was also appointed Chief Steward and Surveyor of the Principality of Wales and Earldom of March, Chief Justice of North Wales and—until the majority of the boy Earl of Pembroke—Chief Justice and Chamberlain of South Wales. The Welsh were inveterate Lancastrians. Shortly after Edward's return to London Henry ap Thomas ap Griffith and Morgan ap Thomas ap Griffith seized the castles of Cardigan and Caermarthen as bases for a full-scale rebellion. The seventeen-year-old Chief Justice dealt with them with impressive speed, recapturing both castles before Christmas.

But Warwick and Clarence remained an insoluble problem. They knew that their very existence threatened the King while they could not forget a most unforgiving Queen. Even had they wished, they were unable to hold back their supporters—a strange mixture of personal followers, secret and not so secret Lancastrians, and energetic opportunists. By March 1470 risings were again breaking out in the North. On 10 March Sir John Conyers, Lord Fitzwalter and Lord Scrope of Bolton were up in arms. The outbreak was recognised as very serious. After an apparently puny affray by Lord Welles and Sir Thomas Dymmock in Lincolnshire the previous month, on 4 March Welles's son Sir Robert had had a proclamation read in all the churches of that county—every man must rally against the King in the names of the Duke of Clarence and the Earl of Warwick.

This time Edward moved much more quickly, smashing the risings and summarily beheading their leaders. Before he died Sir Robert confessed that Clarence and Warwick had been behind him. These two 'great rebels' refused to obey the King's summons without a safe conduct. Having got as far North as Manchester, they then fled down to Devon and embarked for Calais with their wives. At Calais, although the Lieutenant Lord Wenlock was secretly Warwick's friend, they were met with gunfire. The poor young Duchess of Clarence was in labour and miscarried as a result, her stillborn son being buried at sea. The miserable party finally landed at Honfleur, where King Louis was only too pleased to give them refuge.

Edward was prepared to use any means to prevent their return. At the suggestion of the sinister John Tiptoft, Earl of Worcester, twenty of Warwick's men were publicly impaled at Southampton for an example (though the victims seem to have been hanged beforehand). Yet Warwick was far from beaten.

By now he had decided that Clarence would make an impossible King. But there was still a Lancastrian Pretender available—together, Lancastrian faithful and Yorkist disaffected might well restore Henry VI. Louis was enchanted by the prospect and forced Margaret of Anjou to forgive the Earl and ally with him. On 22 July 1470 in Angers Cathedral Warwick knelt on the stone floor before her for a good quarter of an hour, first begging her forgiveness and then swearing loyalty to King Henry. She even consented to her only son, Prince Edward, marrying his younger daughter Anne. The boy was already all too like his ferocious mother, alarmingly haughty and talking of nothing but war and beheading his enemies. However the Earl must subdue England before she and the boy returned—an ultimately fatal miscalculation. Clarence was left with nothing but the right to inherit the throne should Edward of Lancaster fail to beget children.

Meanwhile, in Northern England still more small risings were breaking out once again. They were not especially dangerous, but important enough to keep Edward IV there. Richard was with him, a precociously mature eighteen year old who in August 1470 was appointed Warden of the West Marches against Scotland. But the real danger lay in the South.

The King was at York when he was suddenly informed that on the evening of 13 September the Earl of Warwick, together with the Duke of Clarence and such Lancastrian exiles as the Earls of Oxford and Shrewsbury, had landed in Devon and were making for London. Edward started out for the South. But he had only reached Doncaster when in the middle of the night his minstrels burst into his bedchamber to warn him that the Marquess Montagu—Warwick's brother, formerly Earl of Northumberland—was advancing with a large body of troops to capture him.

The King reacted with his usual decisiveness. Together with Richard, Hastings, his brother-in-law the new Earl Rivers, and a few hundred devoted followers he galloped to King's Lynn in Norfolk. There he commandeered two flat-bottomed merchantmen from Holland to supplement the single small royal ship which he found in the port. Then, still in his armour, he set sail for the Low Countries. Commynes observes 'They did not have a penny between them and scarcely knew where they were going.'

CHAPTER FOUR

THE WHEEL OF FORTUNE

'Truly me repenteth that ever I came into this realm, that should be thus shamefully banished undeserved and causeless: but fortune is so variant, and the wheel so moveable, there nis none constant abiding.'
Sir Thomas Malory, Morte d'Arthur

'the getting of the garland, keeping it, losing and winning again, cost more English blood than has twice the winning of France.'
Sir Thomas More, The History of King Richard the Third

The 're-adeption' or 'second reign' of poor Henry VI now began. He was released from imprisonment in the Tower of London, where he had spent five years. Still 'not so cleanly kept as should seem such a Prince', he was moved to the adjoining palace to receive the homage of the Earl of Warwick, who having unmade him a King now made him a King again. Then, hastily smartened up and put into a blue velvet robe, he was paraded through the streets to St Paul's to give thanks—the Earl carried his train in the cathedral, a scene not without irony. Eventually Henry was installed in his Palace of Westminster as though there had never been a Yorkist interregnum. There were a limited number of reprisals; the impaler Tiptoft was beheaded and several particularly hard-line Yorkist lords were imprisoned. Queen Elizabeth Woodville found sanctuary in Westminster Abbey where after a few weeks she gave birth to her first son by her second marriage, the future Edward V.

The Yorkist cause appeared lost. Edward and Richard's little flotilla, after escaping from pirates only with difficulty, managed to land on the coast of Holland near Alkmaar. Commynes, who actually spoke to men who had seen them, says 'There never was such a beggarly company.' Edward had no money and gave his ship's master 'a robe lined with fine marten's fur, promising to reward him better in the future'. Luckily the Governor of Holland, Louis de Gruthuyse, was well disposed and paid for them to go to the Hague. Even so, Duke Charles (who by now had succeeded Philip the Good) was most unhappy at having these embarrassing refugees in his territory. He 'would rather the King had been dead.'

But Warwick's régime was extremely vulnerable. It had few rewards to offer its supporters, as it could not afford to antagonise too many people by a general re-distribution of estates and offices, while Lancastrian exiles and moderate Yorkists found it hard to trust one another. Dependence on Louis XI was a serious handicap, since the English detested the idea of any alliance with France. Nevertheless

Louis forced Warwick to join him against Burgundy and to declare war on Duke Charles in February 1471. A nobleman first and foremost, and one of those who despised merchants, Warwick simply could not see that this meant the loss of England's chief markets in the Low Countries. It was a mistake which Edward would never have made.

As so often the French King had been too clever by half. The Duke of Burgundy now had no option but to support the Yorkists—the new Anglo-French alliance was too dangerous for him to do anything else.[1] Edward and his brother were summoned to the Burgundian court where Charles gave them a large sum of money 'to assist his return'. It amounted to 50,000 Burgundian florins, roughly £8,000 in English gold of the period. He also hired three or four large ships for him, together with fourteen well-armed Hanseatic vessels. Presumably Richard now became extremely busy organising the expedition. However, we know that he was at Lille in February 1471, with his sister Margaret. It is possible that here he met William Caxton, an English merchant and the future father of English printing, who had recently joined the Duchess's household.

Edward hoped to sail on 2 March, but it was still winter and the North Sea was stormy, a terrifying prospect for the little boats of the period. By 11 March the weather abated and the King's expedition sailed out from Flushing. He made land in Norfolk the following morning, but after a scouting party had been attacked, sailed on to Ravenspur in Yorkshire, a small and long since vanished port at the very mouth of the River Humber, where he disembarked on 14 March in the teeth of a storm. Richard's ships went aground some four miles away. Luckily he and his 300 troops managed to rejoin his brother the next day. Their army was tiny, 2,000 men in all, though among them were Flemish hand-gunners. Besides the King and Gloucester the only prominent Yorkist commanders were Lords Hastings and Rivers.

They were in a desperate situation. If England disliked some of Warwick's measures, it was tired of fighting and of changing Kings. Even Yorkist landowners were frightened that Edward's army was too small. Hostility was evident everywhere. Undaunted, he remembered how Bolingbroke had behaved seventy years before when he came to overthrow Richard II and announced that he merely wanted his Duchy back. Edward proclaimed that he only sought his rightful inheritance, the Dukedom of York, and made his men wear Lancastrian badges. At York the city fathers, led by the Recorder Thomas Conyers and a citizen called Martin de la Mere, refused to admit him but he managed to enter with a dozen or so companions, all sporting the ostrich plumes of the Lancastrian Prince of Wales, and strolled ostentatiously about the streets. Next day the rest of his little army was let in. They found it harder to leave than to enter—the Recorder and de la Mere tried to force Edward to take an oath in the Minster that he had not come to claim the throne. But the zealous burgesses were kept in talk until the expedition had got outside the walls.

Edward and Gloucester then began their progress South. Yorkists rallied to them in increasingly large numbers. By a brilliantly calculated series of marches and counter marches they eluded Warwick's troops and a fortnight after his landing Edward felt sufficiently confident to proclaim himself King again. On 4 April Clarence, having deserted his father-in-law with 4,000 men, was reunited to his brothers at Banbury in an emotional meeting.

Having lured the Lancastrians out of London, Edward was able to enter the capital triumphantly on 11 April, Maundy Thursday. As Commynes points out, 'there were more than 2,000 of his supporters there, hidden in the sanctuaries, including three or four hundred knights and esquires who were very important to him' while his enormous debts 'made his merchant creditors support him' and 'several noblewomen and wives of rich burgesses with whom he had been closely and secretly acquainted won their husbands and kinsmen over to his cause.' He was reunited not only to his wife but to his new son and heir. Commynes comments grimly 'had they shut the gates against him his fate would have been sealed, because the Earl of Warwick was only a day's march behind him.' Henry VI was taken back to the Tower.

Yorkists from all over England now hastened to London. King Edward found himself with an adequate army and an excellent artillery train, ready to fight Warwick, news of whose advance arrived on Holy Saturday—it was learnt that he was marching on London down the road from St Albans and would come through Barnet. The King sent his advance guard to intercept them under Richard. Scouts found the Lancastrians just outside Barnet but it was dark before Edward came up. He was only too willing to give battle to the Earl, before Margaret arrived from France with reinforcements.

Warwick's army bivouacked north of Barnet village, in the positions they would fight the following day. The Earl himself commanded the reserve and an unusually large number of cannon, while his brother, the Marquess Montagu, had the centre and straddled the road. The left was entrusted to the Earl of Oxford behind hedges to the west, and the right to the Duke of Exeter on a slope eastward protected to some extent by a marshy bottom below as well as by a thick hedge. Edward's troops encamped much nearer the enemy than either side realised, due not only to the pitch dark but to an unnaturally thick fog—which locals believed to have been conjured up by the ghost of a wizard, Friar Bungay. Throughout the night Warwick's guns fired ceaselessly, but because of the darkness 'it so fortuned that they always overshot the King's host and hurted them nothing.'

Commynes reports that everyone, commanders included, dismounted and fought on foot in the ensuing battle. The archers and hand-gunmen were unarmoured, which enabled them to get out of the way more quickly. The 'hand-to-hand' infantry were the bill-men, who used an English version of the half-pike, the 'brown bill' whose head still trims country lanes even today; they were protected by light 'sallets', helmets rather like steel sou'westers, and 'jacks'—metal-studded leather coats down to the knees and several layers thick. The gentry generally wore full armour, which contrary to modern belief was surprisingly light; huge elbow pieces, to catch and snap an enemy's weapon were common, together with sallets and chin guards. It had been developed to such a degree that no sword could penetrate it, so the favourite tool of men of rank when dis-mounted was the two-handed pole-axe, with a five-foot metal-plated handle and a blade designed to crush and rip open armour like a modern tin opener—Richard is known to have carried an axe at Barnet, probably one of this sort. (On horseback a shorter weapon was preferred.) Despite bows, hand guns, and cannon, both sides knew that once they got to grips the outcome would be decided by a dreadful slogging match in the mud, everyone hacking, hammer-ing, and stabbing until it was over—one way or the other.

Commynes comments sardonically that Warwick was normally an excessively cautious warrior, who invariably remounted his horse after his men had engaged the enemy, so that he could make a quick escape if things turned out badly. There was never any mercy for defeated leaders in the Wars of the Roses. However, on this occasion his pugnacious brother, the Marquess Montagu, persuaded him to remain on foot—no doubt to boost his troops' morale.[2] The nervous Earl knew that he outnumbered Edward's army of 10,000 by at least half as much again.

The Yorkists began to move at about four o'clock on Easter Sunday morning, after a miserably dank night spent on the wet ground. Richard is said, on questionable authority, to have commanded—in name at least—their right wing which faced Exeter, Lord Hastings their left opposite Oxford and King Edward the centre.[3] Because of the murk they were wrongly aligned, and outflanking was to play a considerable part. In the dark, trudging clumsily through the marshy ground, Richard's men found themselves far to the right of Exeter's hedge and once they were up the slope were able to charge into his flank—soon it was a desperate melee and two of the young Duke's squires were cut down.[4] (According to a Hanseatic merchant, writing on 17 April, Richard was slightly wounded.)[5] On the other wing the Earl of Oxford similarly outflanked the Yorkist left and Hastings's men broke and ran, hotly pursued by the Lancastrians. In the centre, however, there was a sustained and murderous conflict, each side battering grimly away at the other and refusing to give ground. In consequence, the entire battle pivoted until the Lancastrians faced east and the Yorkists west, instead of north and south. Warwick used his reserve to strengthen Exeter, who then managed to stiffen the Lancastrian left wing and hold off Gloucester's onslaught. Edward, who 'fought as much or more than anyone on either side' according to Commynes, was in the thick of the combat in the centre and because of the dense fog could not see what was happening. Meanwhile Hastings's panic-stricken survivors were fleeing down the road towards London, shouting that 'the King was distressed and his field lost.'

Now was the time for Oxford, who had re-formed his troops, to attack Edward from behind and win certain victory. His men marched purposefully up the road in their livery of a star with streamers. They did not realize that the line of battle had swung round and mistook Montagu's centre for the King's troops. In the fog and dim watery light of early morning Montagu's men confused the star with streamers for the Yorkist sun in splendour and shot a lethal arrow volley at their comrades. Oxford and his soldiers at once thought that the battle had been lost and ran for their lives, shouting 'Treason!'

The confusion infected Montagu's centre, which collapsed. The Lancastrian right followed suit. The Marquess was killed. Warwick mounted his horse and rode off, but the 'Proud setter-up and puller-down of Kings' was caught and slain in Wrotham Park as he was trying to reach the safety of Barnet Wood. Edward is said to have given orders to save his life yet it seems unlikely; Commynes states that both men of noble birth and commoners were killed because the King did not give his usual order to 'spare the commons and slay the gentles' since he was furious with ordinary Englishmen for supporting the Earl. Not a man to be blinded by sentiment, he had the corpses of Warwick and Montagu displayed outside St Paul's for several days. Exeter was so badly wounded that the Yorkists thought he was dead and, stripping the unconscious Duke, left him naked on the battlefield—later he somehow reached the sanctuary at Westminster. Only Oxford got away, to fight another day.

Edward IV had shown Gloucester how to outmarch, outmanoeuvre and outfight the most formidable-seeming opponent. Warwick was above all defeated by the sheer speed of the King's tactics. We cannot even guess how Richard felt about the bloody end of the close kins-man with whom he had spent his early teens.

The Yorkists had undoubtedly won a great and glorious victory. But the Lancastrians were far from beaten. On the very same day that Barnet was fought, Queen Margaret and her son landed in Dorset at Weymouth. Adverse winds had delayed her in Normandy for the past three weeks—if it had not been for the weather she would have joined Warwick in time to make him invincible. Horrified by the news of his defeat and death, she almost sailed back to France. However the Duke of Somerset persuaded her that the Yorkists had lost many men and that most of England was still Lancastrian.

Somerset's assessment seemed justified as she rode to Exeter and then by way of Taunton and Wells to Bath; large numbers of West-Country landowners, from Cornwall to Wiltshire and led by the Earl of Devon, rallied to her banner. It was known that the gentry of Wales, of Cheshire and of the Northern Midlands were even more devotedly Lancastrian. If only she could reach the loyal heartland she would win.

Two days after Barnet, Edward heard of her arrival. He at once borrowed as much money as he could from the London merchants and began gathering fresh troops and a bigger artillery train at Windsor, where on 23 April he celebrated St George's Day with his brothers and his Garter Knights. He then learnt that Margaret and her army intended to cross the Severn and link up with the Welsh Lancastrians. A lucky rather than a gifted general—he fought many battles, always on foot, and was never beaten—the King knew enough of strategy to see that she had to be intercepted, at all costs. On 24 April he and his brothers set out to do so.

Somerset and the Lancastrian commanders did not realize just how fast Edward could move. They wasted time collecting guns and a few more men at Bristol, and the Yorkist garrison at Gloucester managed to bar the gates and stop them crossing the Severn. By now aware of their danger, the Lancastrians marched all night to the next crossing place at Tewkesbury, through 'foul country, all in lanes and stony ways, betwixt woods, without any good refreshing'. But Edward and his army were close on their heels, marching almost parallel. The last day of pursuit, Friday 3 May, was one of sweltering heat—'right-an-hot day'. Both sides suffered dreadfully from thirst in an incredible march of over thirty-six miles, since the water in the streams was undrinkable from being muddied by horses and wagons. By the late afternoon the Lancastrian foot could not move another step. They had reached Tewkesbury, but were too exhausted even to try to cross the river under cover of darkness.

Nevertheless, the Duke of Somerset—Edward Beaufort, whose father and brother had already perished in the merciless conflict—was a brave and experienced commander. His troops were loyal and soon refreshed by a proper night's rest. He knew how to make the most of the ground, taking up a strong entrenched position with his 3,000 men on a long, low ridge south of the town of Tewkesbury—it could only be attacked through 'foul lanes and deep dykes, and many hedges, hills and valleys, a right evil place to approach'. He also used his scouts to familiarise himself with this difficult terrain.[6]

Somerset himself commanded the Lancastrian right, the Earl of Devon the left. The centre was nominally under the seventeen-year-old Edward, Prince of Wales, but in reality commanded by the octagenarian yet still extremely formidable Lord Wenlock, a veteran of Henry V's campaigns. They might well have won, if only they had been content to stay on the defensive and rely on their archers as in the old wars in France.

6. *Henry VI, whose murder was either supervised or carried out personally by Richard. From a stained glass window at King's College, Cambridge.*

7.   *Richard's sister, Margaret of York, Duchess of Burgundy. Her noticeably sharp features may well have resembled her brother's. Musée du Louvre, Paris.*

8. *Richard's brother-in-law, Charles the Bold, Duke of Burgundy.*
Gemäldegalerie, Staatliche Museen, Preussischer Kulturbesitz, Berlin.

9. Execution after Tewkesbury of Lancastrians condemned by Richard as Constable of England. On the right is the Prior of St John's. Centrale Bibliotheek, Rijksuniversiteit, Ghent.

The Yorkists numbered about the same, 3,000 combattant troops. King Edward took the centre, Richard the right and Hastings the rearguard.[7] The right was also the advance guard and early on the morning of Saturday 4 May was the first to engage the enemy with arrow and artillery fire. Knowing the tangled terrain below him, Somerset was confident that if he left the high ground and took his men down he could surprise Gloucester's attack from the flank and break it up before it had properly begun. His intelligence failed to inform him that the King had positioned 200 lances in the trees of Tewkesbury Park. Somerset engaged Richard's troops at closer quarters and found a hotter reception than he had expected, being pushed back; as he was about to retreat uphill the squadron concealed in Tewkesbury Park hurtled into his men who 'were greatly dismayed and abashed, and so took them to flight into the park and into the meadow that was near, and into lanes and dykes, where they best hoped to escape the danger.' Edward was now able to overwhelm the Lancastrian divisions one by one, he and Hastings charging up the hill at them. They were already shaken by Somerset's rout and by Gloucester attacking their centre from the flank. Somerset, who had got back safely, went berserk—he rushed up to Wenlock, shouting that he was a traitor for not having supported him properly, and then struck the old man down with his axe. The Lancastrian army disintegrated. But there was no escape, since behind lay the River Avon. About a thousand died in the field which sloped down to it— and was renamed 'Bloody Meadow'. Those who were not hacked to death drowned in the river.

CHAPTER FIVE

FIRST BLOOD

'where his advantage grew, he spared no man's death whose life withstood his purpose.'
> Sir Thomas More, The History of King Richard the Third

'that devil's butcher,
Hard-favour'd Richard?'
> Shakespeare, King Henry VI, Part III

The years 1470 and 1471 were when Richard saw most of Edward IV, fighting at his side, learning how to make and keep allies, how to outwit enemies. His brother taught him a lot. In war, to move fast—the value of engaging one's opponent as soon as possible. In government, how to treat local or personal loyalties with the most delicate consideration, to reward magnates with new titles and confiscated estates, to woo burgesses with municipal privileges and take good care of mercantile interests. In government too, to manipulate Parliament and the law of the land in the service of one's interests.

Edward also showed his young brother the value of murder as a political instrument. Gloucester was an enthusiastic pupil, who speedily made himself useful. If 1471 was the year in which he first saw death in battle, killing and seeing his followers killed at his side, it was also a year when he first sent men to execution without mercy and in which he first committed murder.

Despite Edward's having granted them a free pardon on the Saturday that Tewkesbury was fought, the Duke of Somerset and his party were dragged out of the Abbey on the following Monday. The doomed men, who had no doubt kept their weapons, resisted desperately and there was so much bloodshed that the church was afterwards reconsecrated. They were brought before Richard, in his capacity as Constable of England.[1] Brusquely he condemned them to death. Immediately after he had pronounced sentence they were taken to a block set up in Tewkesbury marketplace and beheaded without further ceremony.

Edward and Richard's admirers argue that Tewkesbury Abbey was not technically a true sanctuary, that they had every right to court-martial 'traitors' taken in battle. Nevertheless, among those beheaded was Henry VI's Lord Treasurer, Fra John Langstrother, the Prior of Clerkenwell. As a professed Knight of Rhodes he was a religious under full vows and therefore canonically immune from the death penalty—he was the only member of his Order to be executed in England until the religious persecution of Henry VIII.[2]

Gloucester has other claims to being his brother's hatchetman. He has been accused of being personally responsible for the deaths of three kinsmen in 1471—the Prince of Wales, Henry VI, and the Bastard of Fauconberg.

On the whole modern opinion is inclined to acquit the young Duke of the murder of Edward of Lancaster after Tewkesbury. At a first glance the contemporary English sources—of which there are very few—seem to provide good grounds for acquittal, agreeing with Commynes that 'the Prince of Wales was killed on the battlefield.' Dr Warkworth (Master of Peterhouse, Cambridge, who wrote about a dozen years later) reports how the boy was overtaken as he fled and slain as 'he cried for succour to his brother-in-law, the Duke of Clarence.' The latter himself, writing only two days afterwards, claims that 'Edward, late called Prince' had been 'slain in plain battle'. *The Historie of the Arrivall of Edward IV in England*, written at the King's command by a Yorkist official within three weeks of the battle, similarly says that 'Edward, called Prince, was taken, fleeing to the townwards [of Tewkesbury] and slain in the field.' So also does the *Tewkesbury Chronicle*. His name heads a list, 'Ded in the Feld', compiled probably just after the battle—'Edward that was called Prynce.' However the Crowland chronicler is ambiguous, stating that Henry VI's son had been slain 'either on the field or after the battle, by the avenging hands of certain persons.'

Save for Warkworth, while they say where Edward of Lancaster died, none of these sources describes how. Obviously Clarence and the Yorkist author of the *Arrivall of Edward IV* would omit anything embarrassing about his death. There is an alternative and horrific account of what really happened, admittedly by chroniclers who wrote a little later. The gap in time is only a matter of thirty years at most, and James Gairdner points out that if the true facts were 'preserved only by tradition till the days of Polydore Vergil and of Hall . . . they are not on that account unworthy of credit.'[3] Dr Hanham (in the course of trying to demolish Gairdner), makes the extremely relevant point that many modern historians who use tape recorders place considerable value on 'tradition', which they have renamed 'oral history'; she also concedes that she has 'probably laid less stress than is just on the importance of living informants . . . It cannot be denied that sometimes evidence may be handed down in a verbal form over a surprisingly long period and with astonishing fidelity.'[4]

Although Horace Walpole cites the Crowland writer's statement in defence of Richard, it could bear precisely the opposite interpretation in the light of oral history. Vergil, whose researches into Richard's career began about 1502, and who almost certainly spoke with men who had actually fought at Tewkesbury, is the first to accuse him of

Edward of Lancaster's murder, together with Clarence and Hastings.[5] Though More does not say that Gloucester did the deed, he implies that with Hastings, Richard 'was one of the smiters of Prince Edward'. Certainly all early-sixteenth-century chroniclers believe that he was implicated.

The most detailed version of the alternative account of how young Edward died 'in the field by Tewkesbury' is given by Hall. The Prince, 'a goodly feminine and well featured young gentleman' was taken prisoner by Richard Croft (the King's former tutor) and brought to his master who had offered a hundred pounds for the boy dead or alive, though promising that if not yet dead his life would be spared. After a long, cold look at his rival, Edward IV asked why he had dared to bring an army against him. The reply was 'to recover my father's Kindom and inheritance.' The King then either pushed him away or struck him with his steel gauntlet, whereupon 'they that stood about—which were George, Duke of Clarence; Richard, Duke of Gloucester; Thomas, Marquess Dorset; and William, Lord Hastings—suddenly murdered' the young Prince.

Most modern historians question the alternative account, though in different ways. Kendall considers that Warkworth was telling most if not all of the truth and that Clarence was probably responsible for killing the boy, if he did not do it himself. Yet Gairdner, however unfashionable, surely carries conviction in arguing that the oral tradition noted down by Vergil and Hall could well have been correct and that it is reasonable to suspect Richard's complicity. Only the historians' attitude of mind has changed since Gairdner wrote—there is no new evidence, and it would be unwise to dismiss the great Victorian's intuition too easily.

There is no doubt at all that Gloucester was implicated in Henry VI's death. Dr Warkworth, of whose testimony as to Prince Edward's end so much is made by Kendall, gives a moving report. 'And the same night that King Edward came to London, King Harry, being in ward in prison in the Tower of London was put to death the 21st day of May on a Tuesday night between eleven and twelve of the clock, being then at the Tower the Duke of Gloucester, brother to King Edward, and many other; and on the morrow he was chested and brought to Paul's and his face was open that every man might see him. And in his lying he bled on the pavement there; and afterwards at the Black Friars was brought, and there he bled new and fresh; and from thence he was carried to Chertsey Abbey in a boat and buried there in Our Lady's Chapel'. As will be seen the fact that Warkworth says that Henry is still buried at Chertsey indicates that he is writing before the reign of Richard III.

It is important that the corpse was supposed to have bled—popular superstition thought it a sure sign of sanctity. Contemporary Englishmen undoubtedly regarded King Henry as very holy indeed. The *Great Chronicle of London* preserves a Londoner's impression; 'after my mind he might say as Christ said to Pilate, *"Regnum meum non est de hoc mundo"*, for God had endowed him with such grace that he chose with Mary Magdalene the life contemplative and refused of Martha the active.' To judge from his behaviour when he ascended the throne, no one was more impressed than Richard Gloucester, who himself plainly came to believe that the last Lancastrian king was a saint. Nonetheless, the *Great Chronicle* adds grimly 'of whose [Henry's] death the common fame then went that the Duke of Gloucester was not all guiltless.' A later tradition reports that he entered St Paul's while the King was lying there, whereupon the corpse bled in witness that the young Duke was its murderer.

Understandably, the *Arrivall of Edward IV*—so often quoted to absolve Richard of guilt at Tewkesbury—states blandly and most unconvincingly that Henry VI 'died of pure displeasure and melancholy'.[6] The Crowland chronicler, also cited to exculpate Richard at Tewkesbury, hints that he had a shrewd idea of what actually happened. 'I will say nothing about how at this time the body of King Henry was found lifeless in the Tower of London. May God have shown mercy to the man who thus dared to lay his sacrilegious hands on the Lord's annointed and have granted him time for repentance. He it was who did the deed deserves the name of tyrant, just as the victim deserves that of glorious martyr.'

Writing a short while after Richard III's own death, the admittedly partisan John Rous says of him 'He caused others to kill the holy man King Henry VI, or as many think, did so by his own hand.' Commynes reports that immediately after Tewkesbury 'the Duke of Gloucester, Edward's brother, who later became King Richard, killed this good man [Henry] with his own hands or at least had him killed in his presence in some hidden place.'[7]

There was good reason to think that the much decried Tudor historians were in this instance very near the truth. More is unequivocal. Richard 'slew with his own hands—as men constantly say—King Henry the Sixth, being prisoner in the Tower, and that without commandment or knowledge of the King [Edward], who would undoubtedly, if he had intended that thing, have appointed that butcherly office to some other than his own born brother'; he adds that, when Richard had killed his cousin, he cried 'Now there is no heir male of King Edward the Third but we of the House of York!' Vergil, Fabyan and Hall say the popular rumour—'the most common fame'—was that Henry was 'stuck with a dagger by the hands of the Duke of Gloucester'.[8] The dagger, or one like it, was still being venerated as a holy relic at Reading Abbey when it was dissolved in 1534.

No one will ever know exactly how Henry VI met his death, but it is certain he died violently. An examination of his skeleton in 1910 found that his skull had been 'much broken'. Tradition has it that the murder was committed in the octagon chamber on the first floor of the Wakefield Tower in the Tower of London. If Edward IV was ultimately responsible, no contemporary or Tudor source says that he was at the Tower on the fatal night. Even Kendall admits Richard's involvement, that Edward sent him 'with a delegation of noblemen to bear an order to Lord Dudley, Constable of the Tower: that feeble candle, the life of Henry the Sixth, was to be snuffed out.' He does not dispute the likelihood of Gloucester having done the deed himself. However he makes no mention of the opprobrium incurred by the Duke as the murderer of an anointed King—something regarded as worse than sacrilege in that extraordinarily superstitious age.

The Bastard of Fauconberg, Thomas Nevill, was Warwick's illegitimate nephew and yet another of Richard's close kindred, being the son of a first cousin. 'Captain' of the Kingmaker's navy, his job had been to prevent reinforcements reaching Edward from Burgundy. The *Great Chronicle of London* tells us that 'having a multitude of rovers' with him, he landed in Kent 'and there a-raised much idle people' and then advanced on London. His ships sailed up the Thames, their cannon firing into the City and burning Aldgate and London Bridge. The Bastard went by land. His original intention had been to rescue Henry VI from the Tower, but he decided to deal with King Edward first. He had brought troops from Calais and was joined by so many recruits that he was rumoured to have more 'than twenty thousand good men well harnessed [armoured].' Warkworth comments that he posed a greater threat to Edward than anything the King had faced at Barnet or Tewkesbury.

What followed smacks of classical Italian Renaissance statecraft, an episode straight from the pages of Guicciardini. Edward, badly outnumbered, sent agents to enlist the help of one of Fauconberg's allies—Nicholas Faunt, Mayor of Canterbury—in persuading him to withdraw to Blackheath. In Warkworth's words, 'And for as much as fair words and promises make fools fain, the Bastard commanded all his host to turn to Blackheath again.' The King seems to have made a secret bargain with him, since Fauconberg then 'stole away from the host' with only 600 horses, and returned to his ships at Sandwich. Here he surrendered to Richard Gloucester, who arrived on 27 May—six days after dispatching Henry VI. As an experienced soldier the Bastard probably expected that he had something to offer Edward, who granted him a free pardon on 10 June. Fauconberg then accompanied Richard to the North on a campaign to pacify the Border, which was still swarming with small bands of Lancastrians besides being plagued by Scots raiders. Meanwhile Nicholas Faunt was hanged, drawn and quartered at Canterbury.

No one has left an account of just what happened between the Duke and the Bastard. All that we know is that Richard had Fauconberg beheaded at Middleham 'notwithstanding he had a charter of pardon' and sent his head South to be displayed on London Bridge 'looking into Kentward'. It is possible that he was caught trying to escape to the Continent, but if so it is curious that he did not do so when he still had the opportunity. One cannot avoid the suspicion that he was led into a trap. As More explains, Gloucester was always 'close and secret, a deep dissembler, lowly of countenance, arrogant of heart, outwardly companionable where he inwardly hated, not hesitating to kiss whom he thought to kill, pitiless and cruel, not for evil will always but oftener for ambition and either for the surety or increase of his position.' The Bastard of Fauconberg never stood a chance with this boy of eighteen. Cesare Borgia could not have done better.[9]

It is true that the young Duke acted as his brother's tool in these killings, and Edward IV must bear much of the responsibility for them. Nevertheless Richard was an alarmingly efficient instrument. He had learnt the political advantages of murder, how to eliminate discreetly anyone who stood in his way. So far there was no reason for him to appreciate its disadvantages.

CHAPTER SIX

THE RIVALRY WITH CLARENCE

'Some wise men also think that his drift, covertly conveyed, lacked not in helping forth his brother of Clarence to his death . . . But of all this point is there no certainty.'
Sir Thomas More, The History of King Richard the Third

'Clarence, beware; thou keep'st me from the light.'
Shakespeare, King Henry VI, Part III

Edward IV had made a triumphal return to London on 21 May 1471. With him rode the two Princes of the Blood—Clarence and Gloucester—three other Dukes, six Earls, sixteen Barons and a whole host of knights and gentlemen, their banners flying, trumpets and kettle-drums sounding. Among the procession was the wretched Margaret of Anjou in an open chariot, adding an almost Roman note to what spectators obviously remembered as the parade of a lifetime. Richard rode at the head of the cortège in his capacity as Constable of England. Even if small groups of Lancastrians still held out, their cause was plainly in ruins and seemed incapable of reviving.

By now the Duke of Gloucester was a strangely mature 18 year old. Indeed he had never had time to be young. There were those terrifying experiences as a little boy, when he heard of his father and brother's horrible end and had to fly into exile, then the menacing conflict for his loyalty between Edward on the one hand and Warwick on the other, then the grim and bloody struggle for survival from which he had just emerged. He had seen dissimulation and treachery at close quarters, how ruthless determination could retrieve a seemingly hopeless cause. He had experienced war and killing at their most savage, finding himself to be both fierce and cruel. He was about to show himself no less ferociously acquisitive, greedy for wealth and possessions on regal scale. But he would not yet reveal himself as equally greedy for power. Richard would never dare to antagonise his all-powerful eldest brother, whom—unlike Clarence—he rightly recognised and feared as a ruler without mercy.

Gloucester was loaded with rewards. He was made Great Chamberlain of England, Steward of the Duchy of Lancaster beyond Trent—which gave him an official residence at Pontefract—Commissioner of Wales, Cornwall and Chester until the Prince of Wales should come of age, and, a little later, Warden of the Forests north of the Trent. He already included among his many great offices that of Warden of the West Marches against Scotland. King Edward was determined to make him Warwick's successor in Northern England, an area not only dangerous on account of its Nevill and Percy loyalties but also as a hotbed of Lancastrianism. Great offices were of little use unless accompanied by great estates. Accordingly, in June Richard received Warwick's castles of Middleham and Sheriff Hutton in Yorkshire and of Penrith in Cumberland, together with all their lands. At the end of 1471 he was granted the estates of the Earl of Oxford and of various other Lancastrian leaders in Essex—it has been estimated that this second grant of lands amounted to approximately 80 manors with an annual income of more than £1,000, an enormous sum for the period.

Meanwhile, after he had captured the Bastard of Fauconberg in June he returned briefly to London. This was in order to attend an assembly of the Lords of the Realm in the Parliament chamber at Westminster, where he paid homage to Edward's infant son, swearing allegiance. Almost at once he left London for his Northern campaign, but came South again in September.

There were important matters which made his return imperative. What was at stake was the rest of Warwick's enormous inheritance. The Northern lands which had belonged to the Kingmaker were easily disposable but not the greater part in the South and Midlands and in the Welsh Marches, because legally they were still the property of his widow (who had taken sanctuary at Beaulieu Abbey in Hampshire). Clarence expected to inherit all her lands through his marriage to her eldest daughter, Isabel. However Richard intended to dispute the inheritance by marrying the younger daughter, Anne, the sixteen-year-old widow of Edward of Lancaster.

Anne had been captured with Margaret of Anjou after Tewkesbury. She had been taken first to Coventry and then to her brother-in-law's London house—which was her father's old mansion in Warwick Lane. It seems likely that Richard visited the Duchess of Clarence in June before going North, and declared his intention of making her sister his wife. He was obviously sincere since Anne was one of the two richest heiresses in England. Clarence had no intention of sharing his mother-in-law's estates and would not concede that Anne was entitled to half. When Gloucester came back to London George told him furiously that he could not marry her.

Richard appealed to the King, who told Clarence to agree to the marriage. George then announced that he did not know where his sister-in-law was. In fact he had hidden her, disguised as a kitchen maid, in one of his retainers' houses in the city. The Crowland chronicler, who gives the only account of these events, tells us that 'the craftiness of the Duke of Gloucester so far prevailed that he discovered the young lady' and had her removed to the sanctuary at the church of St Martin le Grand. She had to spend several months there.

Richard's more imaginative biographers infer that he looked on

Anne as a childhood sweetheart. Sir Clements Markham claims, characteristically, 'Richard III was the only one of our kings who made a true love match. His cousin Anne, the playmate of his childhood, was his first love.' There is no evidence how he regarded her, nor even if their marriage was happy or unhappy. All we can say about Anne, apart from the fact that she was a great heiress, is that she was probably tubercular and that she had had some terrifying experiences. We know also that her ruthlessly determined suitor was virile enough and had already fathered at least two bastards—John of Gloucester and Katherine Plantagenet (though we do not know much about them, let alone their mother or mothers' names).[1]

Edward IV was naturally anxious to avoid a bitter quarrel between his formidable brothers. In the winter of 1471-2 he ordered them to discuss their differences before the Royal Council. The Crowland chronicler, who may well have been present, says that even the laywers there were astonished by the acuteness of Richard and George's arguments and their ability to find precedents; he adds that the three brothers were so gifted that if only they could have remained loyal to each other they would have been invincible. The Council withheld judgement.

Clarence would not give way. In mid-February 1472 Sir John Paston writes that 'Yesterday the King, the Queen, My Lords of Clarence and Gloucester went to Sheen to pardon [i.e., to Confession], men say not in all charity; what will fall men cannot say. The King entreateth My Lord of Clarence for My Lord of Gloucester and, as it is said, he answereth that he may well have My Lady his sister-in-law, but they shall part no livelihood, as he saith. So what will fall cannot I say.'

So forceful and subtle a young man as Richard immediately seized the opportunity which George, perhaps in a fit of anger, had given him. He married Anne quickly. The wedding took place at Westminster, either at the end of February or in March 1472. Such was his haste that he did not wait for the Papal dispensation necessary for him to marry a cousin, though negotiating a shrewd marriage settlement which gave him his wife's lands should the marriage be annulled on grounds of consanguinity. He took Anne home to Middleham, which had by now become a favourite residence, and continued to bargain. He was clever enough to see that in the end Edward would have to decide the terms. He also knew that he must not show himself to be too greedy, like Clarence.

There were more quarrels between the two brothers, especially in the late autumn of 1472. But nothing was decided. The unfortunate dowager Countess of Warwick—whose late husband's titles had now been appropriated by George—petitioned Parliament from her sanctuary at Beaulieu, asking for her lands to be returned to her. She wrote in her own hand, 'in the absence of clerks', not only to the King but to the Queen, to the Duchess of York and to many other royal and noble ladies. The poor woman also complained about the Abbot of Beaulieu's 'guard or strait keeping of her person, which was and is to her heart's grievance'. The following year she was lured out of Beaulieu and, escorted by one of Richard's men—Sir James Tyrell, of whom more will be heard—was taken North to Middleham. Rous says she went hoping to find refuge with her son-in-law, but that he kept her a virtual prisoner for as long as she lived. It is likely that he thought she really might recover her estates and planned to get his hands on them through her. There were certainly rumours that it was just what would happen—'and of this divers folks marvel greatly'.

Duke George was infuriated. Probably 'false, fleeting, perjured Clarence' dabbled in treason yet again. That unconquerable Lancastrian, the Earl of Oxford, who had escaped from Barnet, seized St Michael's Mount on the Cornish coast in the autumn of 1473 and raised his standard. There were rumours that George was in some way involved. About this time Sir John Paston noticed how members of Edward's household were sending for their armour as if they expected trouble. He commented that the 'Duke of Clarence maketh himself big in that he can, showing as he would but deal with the Duke of Gloucester. But the King intendeth to be as big as they both and to be a stifler between them. And some think that under this there be some other thing intended, and some treason conspired.' In the event Edward's men quickly sealed off the Mount, starving Oxford into surrender and imprisonment by the following January. In itself it was not a particularly alarming episode. What was disturbing, however, was that Oxford was said to have shown Louis XI a list of names of those ready to support him and that it included a Duke's. No doubt Richard was far from displeased by such insinuations about his brother of Clarence.

Edward IV may have suspected George, but was not yet prepared to destroy him. He worked hard to reconcile him with Gloucester. In May 1474 an iniquitous Act of Parliament took away from Lady Warwick all rights to her own property, ordaining it should be treated as though she 'were now naturally dead'. The wrangling continued for nearly another year and only in February 1475 was a settlement finally agreed. Details of it have not survived but Richard appears to have done very well indeed. Besides the Nevill and Montagu estates in the North he secured the Salisbury lands and the Lordships in the Welsh Marches. Clarence kept the Beauchamp and Despenser estates, together with his late father-in-law's splendid London mansion. Throughout, Gloucester had shown himself as flexible as he was determined, even surrendering the office of Great Chamberlain to George at the King's request. He knew that Edward IV's favour must be retained, whatever the cost.

It was about this time that Richard Gloucester adopted his famous motto, '*Loyauté me lie*' (loyalty binds me), of which he was obviously proud and which he sometimes wrote after his signature—even during the reign of his luckless nephew. There is no need to question his loyalty to Edward. He was far too astute not to realize that the Yorkist family simply could not afford to intrigue against its head—at any rate not while the King remained alive and formidable. He had seen how Edward was unbeatable, both as a soldier and as a politician, and that he was supremely ruthless. As Machiavelli observes, 'It is necessary for a prince who wants to survive to know how to do wrong.' It is worth emphasising that it was the King who gave Gloucester his first lessons in political murder. Disloyalty to such a brother could lead only to disaster, while fidelity was sure to procure rich rewards.

On the other hand, Richard's brutally realistic loyalty is by no means a proof—as has often been argued—that he did not covet the crown. More says some discerning contemporaries suspected that 'he long time forethought to be King in case that the King his brother (whose life he looked that evil diet should shorten) should happen to decease (as indeed he did) while his children were young.' Sir Thomas admits that this would never be known for certain, but plainly he considered it quite possible.

Gloucester also adopted a badge, his famous device of a white boar with golden tusks and golden bristles. There is no record of the reason for his choice. If we knew, it might well explain how he saw himself. Admittedly, members of the House of York had borne a boar before, but it had been blue and not white. Perhaps, in the symbolism so dear to the fifteenth century, the colour was intended to represent purity of heart and loyalty. As for the animal, it was pre-eminently an emblem of ferocity; Malory's Sir Gawain was 'as brim [fierce] as any boar'. The great seventeenth-century herald, Guillim, describes its significance in terms which might just possibly be thought to have been inspired by Richard's reputation, but certainly reflect what late mediaeval Englishmen thought of the boar. He is 'the most absolute champion among beasts' and 'so cruel and stomachful in his fight, that he foameth all the while for rage'. Guillim continues, 'The bearing of the boar in arms betokeneth a man of a bold spirit, skilful, politic in warlike feats, and one of that high resolution that he will rather die valorously in the field, than he will secure himself by ignominious flight.' These qualities were undoubtedly cultivated by the Duke.[2]

The failure of Oxford had shown even Clarence that he had little to hope from Lancastrian intrigues. But by now his brother the King was setting on foot a 'great enterprise' which was so exciting that for a while even George seems to have forgotten his discontent. Edward IV intended to revive the traditions of Henry V and launch an invasion across the English Channel—after all, he styled himself King of France and had been born in Normandy. He was too practical to hope to reconquer the lost kingdom, but there was an excellent possibility that he might gain some territory and even win a little glory. At the very least he could stop Louis XI from supporting Lancastrian intrigues. Edward's brother-in-law, Charles of Burgundy, was ready to revive the alliance with which Henry V had all but dispossessed the Valois, while the prospect of a lucrative raiding expedition into France had a deep appeal for most Englishmen—many of their forefathers, and even some still alive, had made their fortunes out of French plunder. When the King first discussed the matter with Parliament in 1472 he was immediately voted enough money to pay for 13,000 archers, though in the event it proved too difficult to levy these special taxes. However Edward managed to obtain another grant from Parliament, besides obtaining certain 'benevolences', or more or less forced loans, which he solicited personally from his richer subjects—as Gairdner says, 'curious stories are told of his success with wealthy widows.'

By the summer of 1475 the English expeditionary force was ready. It consisted of nearly 12,000 picked troops, including almost the entire English nobility. Richard brought 120 lancers and 1,000 archers—perhaps 1,360 men in all, since a 'lance' was a unit comprising a man-at-arms and two armed valets. He would also have taken a personal retinue of gentlemen and servants to wait on him during the campaign. Commynes undoubtedly reflects the opinion of his terrified master, Louis XI, when he tells us that the force was 'the largest, best disciplined, best mounted and best equipped army with which any English King ever invaded France.' The Milanese ambassador reported that Louis was so appalled that he 'has almost lost his wits.' On 4 July the English crossed to Calais. No doubt many of them looked forward to a second Agincourt.

Edward IV had every intention of fighting a full-scale war. But, as the shrewd and extremely knowledgeable Commynes afterwards suspected, the English King had by now grown too self indulgent—too fond of 'ease and pleasure'—to relish the prospect of a long-drawn-out conflict. Moreover it was already after mid-summer, dangerously late to start campaigning. Most serious of all, the Duke of Burgundy was busy in Germany, fighting to install his candidate for the Archbishopric of Cologne; when Duke Charles joined the English at Calais on 14 July, he brought only his personal bodyguard since the bulk of his troops were occupied in plundering Lorraine and hopelessly out of control—not quite a month later he said goodbye to Edward in order to go campaigning in Lorraine himself. Meanwhile Louis was advancing to meet the invaders with a large army.

Always at his wiliest when threatened, the French King had let Edward know that he was prepared to negotiate and would offer very attractive terms. Disheartened by the inadequacy of Burgundian assistance, the English King consulted his magnates as soon as Charles left and then decided to see what Louis XI had to offer. Among the few who are known to have opposed such a step was

Richard Gloucester; the twenty-three-year-old veteran of the campaign of 1471 plainly believed in war. But the French King was far too cunning not to be able to overcome all opposition when there was so much at stake. At Amiens a splendid entertainment was laid on for the entire English army—there were tables at the gates laden with wine and taverns where the troops could eat and drink free of charge. After three days most of them had got so drunk on free wine and gone on the rampage to such an extent that the infuriated Edward had to eject them from the town. This did nothing towards making him want to fight. On 29 August the two Kings met at Picquigny near Amiens, on a specially built bridge over the river. Commynes was present and says that Edward, who was accompanied by Clarence but not Gloucester, looked truly regal. 'Indeed I do not remember ever having seen such a fine looking man as he was when My Lord of Warwick made him flee from England,' he observes, but adds ominously that by now 'he was beginning to grow fat.' He also noted how the English King spoke 'very good French'. An agreement was quickly reached. In return for 75,000 crowns paid down and further annual payments of 50,000, Edward would leave French soil peacefully, English merchants would no longer suffer from French trade restrictions, and the infant Dauphin was betrothed to his eldest daughter. Both monarchs pledged themselves to help one another against rebellious subjects, and the French were allowed to ransom Margaret of Anjou. By 18 September Edward had left Calais. Louis XI joked 'I chased the English out of France far more easily than my father did—he had to do so by force of arms, but I simply used meat pies and good wine.'

Interestingly, Commynes tells us that at first Richard had been against the treaty. It is an exaggeration to guess, with Professor Myers, that he was 'honest and patriotic, as in the negotiations at Picquigny, when most of those around were corrupt'. We simply do not know his motives or what he felt, only that to begin with he did not like the treaty. We do know that, young as he was, he was clearly a realist. After Picquigny he visited Louis at Amiens and accepted magnificent presents, which included some fine plate and several superb horses.[3] He probably sailed from Calais with his brothers on 18 September. It was the end of his one visit to France.

Soon after, he was back at Middleham. Here he seems to have spent most of the next two years, though at the end of 1475 he was appointed a commissioner to inquire into treason and heresy in Dorset and Wiltshire. But his long-running quarrel with the Duke of Clarence was far from over, even if it now took the form of supporting the King against George's dissatisfaction.

For Clarence, that 'quicksand of deceit' as Shakespeare calls him, was impossible. He has bequeathed the impression of a golden boy, with all the good looks, splendid physique and glamorous charm of his elder brother. Rous describes him as 'right witty and well visaged', More as 'a goodly and well featured prince'. His appearance was so unmistakeably regal that it alarmed the Queen. Moreover, he seems to have been an unusually gifted speaker—Mancini heard he was 'a master of popular eloquence'. He was brave and he was daring. But he was also chronically unstable, vacillating to a degree which indicates serious neurosis and perhaps paranoia. (His younger brother may well have shared the same affliction though he never let it master his relations with Edward.) Professor Kendall suggests that Duke George's difficult temperament owed something to being spoilt as a child at Fotheringay by his sister Margaret, but this is mere speculation, even if there is evidence that they were fond of each other. A simpler, much more likely, explanation is that he suffered from a 'second-son' complex, a phenomen not quite extinct even today among modern English families of great wealth and rank who still believe in primogeniture.

In the last years of Clarence's stormy career Richard stayed mainly in the North. He now had a family, if a very small one, his son Edward of Middleham having been born in late 1473 or early 1474.[4] According to tradition the birth took place in the round tower at the south-west corner of Middleham Castle wall now known as 'The Prince's Tower'. He was given a 'mistress of the nursery', one Anne Idley whom Richard (in a letter to Sir William Stonor) calls 'our right well beloved servant'. Little Edward took on desperate importance in an age obsessed by dynastic pretensions. He had a wretchedly unhealthy inheritance. His aunt would die in childbirth, his mother would die in her twenties, and we know how sickly had been his father's own childhood. Richard therefore had something to distract him from his feud with Clarence—though the birth of an heir made him still more ambitious.

Clarence may have been disappointed by the outcome of 'the great enterprise of France'. An even worse disappointment awaited him. On 22 December 1476 the Duchess of Clarence died after a protracted illness in consequence of bearing a second son, and only ten days later Charles of Burgundy fell in battle against the Swiss. His widow urged Edward IV to let George marry her twenty-year-old step-daughter Mary, the heiress to Burgundy. But, the Crowland writer informs us, 'so high an exaltation of his ungrateful brother as that contemplated displeased the King. He made every possible objection and did everything he could to stop the marriage.' Edward was successful and Mary later married the Archduke Maximilian.[5]

Understandably Clarence was furious and, Russell continues, the two began 'to regard each other in a most unbrotherly way.' Courtiers were seen 'running to and fro, from one to the other, repeating every remark uttered by the brothers, even if they had said them in the most private rooms.' Edward also refused to let Clarence marry a Scottish princess. The Queen made matters worse by trying to obtain Mary's hand for her brother Lord Rivers—a proposal contemptuously dismissed by the Burgundian court, much to Elizabeth's humiliation. It increased her dislike of her brother-in-law, already strong enough. More comments 'women commonly, not of malice but of nature, hate them whom their husbands love.'

Duke George began to behave in a fashion which bordered on lunacy. He put about rumours that Edward was a bastard and had no right to the throne—rumours which would one day inspire Richard—and seems to have tried to foment armed disturbances in East Anglia. He refused ostentatiously to eat or drink during his rare visits to court, insinuating that he was frightened of being poisoned. He also claimed that his wife had been murdered. In April 1477 he sent nearly a hundred men to abduct a former waiting woman of the late Duchess, Ankarette Twynhoe, who was now in the Queen's service. This clearly very respectable lady was accused of administering 'a venomous drink, of ale mixed with poison' to the Duchess of Clarence. She was beaten, robbed of her jewellery, and then dragged off without a warrant from her home in Somerset to Clarence's castle at Warwick. Here she was hanged within twenty-four hours, after being condemned by a jury bullied into acquiescience by the Duke. In addition, with suicidal foolhardiness, he claimed that his wife had been bewitched by the Queen. (A charge of which Richard discreetly took note.)

Already angry, Edward struck back in similar fashion. He arrested an astronomer of evil repute—'also known to be a great necromancer'—Dr John Stacey of Merton College, Oxford and had him tortured till he admitted that he had cast horoscopes of the King and his son to learn when they would die. Stacey implicated a member of Clarence's household, Thomas Burdett—'a merchant dwelling in Cheapside, at the sign of the Crown, which is now the sign of the Flower-de-luce, over against Soper Lane', More remembered—on a plainly trumped-up charge. Both were found guilty of having 'imagined and compassed' the deaths of King Edward and the Prince of Wales, Burdett being additionally and more plausibly found guilty of inciting rebellion. Both were hanged at Tyburn on 20 May 1477, protesting their innocence. Their execution was clearly meant as a last warning to George. Unabashed, the Duke burst in on a Royal Council at Westminster when Edward was absent and insisted on having read out Stacey's and Burdett's denials. He had gone too far. By the end of the following month he was in the Tower.

Clarence's trial took place at Westminster in January 1478. Richard was among those present. The King told the Lords of George's scheming to destroy him and his family, of a 'much higher, much more malicious, more un-natural and loathly treason' than ever before, declared him 'incorrigible' and demanded a sentence of high treason. Accordingly Clarence was condemned to death and his children forfeited their inheritance. His mother, Duchess Cicely, protested at a public execution, so on 18 February he was murdered in

10. The Boar hat badge of one of Richard's followers. Found in the moat at Middleham. Yorkshire Museum, York.

11. Another of Richard's favourite residences in the North, Pontefract Castle where Edward V's uncle, Earl Rivers, and half-brother, Lord Richard Grey, were executed. Pontefract Public Library.

12. *Edward IV c. 1471. The man on the left wearing the Garter has been tentatively identified as Richard. British Library, London.*

13. *A staunch supporter, John Howard, 1st Duke of Norfolk, who was killed at Bosworth. A stained glass window, no longer in existence, formerly at Tendring Hall, Suffolk.*

14. *James III of Scotland with the future James IV, by Hugo van der Goes. (The boy was formerly believed to be Alexander, Duke of Albany.) Royal Collection.*

15. *Richard's London residence when Duke of Gloucester, Crosby Place in Bishopsgate. The building was later moved to Chelsea.*

the Tower, almost certainly drowned in a butt of Malmsey—Mancini heard that he had been 'plunged into a jar of sweet Falernian', Commynes says specifically that it was Malmsey, and his daughter afterwards wore a little wine cask at a bracelet on her wrist in memory of him. By a grim irony he was buried at Tewkesbury Abbey. He was still only twenty-eight.[6]

It was a horrible way to die. One contemporary foreign source, Molinet, says that the Duke himself suggested it to his brother— perhaps he had meant it as a joke. Beheading in private, strangling or smothering, would surely have been preferable. (Or drowning at sea like their brother-in-law, the Duke of Exeter, whose murder has never been solved.) Not even the wildest legends of the Borgias contain so exotically cruel and inhuman a killing. Beyond question there was a dark and sinister side to Edward IV. The Crowland writer tells us that he believed the King 'inwardly repented very often' Clarence's death, while More says 'piteously he bewailed and re-pented it.' Yet Polydore Vergil complains that, though he talked with many people who knew the court in those days, he could never obtain a convincing account of Edward's true motives.[7] We may guess that, like Machiavelli, the King thought that 'a Prince, so long as he keeps his subjects united and loyal, should not worry about being called cruel.'

The Duke of Gloucester's feelings about George's end are un-known. Mancini reports he was so overcome by grief that he could not hide it. More, while admitting that in public he opposed Clar-ence's killing, is not so sure. 'Some wise men also think that his drift, covertly conveyed, lacked not in helping forth his brother to his death, which he resisted openly, howbeit somewhat (as men deemed) more faintly than he that were heartily minded to his wel-fare.' Sir Thomas adds that the same observers thought it quite possible he was glad to see George out of the way in case it became feasible to aim at the throne. Vergil's information, that the King frequently lamented how no one had pleaded for Clarence's life, is significant; the youngest of the three brothers had not bothered.

Richard's anger was real enough, but it was anger at the triumph of the Queen and her kindred—even if he had stood aside and let them persuade Edward to destroy George. Undoubtedly his interces-sion would have saved him. One can only deduce that his failure to do so was deliberate. It is true that he would not obtain the rest of the Warwick estates, which went to the Crown. What he did gain was to become the nearest adult male in line of succession.

Gloucester had won his battle with Clarence. Three days before his uncle's bizarre death, little Edward of Middleham received one of his titles being made Earl of Salisbury. Three days after it Richard became again Great Chamberlain of England, an office which he had surrendered some years previously to his late brother at the King's request. At the very least this indicates a robustly unsentimental attitude.[8] However, as Francis Bacon observes of the Plantagenets, 'it was a race often dipped in their own blood.'

CHAPTER SEVEN

RICHARD IN THE NORTH

*'Free was he called of spending and somewhat above his power liberal;
with large gifts he got him unsteadfast friendship.'*
    Sir Thomas More, The History of King Richard the Third

*'He kept to his own domains and strove to make himself popular with
the people round about by granting favours and in his administration
of justice.'*
    Dominic Mancini, De Occupatione Regni Anglie
    per Riccardum Tercium

In the North Richard Gloucester became the mightiest subject that
any English King has ever had. By the end of his time there, not
even John of Gaunt or the Kingmaker had possessed more power or
independence. It was not just because of his wide lands and many
offices. It was a considerable achievement, since Northcountrymen
were not easy to govern and the region held ancient loyalties to
strongly entrenched families. Yet one may detect shortcomings.

Beyond question the Duke's overall administration was brilliantly
successful. It laid the foundation of the Council of the North, which
he set up when he was King and which lasted until Charles I's time.
This enabled Northerners' problems to be taken care of on the spot
instead of being referred to London. Always suspicious of Southerners, the Northcountry people must nonetheless have been flattered
that Richard so seldom left them, not even to go to court which—
Mancini heard—'he rarely visited.' There is no evidence that he
graced Gloucester with his presence before he became King nor that
he ever went to his enormous estates in South Wales. As Anne's
husband the Nevill's clan, with their countless retainers, accepted
him as a kinsman and gave him their loyalty. He strove consciously
to be worthy of it. Like his Nevill grandfather, he immersed himself
in Border politics, guarding his folk against Scots raiders. One may
guess that he took on Northcountry qualities, perhaps mannerisms;
conceivably a Yorkshire accent was among them. He was always on
ceaseless progress throughout the region. It is indisputable that his
firm hand and employment of Northern officials won him golden
opinions and devoted servants among the townsmen and among
some of the gentry. But in the end Gloucester's dependence on the
North and, above all, his omnipresence there were to help contribute
to his downfall.

The North—England north of the river Trent—was a bleak, often
rugged country. West of the Pennine Chain, the Lakeland hills of
Cumberland and Westmorland and the sandy wastes and moors of

Lancashire were generally poor and sparsely populated, though with pockets of good farmland. East of the Pennines, it was much more varied, rich wolds alternating with vast tracts of desolate moorland— even Derbyshire had its moors. York, the Northern capital, was large, rich and prosperous but the other two principal cities, Durham of the Prince Bishops and Carlisle, were comparatively small—Carlisle's walls being 'in compass scant a mile' according to Leland.

As a race the Northerners were all but intractable—in 1489 a mob lynched the Earl of Northumberland for failing to cut their taxes. They were hard men, harsh and dour. They grew rougher and more warlike still towards the Border, Shaftoes and Fenwicks being a byword for ferocity, a society organised for war. Their squires lived in fortified 'peel' towers, not just to defend themselves from the Scots but as protection against their neighbours. Robbery, rustling, arson and manslaughter were endemic. The South dreaded them. A proverb ran:

> 'Out of the North
> All ill comes forth.'

Gloucester was of course supreme in Cumberland, Westmorland, and West Yorkshire, where the bulk of his estates lay. (A local speciality there was the 'Carlisle axe', a peculiarly vicious form of halberd.) In addition, although Warden of only the West Marches against Scotland, he had tacit authority over Lord Northumberland, who was the Warden of the East and Middle Marches. And, as Steward of the Duchy of Lancaster, Richard was all powerful in much of Lancashire as well. In substance therefore he was more or less viceroy of England North of Trent. Yet before he became King he would strengthen his position even further.

The Duke was interested in every aspect of his new domain, down to its mineral wealth. He fell victim to the sales patter of some enterprising German miners—though one source says it was a certain George Willarby—who convinced him that silver would be found next to local deposits of copper. In 1475 he obtained the custody of mines in Westmorland from Edward IV, and he appears to have had copper mines operating at Keswick and Alston in Cumberland and also in Northumberland (jointly with the Earl). Ten per cent of the silver was to go to the King. There is no record of any being found.[1]

Understandably, Gloucester was frequently at York, an easy ride from his castle of Sheriff Hutton. The city boasted 12,000 inhabitants and sixty churches—with nine more outside the walls—as evidence of its prosperity. It contained countless artisans and tradesmen and still more merchants who, via the River Ouse and Kingston upon Hull, traded with the Low Countries, Germany, and the Baltic. The Duke took calculated pains to flatter them all, dealing with such petty matters as the removing of illegal fish traps from the local rivers, and intervening in a disputed election for Mayor. Sometimes he managed to have them exempted from taxes. In 1476 when the King wanted to punish the city for riots, he persuaded him to relent. On one occasion he even sent a member of his household to be tried by the Mayor and Corporation for insulting a citizen of York.

Richard also made a point of being present at the chief event in the city's year. This was the Mystery Plays, which were performed by the guilds on Corpus Christi—a feast falling between late May and June. As many as 600 players took part in fifty or more scenes staged on wagons in the streets around the Minster.[2] In 1477 the Duke and his Duchess tactfully joined the Corpus Christi Guild, one of the richest in York since it had close connections with the wealthy Merchant Adventurers Company. Graciously they walked in the guild's procession when it escorted the Host in its silver and beryl pyx to the great cathedral, led by priests in gorgeous vestments and acolytes carrying candles and burning incense as they chanted. Richard was never averse to a procession of this sort, having a marked taste for formal piety.

His modern defenders make much of his popularity in York. But however rich its citizens may have been, they were politically negligible even though they paid good taxes and supplied soldiers. It is a cliché among historians of the Wars of the Roses that the cities took little part in the struggle. The Duke should have concentrated his energies on winning more friends among the magnates.

Durham had considerable status as the capital of what was almost an independent country, a palatine bishopric comprising Co. Durham itself together with parts of Northumberland and some places in Yorkshire. It was a buffer state between England and Scotland over which the Prince Bishop ruled like a King, striking his own money. It was frequently attacked by the Scots and, if he had little say in its administration, Gloucester had cause to be concerned about its military situation.

For one of the Duke's problems was that his fief was a frontier land. Every so often Scots raiders struck deep into it, killing, plundering, burning, driving off cattle, in hit-and-run attacks. While York was too far south for them, Durham and Carlisle had always to be prepared for such irruptions, the people round about depending on fortified peel towers and *bastles* (i.e., bastilles) for protection. Richard had to be constantly on progress, not just to dispense justice among his violently quarrelsome subjects, but in order to organise the defences against invasion.

Carlisle, in Cumberland and only a few miles from the Border, was unmistakeably a frontier town. Built of red sandstone it possessed an imposing cathedral and a prosperous market but was dominated by the huge castle on its bluff which was intended—perhaps unrealistically—to strike fear into Scots. The latter, popularly known as 'Moss Troopers', terrorised the local countryside, sallying forth from hidden fastnesses in the 'Debatable Land', as the wild moors and marshes of the Solway Moss were called. Gloucester had to pay many visits to Carlisle.

A little town which he also visited on a number of occasions was Scarborough in Yorkshire. Like York it had once been controlled by the Earl of Northumberland, but Richard exchanged it for some of his wife's estates. He developed close links with it and may even have had a house there instead of using the great castle on the cliffs over the North Sea. It was the nearest port to Sheriff Hutton, and a fast horseman could reach it in a few hours. When he became King, Gloucester made it into a county of its own, an extraordinary distinction. The reason for his interest was undoubtedly privateering. The Scots raided by sea as well as by land, even in peacetime, chiefly from Leith, and the English retaliated. The Duke took his office of Lord High Admiral very seriously indeed. In the South he delegated his legal work to a Dr William Godyer, who heard cases appertaining to the sea on a Thames-side quay in Southwark. Here in the North Richard was able to play an active role and fitted out his own ships— in 1474 one of them, the *May Flower*, captured a vessel called *The Yellow Carvel* which belonged to the King of Scots and an embassy had to be sent to James III to apologise. Privateering was a nasty, cruel business, captured crews being generally thrown overboard without mercy. There is no record of the Duke sailing on any of these expeditions.

Most warfare waged by Richard was on land. In April 1474 the Duke of Albany, brother to the Scots King, prepared to repulse the Duke of Gloucester, who was rumoured to be about to raid either the West or the Middle Marches of Scotland. This particular raid does not seem to have taken place. (A few years later Richard was to meet Albany in very different circumstances.) But hostilities between English and Scots were perennial.

No great Northern lord can have liked having a Royal Duke, and an unusually formidable one, on his doorstep. Not only was Gloucester the King's brother, but through his mother and wife he was a Nevill as well, and if he had acquired Nevill lands he had also inherited Nevill feuds—something which he may not have quite understood. Even minor gentry must have been unsettled by so brutal a transference of loyalties as that which took place after the Yorkist triumph. Richard's presence constituted nothing less than a revolution—social and administrative as well as dynastic. It is logical to suspect that conservative Northern magnates were only too anxious to be rid of this meddlesome interloper, but because of the fear he inspired they hid their resentment under a mask of friendship and co-operation. The fact that he trusted them until the very last indicates a serious inability to judge his fellow men.

Above all, Gloucester misjudged the Percys. Until the rise of the Nevills they had been paramount in Northern England. As Lancastrians they had lost their Earldom of Northumberland with the third

Earl, who fell at Towton; many other members of the family had also died fighting against the House of York in the recent wars. Henry, the fourth Earl—six years older than Richard—had seen the inside of both the Fleet prison and the Tower before being restored to his lands and honours in 1469. Timid and indecisive, Lord Northumberland was quite ready to co-operate with Edward IV's all-powerful brother. But it was surely unrealistic to expect him, a genuine, canny Northcountryman, to be unshakeably loyal to someone who, apart from everything else, was a self-made, imitation Northerner, and who must have had irritating Southern ways. Furthermore, Gloucester was regarded as an ally by his wife's Nevill kindred—the very last association to recommend him to a Percy. Yet the Duke obviously trusted the Earl. It surely needed excessive self confidence to do so. Henry Percy was almost as supreme in the North East as Gloucester was in the North West and in addition commanded a deep, traditional, respect throughout the North as a whole. The Duke took the greatest pains to be tactful, acting jointly with him whenever possible. But even if there was a species of condominium and if he was accorded a second-in-command's rank, it was inevitable that Henry of Northumberland should resent Richard's primacy. It is plain that he particularly resented the Duke's influence in York, where once his forebears's wishes had always been respected; nowadays the citizens took every opportunity to appeal against him to Richard, who invariably supported them. Gloucester and Northumberland were always vying with one another, though perhaps they did not admit it to themselves. Forseeably—though not by the Duke—the Earl would eventually betray his rival.

Richard showed still more baseless sang-froid about another magnate, who was what would today be termed an outstanding security risk. Thomas, second Lord Stanley, born in 1435, belonged to a comparatively new great family which was still rising. During recent years it had acquired large estates in Cheshire, Lancashire, and Derbyshire. Its present head, once Warwick's brother-in-law, had twice switched his allegiance from York to Lancaster and then back again. As if that were not enough, his new wife was one of the last surviving Beauforts—Margaret, Countess of Richmond and mother to Henry Tudor. Yet however obviously a natural traitor, the 'wily fox' was always too clever for Gloucester. In the end Thomas Stanley would kill him, or see that someone else did.[3]

Henry, fourth Lord Scrope of Bolton, was one of the rare Northern magnates who might reasonably have been expected to be faithful to Gloucester. Born the same year as Stanley, he had an impeccably Yorkist background; not only had he fought with the King at Towton, but his grandfather had been executed in 1415 with Richard's grandfather for plotting against Henry V. Admittedly he had compromised briefly with Warwick in 1470, but had quickly returned to being Edward IV's loyal and useful servant. Nevertheless he bore a grudge;

he resented the failure to give him back the Lordship of Man, confiscated from his family at the beginning of the century and now held by the Stanleys—doubtless Gloucester often heard about this when visiting Scrope at his splendid stronghold of Bolton. As with Northumberland, the Duke clearly had complete trust in him.[4]

Another important magnate was Lord Greystoke, whose lands were scattered all over Cumberland and Northumberland. Apparently he was helpful enough. However, having been born the year before Agincourt, Ralph Greystoke had reached what was then considered a great age by the time Richard arrived in the North.

Not only the great families who retained their power constituted a potential danger. The Cliffords, who had once held sway throughout the Lake District and in much of Western Yorkshire, were old enemies of the House of York, long dispossessed. The tenth Lord Clifford had fallen in the battle against Gloucester's father, while the thirteenth—known as the 'black' or the 'butcher'—slaughtered the Duke's brother Rutland on the bridge at Wakefield, before being killed and attainted himself. Clifford's son Henry, only three years younger than Gloucester, was brought up secretly in remote Yorkshire or Lakeland farmhouses, so humbly that he could neither read nor write; the 'shepherd lord' would not recover his inheritance until after Bosworth. Meanwhile Richard occupied the Clifford Barony of Westmorland, the Clifford hereditary Sheriffdom of Cumberland and the Clifford family home at Skipton-in-Craven in the Pennines. Privately many North-Western gentry must have resented such a usurpation and being forced to abandon their traditional loyalties. And rumours circulated widely that there was still a Clifford heir in hiding.

The North was in fact full of danger. Over large areas nobility and gentry were unhappy, seriously unsettled, and they were the people who did the fighting. But, judging from his behaviour when King, Richard trusted almost implicitly anyone who came from the North. His administration there is cited by most historians, hostile or friendly, as evidence that he would have made an excellent monarch had he survived. Nevertheless, his failure to inspire loyalty among its magnates indicates a disastrous incapacity to make good friends.

The men who worked most closely with Richard in the North were Lords Northumberland, Stanley, Scrope, Greystoke and Lovell, Sir Richard Ratcliff, Sir Ralph Assheton, Sir James Tyrell, Sir Thomas Makenfield, Sir Thomas Everingham, Sir John Conyers, Sir John Savile, and Messrs Fairfax, Kendall, Harrington, Metcalfe and Pygott. These, with various unknown lawyers, were his administration's principal officers. Not all came from the North. Lovell was from Northamptonshire and Tyrell from Suffolk while Kendall, a 'household man' of the House of York, may possibly have originated from the West Country. But despite these exceptions it is clear that

Gloucester had a predilection for Northerners—it was to become increasingly apparent after he became King.

Naturally the Duke had as many dealings with the Lords Spiritual as with the Lords Temporal. Senior clerics were no less professional administrators than churchmen. Among the Archbishops of York, George Nevill—the Kingmaker's brother and Richard's near kinsman—was completely broken when he was released from imprisonment, to die in 1476; 'such goods as were gathered with sine were lost with sorrow', his very mitre being broken up and its jewels set in a crown. Despite being a former Chancellor of Queen Margaret's household and tutor to Prince Edward, who had once been suspended for Lancastrian sympathies, his successor Lawrence Booth gave no trouble. The humbly born Thomas Rotherham who succeeded Booth in 1480 gave useful assistance, although Lord Chancellor of England and more often in London than in York; one day Richard would put him in prison. At Durham William Dudley, a former Dean of Windsor, was to send his troops to fight for the Duke against the Scots on three occasions. At Carlisle John Story was a gifted administrator and well thought of at court, being appointed an executor of Edward IV's will; he acted as envoy to the Scots in 1471. Among the Bishops of Lincoln was John Russell, who was to be Richard's Lord Chancellor and (almost certainly) would write the continuation to the Crowland Chronicle.

Gloucester made a point of being on very amiable terms with religious houses. In particular he gave offerings to Our Lady of Jervaulx and to shrines at Fountains Abbey and at Coverham Abbey. (Leland notes 'there was good singing in Coverham'—perhaps it was the same in Richard's time.) The Duke presented £20 to the Abbot and Canons of Coverham to help them rebuild their church. All three were mitred Abbots and men of considerable influence, even if they did not sit in the House of Lords.

Richard was an ostentatiously munificent benefactor of the clergy. He paid for repairs at churches near his Yorkshire houses, among them Skipton-in-Craven and Sheriff Hutton where he built a new chapel. He did still more at Middleham, where he converted the parish church into a 'college' with a dean, six chaplains, four clerks and six choristers; their function was to celebrate Masses for the King and Queen and their children, for himself and his wife and son, his mother and sisters—for their 'good estate' when alive and for their souls when dead. The Masses were also for the souls of his father and dead brothers and sisters. There was an altar for each of Gloucester's favourite saints at this time, a fairly conventional selection—the Blessed Virgin, St George, St Catherine, St Cuthbert and St Barbara—apart from St Ninian.[5] He intended to found a similar but larger college at Barnard Castle, though this does not seem to have materialised; it was to have been dedicated to St Margaret and St

Ninian. (His devotion to the latter was perhaps a souvenir of some raid into Dumfriesshire.)

It has long been suggested—and almost equally long denied—that there may be significance in the fact that the licences for these foundations were both obtained on 21 February 1478. This was precisely three days after Clarence's killing, and also the same day that Gloucester acquired Clarence's office of Great Chamberlain. Whether there is any connection between the two events, Richard certainly believed that it was not just 'an holy and wholesome thing to pray for the dead', but a means of buying forgiveness for sins.

The Duke built on a large scale at his many residences. He had a string of mighty houses in his vast Northern territories, to serve as centres of local influence and to facilitate his constant journeying— not only he, but his large retinue as well, had to be accommodated and provided with fresh horses—and he was constantly improving his residences. For a time he also possessed a house in the South, Sudeley Castle in Gloucestershire, to which he added a superb great hall lit by huge Perpendicular windows with delicate tracery, though there is no evidence that he ever visited it. His real home, in so far as he had one at all, was divided between Middleham and Sheriff Hutton.

Middleham has already been described. Its rival, Sheriff Hutton, was closer to York and Scarborough. Only a few fragments remain of this once palatial house and a farm has been built inside its walls. Not even seventeenth-century prints preserve a glimpse of its splendours. Fortunately it was visited by Leland fifty years after Richard's death. He tells us 'The castle of Sheriff Hutton, as I learned there, was builded by Ralph of Raby, the first Earl of Westmorland of the Nevills [Gloucester's grandfather] . . . I marked in the forefront of the first area of the castle [it]self three great and high towers of which the gatehouse was the middle. In the second area there be a five or six towers, and the stately stair up to the hall is very magnificent, and so is the hall itself, and all the residue of the house, in so much that I saw no house in the North so like a princely lodgings.' Sheriff Hutton was the nexus of a group of princely manors which all belonged to Richard.

Another castle of which the Duke seems to have been fond was Pontefract in the West Riding, the southernmost of his Northern residences. He was also partial to Skipton-in-Craven, and to Barnard Castle in the extreme south west of Co. Durham. Built on a steep bank a hundred feet above the River Tees, the latter was almost as palatial as Sheriff Hutton, with two inner courtyards and, according to Leland, towers of 'great lodging'. With its outbuildings it was reputed to cover almost seven acres. Barnard Castle was at the foot of the Pennines and a useful staging place on the long ride from Middleham to Penrith. Constructed of red sandstone like Carlisle, eighteen miles away, Penrith was yet another of Warwick's former castles to which Richard grew attached. Here too he repaired the local church. Even today its windows preserve portraits said dubiously to be of his father and mother and of himself as King, and an inn in the town is still called The Gloucester Arms.

In addition the Duke must frequently have stayed with his subjects whether at the mansions of great lords, at Bishops' palaces or at abbeys. When he visited York, he usually seems to have been the guest of the Augustinian friars at Lendal. We know that he was not above sleeping at ordinary inns. Yet undoubtedly he preferred splendour, demanding magnificence in his own dwellings. Although he seldom came to London, sometime after 1475 he purchased Crosby Place in Bishopsgate which had been recently built by a rich woolman, Sir John Crosby. 'Very large and beautiful and the highest at that time in London', the Elizabethan antiquary John Stow informs us. (Forty years later it was bought by Thomas More—perhaps its ownership had something to do with his fascination with Richard.)

As Mancini says, Gloucester rarely went to court. The Italian believed that this absence was deliberate, to 'avoid the Queen's jealousy', which sounds likely enough. The Woodvilles were steadily increasing their already substantial power and influence. They consisted of Elizabeth's two sons, the Marquess of Dorset and Richard Grey—generally known as 'Lord Richard'—together with her brothers, Anthony, Earl Rivers, Sir Edward Woodville, Richard Woodville, and Lionel Woodville who was Bishop of Salisbury. In addition some, though not all of her brothers-in-law belonged to the party, which had acquired such useful recruits as Sir Thomas Vaughan, tutor to the Prince of Wales. Dorset and Sir Edward were reasonably formidable, but the real leader was Rivers.

Lord Rivers was an undeniably attractive figure, chivalrous, cultivated and travelled, a patron of letters, something of a mystic, and even a poet. Mancini gathered that 'Rivers was always thought of as a generous, sensible and fair minded man, who had shown his quality throughout every possible change of fortune. However successful, he had never harmed anyone but indeed had done many kind actions.' All these virtues did not stop Lord Rivers from being both ambitious and ruthless, and in the right circumstances he would obviously make the most of having 'the care and direction of the King's son'. In contrast to the Earl, the other three brothers were hated by everybody, not simply for their greed and lack of scruple but as upstarts. The 'old nobility' in particular detested them. Moreover, according to Mancini, the whole of England blamed them for the destruction of Clarence.

The Woodvilles and Greys were not the only people with influence at court. There were two much respected prelates. One was Richard's neighbour, the Archbishop of York and Lord Chancellor, Thomas Rotherham. The other was the even more formidable John Morton,

Bishop of Ely, who was More's future patron. And above all there was Hastings, Chamberlain of the Royal Household.

William, Lord Hastings was Edward IV's oldest and closest friend. Probably that alone was enough to make Elizabeth Woodville his enemy. 'Hastings against whom the Queen especially grudged for the favour the King bare him,' explains More. She also suspected he was a bad influence on her husband, 'familiar with the King in wanton company'. (She may well have been right; after his death Richard's propagandists would claim that the Chamberlain encouraged Edward 'by his evil company and sinister procuring . . . in vicious living and inordinate abusing of his body'.) Furthermore he had been a firm friend of Clarence; it was he who persuaded the Duke to come over from Warwick in 1471. He thought of himself as no less of a friend of Gloucester, his old comrade in arms—we know from More that Richard had a very high opinion of him. On the other hand there was venomously bad blood between Hastings and Dorset, if Mancini is to be believed. 'He maintained a deadly feud with the Queen's son,' we are told, 'on account of the mistresses they were always trying to steal or seduce from each other.' To cap everything, he was Governor of Calais, a post of vital importance which the Woodvilles coveted. While aware how much his wife loathed the man, Edward IV was unwilling to throw him over after a friendship of twenty years. It is true that on one occasion Rivers managed to slander him so convincingly that the Chamberlain found himself 'far fallen into the King's indignation and stood in great fear of himself' but 'it lasted not long.' (We only know of this incident from More.)

In 1480 Lord Hastings was fifty—approaching old age by fifteenth-century reckoning—a soldierly mixture of bravery, bluffness and frivolity, not very intelligent. But for all his failings he was deeply respected for his honesty and shining loyalty to the House of York, and one of the most influential men in England. Everyone except the Woodvilles liked Hastings. He was especially popular with the 'old nobility' who regarded him as their spokesman at court against the Queen and her kin.[6] (The phrase 'old nobility' was really a party label and simply meant those noblemen who disliked the Woodvilles and Greys. Far from being old, an entire new Yorkist peerage had been created; during his reign Edward made four Dukes, two Marquesses, eleven Earls, two Viscounts and six Barons—endowing them with the estates of peers who had backed the losing side.)

By the early 1480s it must have been obvious that Edward IV was going to pieces. At Picquigny Commynes had noticed that the King was putting on weight. Mancini, writing of his last years, tells us how Edward 'was most immoderate with his food and drink. I have heard that he used to take purges just for the pleasure of being able to stuff his stomach again. Because of his indulgence and because of the idleness to which he became so prone after regaining the Crown, he developed a huge stomach—although previously he had not only been tall but lean as well and led a strenuous life.' His womanising was equally out of control. Mancini also informs us that the King 'was lustful to an extreme degree and most insulting to the many women he seduced. As soon as he had satisfied his lust he abandoned them, handing them over to other courtiers, much against their will. Married and unmarried, noblewomen and wenches, he made no distinction, though at least he never raped anyone. He got them all through money or promises and having had them said goodbye to them.'

The Duke of Gloucester's devotion to the North Country can in part be explained by the fact that he saw it as a refuge. It is easy to believe that not only did he fear the Woodvilles, but that he was worried how he might be treated during his nephew's reign. It could be very dangerous to be the King's uncle as the two previous Dukes of Gloucester had discovered and, as has already been suggested, Richard may have shared Clarence's paranoia. He must also have seen the North as a power base. More knew many contemporaries who suspected that Richard had made plans to seize the throne should his nephews still be children on the death of Edward IV— 'whose life he looked that evil diet should shorten'.

This possibility did not occur to the King. In the final years of his reign he was devoting what remained of his energy to the situation in Scotland. Here the incompetence of James III offered considerable opportunities to the English. James had been seduced from the policy of friendship towards England by the ever industrious Louis XI and was turning a blind eye on large-scale raids over the border by his subjects, despite Edward's complaints. By the spring of 1480 Scots raiding had become intolerable. On 12 May the Duke of Gloucester was appointed Lieutenant-General in the North with powers to raise troops. Nevertheless the Earl of Angus—the redoubtable Archibald 'Bell-the-Cat'—overran and sacked Bamburgh on the Northumbrian coast. Gloucester retaliated in September with a counter raid, presumably killing, burning, and laying waste as the custom was. For the moment this quieted matters, but in November Edward decided that he would have to invade Scotland the following summer—'to make against the Scots rigorous and cruel war.'[7] During the winter of 1480–81 the Duke strengthened the walls of Carlisle, reinforced every garrison on the Border and called out levies for the coming campaign. He also assembled ships. In March 1481 he went down to London to discuss invasion plans.

Naval operations, based on both Scarborough and Newcastle, were entrusted to Lord Howard—the King's 'Lieutenant and Captain at Sea'. The future Duke of Norfolk, who was already over sixty and a veteran of the last campaigns of the Hundred Years War, had been an unwavering Yorkist from the very beginning. Knighted by Edward at Towton, he had remained uncompromisingly faithful during Henry VI's second reign, joining Edward as soon as he returned in 1471. He was one of the King's most useful servants, though violent-tempered and overbearing. Gloucester's association as Admiral with old 'Jockey'—or 'Jacky'—Howard plainly made for an enduring friendship which would have important consequences. Despite his age Howard was still ruthlessly ambitious, still an up-and-coming man. (He features, sometimes unpleasantly, in the *Paston Letters*.)[8] A very experienced sailor who had already fought and won several naval battles, on this occasion he proved a devastatingly effective 'Captain at Sea'. He had an excellent fleet crewed by 3,000 men, some of whom were equipped with brass hand guns specially brought over from the Calais arsenal. In May 1482, in his flagship *Mary Howard*, he took his ships openly into the Firth of Forth, appearing off Pittenweem and then off Leith. As soon as he located it, he sailed straight at the enemy fleet which he routed completely, capturing eight of its largest vessels and sinking the rest. Before sailing for home, he destroyed the little Port of Blackness on the North coast of the Firth. However, he had much less success on a second voyage into the Firth later that summer—by now the Scots knew better than to engage Lord Howard at sea.

It is likely that Gloucester personally directed naval operations on the West coast, in his capacity as Admiral. Here his trusted servant Sir Richard Ratcliff commanded a flotilla, which kept guard against Scots warships and privateers.

By contrast, the campaign on land was disappointing, even though Richard had the assistance of Lords Northumberland and Stanley. Edward was unexpectedly detained in the South by alarming disturbances and riots, which were caused by the savage taxes he was levying to pay for the war. Fat, overweight, jaded and tired, the King postponed the invasion. Meanwhile his brother besieged Berwick, which controlled the main road over the Eastern Border, but although it had only a small garrison it was defended by Archibald 'Bell-the-Cat'. Despite being invested by land and sea for the rest of the year and throughout the winter by Stanley, Archibald managed to hold the town—by the spring of 1482 merely the outer wall had fallen. At the same time James III had raised a large army in readiness for the English onslaught and during 1481 launched three separate attacks over the Border, burning some small towns and taking many English prisoners. They appear to have been intercepted and beaten back into Scotland by Gloucester and Northumberland, who followed them to burn and lay waste a wide area before retreating.

During the hard winter of 1481–82 the Duke was occupied in putting down riots all over the North in protest against the crushing war taxation. The Scots kept up their usual hit-and-run raids. However, in May 1482 Gloucester again swept over the Border, to storm and sack the not insignificant town of Dumfries.

If the main business was the continuing siege of Berwick, it was interrupted by countless little battles and skirmishes. While few details have survived, it seems that so much fighting gave the Duke a considerable military reputation. One long-forgotten battle, Hutton Field near Berwick, may have been a last Scots effort to relieve the town. Here old Sir Ralph Assheton—'The Black Knight of Ashton'— did such excellent service that Richard created him a Banneret on the spot. The Black Knight would do him even better service the following year.[9]

However the entire situation on the Border had been changed by the arrival in England of James III's brother at the end of 1482. The King of Scots was despised by his nobility, on account of excessively artistic tastes and low-born favourites, and was therefore vulnerable. At the same time his brother Alexander, Duke of Albany was consumed by ambition and suffered from a classic 'second-son' complex—Kendall's amusing phrase 'Clarence in a kilt' is probably very near the mark. And Albany was a much tougher and more resourceful character than King James. When imprisoned in 1479 in a high tower, he persuaded a 'chamber child' [valet] to help him kill the guards and escape; the boy fell from the tower, breaking his leg, so the Duke reached a ship to France and safety carrying him in his arms. He came to England at the invitation of Edward IV, who promised to help him if he would annul his marriage to the girl he had just wed in France at Louis XI's behest and marry Edward's daughter Cecily. In June 1482, in a treaty at Fotheringay, Albany pledged himself to surrender Berwick and other Border lands, to recognise English overlordship of Scotland, to abandon the 'auld alliance' with France and to marry Princess Cecily. In return the English recognised him as 'Alexander IV' and promised to help him oust James. There began a brief but fascinating partnership between the two ruthless brothers of two reigning monarchs. Richard Gloucester's ambition could well have been fuelled by that of Alexander Albany.

On 12 June 1482 Richard was again appointed Lieutenant-General in the North. By July the new hammer of the Scots and 'King Alexander' were ready to invade Scotland with 20,000 men, including Northumberland and Stanley.[10] They marched over the Border, devastating Berwickshire and Roxburghshire as they went. At Berwick the townsmen surrendered as soon as they saw the vast host, only the citadel holding out. By an extraordinary piece of luck, the invasion coincided with the Scots lords' decision to arrest James III on 22 July and imprison him in Edinburgh Castle. In consequence Gloucester was able to occupy the city of Edinburgh, without striking a blow, at the end of the month.

Richard's object was not so much to defeat the Scots—who in any case were already in total disarray—but to install 'Alexander IV' as a client King. However the latter needed time in which to build up support for his usurpation; accordingly, just like Edward IV in 1471,

Albany denied any designs on the Scots Crown and announced that he had merely come to reclaim his Duchy. He also asked Gloucester to leave Edinburgh. The Scots nobles then sued for peace with England. While emphasising that he had no full authority, Richard insisted on the immediate surrender of Berwick and on repayment of the dowry of Princess Cecily, who had once been betrothed to James III's son and heir as well as to Albany. The Scots quickly agreed to everything, even to the marriage of James's sister to Lord Rivers, one concession which no doubt did not exactly delight the Duke of Gloucester. After barely a fortnight's occupation at most, he retreated from Edinburgh and marched back to Berwick, whose citadel surrendered to him on 24 August. Even before the surrender he disbanded all save 1,700 men of his army in confident anticipation.

In the event, the Duke of Albany became briefly Lieutenant-General [Regent] of Scotland, but was ousted by King James before the year was out. Instead of the subservient Scots régime for which he hoped, Gloucester had merely obtained Berwick and a short truce. He had thrown away the chance of obtaining what could have been far more advantageous terms—and the occupation of Edinburgh had been made possible only because of a rare moment of Scots weakness. He had in fact misjudged Albany's ability and the whole political situation in Scotland.

The Crowland chronicler thought that Edward IV was privately furious at such an opportunity being lost. 'What he [Richard] achieved by this expedition . . . he needlessly squandered.' He adds that to keep and defend Berwick was a ruinously costly business. Beyond question Gloucester had shown remarkably poor political judgement—perhaps he was carried away by a megalomaniac chimera of subduing all Scotland. However, English joy at having occupied the enemy capital and at what appeared superficially to be a great victory no doubt mollified his brother to some extent. All over England there were salvos from cannon and bonfires, in celebration.

For the war with Scotland of 1480–83 was seen as much more than a mere Border skirmish, even if there had been no pitched battles. Englishmen regarded it as a full-scale conflict with a foreign power. They had been driven out of France by Charles VII and then tricked out of it at Picquigny by Louis XI, and Richard had won the first English victory over foreigners since the days of Old Talbot's triumphs—if anything, they hated the Scots more than the French. In the autumn of 1482 most Englishmen considered the Duke of Gloucester a national hero.

At thirty Richard was a slightly built, very short and thin man with slender limbs. He bore a striking resemblance to his 'most dread and dear father' the Duke of York; if More is to be believed, Richard's propagandist Dr Sha saw in him 'the sure undoubted image, the plain express likeness of the noble Duke, whose remembrance can never die while he lives.' To judge from a comparison between the

Society of Antiquaries' portrait of him and a series of contemporary miniatures of Margaret of York, he also had some resemblance to his sister—a small woman with sharp, peaked features. Almost all contemporary descriptions testify that Gloucester was unusually small—physically it was his most noticeable characteristic. Rous speaks of 'his little body and feeble strength', and Vergil says he was 'little of stature'. (One guesses at a height of five feet six inches, at most.) Probably the irregularity of his shoulders and deformed arm were barely apparent, no doubt disguised by the tailor's art. He had undeniably good features, but to judge from surviving portraits, they always wore an oddly restless and distracted look. Sir Thomas, who had spoken to many people who remembered the Duke, tells us he was 'hard favoured of visage and such as in princes is called warlike, in other men otherwise.' Polydore Vergil is more specific—he had a 'short and sour countenance'. (A figure in a Flemish miniature of about 1470, tentatively identified as Gloucester, shows a strangely sharp and acid face.) The Crowland writer, describing his appearance at Bosworth, speaks of 'a countenance which, always attenuated was on this occasion more livid and ghastly than usual.' Making allowances for partisan exaggeration, it is reasonable to deduce from this eyewitness testimony that Richard's face was oddly thin and pale with almost feverishly bright eyes. Vergil adds that when the Duke was thinking he would constantly bite his lip and toy with the dagger at his belt—drawing it half out of the sheath and then thrusting it back again.

One has then the impression of a tense, highly strung—perhaps neurotic—little creature, wiry, full of energy and quick in his movements, with a harsh, aggressive expression. It is probable that he was impatient, easily irritated. More pictures him in a rage 'with a wonderfully sour angry countenance, knitting the brows, frowning, and fretting and gnawing on his lip'. However Sir Thomas also makes it clear that Richard had plenty of charm if he cared to use it, with an amiable and unassuming manner—on occasion he could be 'merry' and 'companionable'. Even Rous admits that he had 'a smooth front'. But since More describes him as 'close and secret', and Mancini confirms that he was renowned for concealing his real thoughts, one may guess that normally he was reserved and uncommunicative. It is obvious that the Duke of Gloucester was an alarmingly forceful personality—Vergil describes him as 'a man much to be feared for circumspection and celerity' while the Crowland chronicler says that he was swift and alert, with an 'overweening mind'.[11]

We know almost nothing of his personal tastes. As with his houses, a love of ostentation is discernible in his indulgence in fine clothes. This is by no means invariably the case among great lords of his time—Louis XI was renowned for his shabbiness—though admittedly Edward IV always dressed with the utmost splendour. It is reasonable to speculate that the Duke may have been trying to compensate for his unimpressive physique. Like Edward, he was a keen hunting man, though he does not seem to have shared his brother's weakness for whoring. He also had a passion for hawking, that most dramatic and savage of field sports; when he became King he bought goshawks, peregrines and lanner falcons all over England and Wales and sent a man 'beyond seas' to purchase birds of prey—presumably the magnificent gerfalcons. Entertainments listed in his household accounts indicate that he was not unconvivial. Probably he was one of those men who are happiest when working—in his case at politics, administration, and soldiering.

His reading, as with most noblemen of the age, is likely to have been very limited. (Almost certainly he read aloud to himself, since this was then the custom.) Apart from religious works, few books which belonged to Richard have been identified. Among them are Aegidius on statecraft, a *Tristan*, William of Worcester's collection of documents about Normandy, and the so-called *Chronicle of John of Brompton*; the last was a history of Britain supposedly written by an Abbot of Jervaulx, a monastery known to the Duke since childhood and where he maintained a stable of horses. Two others were clearly favourites. A book of tales, including two by Chaucer, bears the inscription '*tant le desiree R. Gloucestre*' in his own hand, while an English translation of Vegetius's *De Re Militari*—the standard treatise on war for mediaeval man—is the only illuminated manuscript which is known to have been commissioned by him.

Yet it is not too fanciful to discern an enthusiasm for the fashionable literature of the day. To some extent—in his own eyes at any rate—Richard seems to have modelled himself on the heroes of the knightly romance. Indeed his own death can be seen as positively Arthurian; it is ironical that the *Morte d'Arthur* was printed during the last weeks of his life. His motto and badge, his interest in heraldry, all reveal the obsession with chivalry displayed by most great princes at that time.

By now the Duke of Gloucester had clearly acquired a considerable reputation as a military commander. 'A courageous and most daring prince', the Crowland chronicler calls him. 'In warfare such was his renown that any difficult or dangerous task necessary for the safety of the realm was entrusted to his direction and generalship' says Mancini. 'No evil captain was he in the war, as to which his disposition was more meat than for peace' comments More, who adds that the Duke had both defeats and victories but never for want of bravery or ability. Yet while contemporary Englishmen hailed Richard as a hero for his exploits on the Border, he never actually commanded an army in a pitched battle until Bosworth. All his experience was of raiding and guerilla warfare, and ultimately it failed him. Professor Charles Ross, the most authoritative historian of the Wars of the Roses, admits that the Duke's gifts as a soldier have been inflated— 'His military ability remains an open question.'

Perhaps Richard reveals a little of himself in the pattern of his religious life, which has never been properly examined. He must have absorbed something of his mother's piety to judge from his spiritual reading. Some years ago a manuscript English Bible, Wycliff's translation, was discovered in a New York library. Its history is unknown but the name 'Richard Gloucester' is written in it in his hand. If one is going too far in ascribing his desire to read a forbidden work—forbidden in the vernacular—to fear of personal damnation, it at least shows intense curiosity in the meaning of his religion. He was certainly no Lollard, and impeccably Catholic in believing in penance and atonement, in the efficacy of good works and the intercession of saints. He venerated relics, and was constantly going on pilgrimage, visiting shrines barefoot, taking part in religious processions and endowing chantries to pray for souls of his dead kindred. Plainly the next world was very real to him. The fact that none of this inhibited a complete lack of scruple indicates a certain ability to lose touch with reality and a weakness for self-deception. But Milton (in *Eikonoklastes*) was very wide of the mark in discerning in Richard 'a deep dissembler, not of his affections only, but of his religion'.

At the end of 1482 the Duke of Gloucester rode down to London to receive a hero's welcome and to spend Christmas with his brother and attend the forthcoming Parliament. It is more than likely that during his stay at court he was unpleasantly reminded yet again of just how dangerous were the Queen and the Woodvilles, and that he tried to strengthen his links with the anti-Woodville faction. More says specifically that 'he was well aware of, and helped to maintain a long-continued grudge and heart-burning between the Queen's kindred and the King's blood'—the latter being Hastings and the 'old nobility'.

When Parliament met in January 1483, it was full of praise for the Duke's conduct of the war with Scotland. At the King's request it passed legislation to give him the hereditary Wardenship of the West Marches, a hereditary right to the office of Constable of Carlisle (together with the castle and to all Crown lands in Cumberland, besides virtually regal powers over the county and also over the thirty miles of Scots Border country he now controlled—with the same powers over any more Scots territory he might overrun. He was even authorised to naturalise Scots as Englishmen under his own seal, receiving exactly the same palatine powers as the Prince Bishop of Durham. He had been given, in fact if not name, an independent principality of his own in the North West.

For the Earl of Northumberland all this must have been very bitter news indeed. It looked as though the Percys had finally—and permanently—lost their position as the leading family of the North of England.

It was typical of Gloucester that he should ask Parliament to exempt the Northern counties from the latest round of taxation. As More discerned, he was prodigal in buying unreliable support. It was not a realistic policy, could not be continued when he became King, and would end only in disappointed expectations and unpopularity.

In the last days of February he said a no doubt grateful goodbye to Edward IV, who must have been failing visibly. He never saw him again. There may be some truth in stories of the King's dejection at his setbacks in foreign policy, the opportunity missed in Scotland and the realization that Louis XI had acquired half Burgundy by betrothing the Dauphin to its heiress, and by his reconciliation to the titular Habsburg Duke at the Treaty of Arras. In any case gluttony and whoring had ruined his once magnificent constitution. The Crowland writer refers to him at this time as 'a man of such corpulence and so fond of boon companionship, vanities, debauchery, extravagance and sensual enjoyments'.

The French chronicler Basin records that on Good Friday 1483 Edward suffered a terrible fit of indigestion, from stuffing himself with fruit and vegetables. Mancini, who was then in London, recounts how just after Easter the King went in a small boat to watch some fishing, presumably on the Thames 'Being a tall and very fat man, though not exactly mis-shapen, he let the damp cold chill his guts . . . and caught a sickness from which he never recovered.' Shortly after the fishing expedition he seems to have had a stroke—Commynes says it was an apoplexy—but his doctors could not diagnose what was wrong. Nevertheless, Edward himself soon 'perceived his natural strength so sore enfeebled that he despaired all recovery.' Not long before he died, he summoned Hastings and the Woodvilles to his bedside, begging them to be reconciled—he was so weak that he could not stay sitting up and finished his plea lying on his side. Everyone shed tears and shook hands, even Dorset. Edward IV died on 9 April 1483. 'I was the King and kept you from your foe,' wrote the poet laureate Skelton in his funeral elegy.

The news reached Richard, apparently at Middleham, two days later. It was brought by one of Hastings's men, who must have ridden like the wind. Having seen a good deal of his brother in recent months, the Duke cannot have been entirely surprised.[12]

More tells of an ominous incident. The 'same night that King Edward died, one called Mistlebrook, long ere the day sprung, came in great haste to the house of one Pottyer dwelling in Redcross Street without Cripplegate; and when he was with hasty rapping quickly let in, the said Mistlebrook showed unto Pottyer that King Edward was departed. "By my troth, man," quoth Pottyer, "then will my master the Duke of Gloucester be King." ' Sir Thomas adds (in his Latin version of the *History*) that he heard this story from his father, who was then living in Milk Street in the same ward as Redcross Street. William Mistlebrook and Richard Pottyer undoubtedly existed and have been identified by modern historians; shortly after Gloucester had indeed become King, the latter was appointed an attorney of the Duchy of Lancaster in Chancery—hitherto he may have been the Duke's attorney in Chancery. Plainly Pottyer knew his master only too well.

CHAPTER EIGHT

PROTECTOR AND DEFENDER

'Richard, Brother and Uncle of Kings, Duke of Gloucester, Protector, Defender, Great Chamberlain, Constable and Admiral of England.'
A proclamation of June 1483

'I pray God he may prove a Protector, rather than a destroyer.''
Sir Thomas More, The History of King Richard the Third

A power struggle was inevitable. During Henry VI's minority Humphrey, Duke of Gloucester, had been titular Protector, but the government had really been controlled by the Beauforts. The Woodvilles intended to do the same, to rule England during the minority of Edward V; probably they hoped to recreate the régime, under Elizabeth's control, which had briefly existed in 1475 during his father's absence in France. Neither they nor the twelve-year-old King ever stood a chance against Richard, who was to bring off one of the most brilliant double *coups d'état* in history.

At the beginning the Woodvilles were apparently unassailable and should have come to an arrangement with Gloucester without too much difficulty. Yet within three weeks they had been outwitted and destroyed and Richard was an all powerful Protector—within another seven he was King. Few seizures of power have gone off with such smooth precision. The most plausible inference is, as both Mancini and More suggest, that Gloucester had long been preparing for it.[1]

At least one great nobleman knew which way the wind would blow. More states that—'as I have for certain been informed'—the Duke of Buckingham despatched a trusted agent called Persivell to Richard at York as soon as Edward IV died. Gloucester 'caused him in the dead of night after all other folk departed to be brought unto him in his secret chamber.' The messenger told him that his master was ready to help him in any way he wanted, with 'a thousand good fellows if need be'. He was sent back to Buckingham, still at his principal estate in Brecon with thanks and secret instructions.

As he played so important a part in subsequent events, it is necessary to know something of Henry Stafford, Duke of Buckingham. Like the House of York he was doubly descended from Edward III (through Thomas of Lancaster and John of Gaunt). His father and his maternal grandfather—the second Duke of Somerset—had both perished at St Albans in 1455, his other grandfather at Northampton in 1460, while all his Beaufort uncles had been slain. After the shadowy figure of Henry Tudor, Buckingham was therefore the Beaufort heir to the throne. With such a background he had been understandably mistrusted by Edward IV. And ever since being forcibly married to a Woodville at the age of eleven he had detested his in-laws with a venomous hatred which was reciprocated. As the greatest of the 'old nobility', he was their natural enemy. Besides resenting the deliberate exclusion from public life which he had had to suffer under the late King, the Duke coveted the vast Bohun estates, to which he had an arguable claim. Desperately haughty and ambitious—'a proud minded man and evilly could bear the glory of another'—he was furious at the way he had been treated. Moreover it is likely that he secretly regarded the pretensions of the House of York as being no less upstart than those of the House of Woodville, and he would be just as ready to pull down Richard III as Edward V—probably he had always been a Lancastrian at heart. His motto *souvent me souvient* ('often I remember') is ominously revealing—he laboured under a permanent grudge. However, at the moment he was motivated principally by hatred of the Woodvilles.[2]

Not quite thirty—only a little younger than Richard—'Harry Buckingham' as he signed himself, was not only immensely rich, but very clever and very enterprising. More heard that he was strikingly handsome and impressive in appearance, and a marvellously persuasive speaker. He seems to have possessed genuine personal magnetism. Undoubtedly Gloucester was to succumb to his charm. It was yet another instance of Richard's fatal inability to judge men, for among Buckingham's many gifts was that of concealing his true feelings.

As has been said, the Woodvilles must have seemed in a very strong position indeed in the weeks after Edward IV's death. They were in the South and the Duke of Gloucester was in the North. Their leader, the tough and able Lord Rivers—'as valiant of hand as politic in counsel'—already had custody of Edward V, as his Governor. In London Dorset, their second-in-command, took possession of the Royal Treasury at the Tower, and on the coast Sir Edward Woodville was appointed Captain of the King's Ships. Above all, their party was in a majority on the Council, which met despite Richard's absence, and which was perfectly legal. 'We are quite important enough to make laws and govern by ourselves, without the King's uncle' announced Dorset. Some members of the Council, led by Lord Hastings—still Lord Chamberlain—proposed that Gloucester should be made Protector as stipulated in Edward IV's will. But the Woodville party insisted that the Council as a whole must rule; while the Duke of Gloucester might belong to it, he could only be 'chief councillor'. They argued, perhaps rather unskilfully, that if the entire administration were entrusted to one man he might try to usurp the throne. The Council also fixed the date of the Coronation for Sunday 4 May.

Unfortunately, power had gone to the Marquess of Dorset's head.

He was issuing orders in his name and in that of Rivers, describing themselves as 'Brother Uterine to the King' and 'Uncle to the King'. The rest of the Council grew resentful. Hastings burst out furiously that the blood of the Queen's kindred was too base for them to govern the realm. When it was suggested that Edward V should be escorted to London by a large army, the Lord Chamberlain demanded to know if it was intended for 'use against the people of England' and threatened to withdraw to his garrison at Calais. Privately he sent frantic letters and messages to Richard, warning him that he must act quickly if he hoped to regain control of the government from the Woodvilles.

All the 'old nobility', and not only Buckingham and Hastings, were anxious to block a Woodville takeover. Skilfully Gloucester warned everyone who disliked the Woodvilles—'some by mouth, some by writing and secret messengers'—that they were all in danger if 'our well-proved ill-willers' got control of the King and the government. Indeed, save for the threat by the Woodvilles the English magnates might very well have tried to limit his powers as Protector, as had been done with Duke Humphrey sixty years previously. But in the circumstances they could not afford to bargain and they therefore accepted Richard's leadership. As for the rest of the country, he set about arousing widespread indignation by fabricating rumours of plots by the Queen's kindred.

At the same time the Duke wrote disarmingly to the Council. He stressed how he had always been loyal to his brother and promised to be equally loyal, not only to Edward V but to any sister who might succeed him—should the boy die, 'which God forbid'. He was ready to defend them with his life. He also begged the Council to remember his claims when deciding the new government, citing his own rights and Edward IVs will. Richard ensured that his letter was widely circulated. It made a noticeable impression on public opinion which began to support him 'openly and loudly', according to Mancini—'it was commonly said by everyone that the Duke ought to have the government.'

Gloucester's most urgent problem was to stop the King reaching London ahead of him. If he were crowned the Woodvilles would be able to argue that this precluded a Protector, as had happened after the crowning of the young Henry VI, when the then Protector's powers had at once passed to the Council. Edward was at Ludlow, where he had been spending his childhood, together with his uncle, Earl Rivers. We now know that their only hope would have been to hasten to the capital as fast as possible or to gather a large army. But they delayed to celebrate St George's Day, the festival of the Knights of the Garter, on 23 April. More alleges that Richard's agents tricked the Queen—presumably already alarmed by Hastings's outburst—into sending word to Rivers not to bring too big an escort in case it should provoke a hostile reaction. In the event, when the King set out unhurriedly for London on 24 April he did so with 'a sober company' of some 2,000 men, though most of these were probably unarmed servants. Gloucester and Buckingham had written to ask if they might join him *en route* and accompany him when he made his ceremonial entry into his capital. They 'wrote unto the King so reverently and to the Queen's friends there so lovingly', More tells us, that Rivers agreed to meet them at Northampton.

Meanwhile, Richard, in black from head to foot and attended by 300 retainers similarly clad, took part in a Requiem for Edward IV at York Minister on 20 April. During the Mass he wept, shedding 'plenteous tears'. After it was over he took the oath of fealty to the new King, making all the Northern nobility present swear allegiance. Then, probably on the same day, he and his men rode South in their mourning. Through Persivell he had again been in contact with the Duke of Buckingham, whom he told to rendez-vous with him at Northampton, but to bring only 300 men instead of 'a thousand good fellows'—no doubt to avoid arousing suspicion.

Lord Rivers and his nephew reached Northampton on Tuesday 29 April. But when Gloucester and Buckingham rode in that afternoon, the royal party had already gone on to Stony Stratford, fourteen miles further south. Plainly Rivers was in no mood to wait—he had been joined at Northampton by the King's younger half-brother, Lord Richard Grey, who may well have brought a letter from Dorset urging him to make haste. Hearing of the Dukes' arrival, Rivers went back with a small escort to explain to them that he had gone on to Stony Stratford only because there was not enough accommodation in Northampton for both retinues. Tactfully he addressed Richard as 'My Lord Protector', although everyone knew very well that he and his followers were determined to deny the office to the Duke. For their part Gloucester and Buckingham greeted him with the utmost amiability and friendliness, inviting him to stay for supper—he could spend the night at the inn next door.

According to Mancini, Lord Rivers and Gloucester 'passed a great part of the night in conviviality' before going to bed. (In striking contrast to the 'austere' image of the Duke created by modern historians.) More on the other hand implies that they merely spent the evening together, Gloucester making Rivers 'friendly cheer' and then saying goodnight 'very familiar, with great courtesy'. But he adds that after the Earl had retired, Richard and Buckingham sat up talking until dawn, with a few trusted friends, including Richard Ratcliff.

The inn in which Rivers and his men were staying must have been the usual rambling half-timbered structure of the period, very like the Tabard in *The Canterbury Tales*. Its guests would be dispersed in sleeping quarters up and down many long galleries. In 'the dawning of the day' the two Dukes—who had apparently not been to bed—sent orders to their men to muster as quietly as possible. They then obtained the keys of Rivers's inn and locked all the outer doors, besides setting up road blocks on the route to Stony Stratford so that no one could pass. When the Earl awoke and found himself shut in, he 'marvellously disliked it.' But he put on a brave face and went to Gloucester and Buckingham, demanding to know what was happening. Their answer was to accuse him of trying to turn young Edward against them, after which they arrested him.

The two Dukes then took their entire force and galloped the fourteen miles to Stony Stratford as fast as possible. There they found the little King already on horseback and about to leave. He was with Richard Grey and two gentlemen of his household—his aged Chamberlain, Sir Thomas Vaughan, a veteran Yorkist who had carried him in state processions when he was a baby, and Sir Richard Haute, yet another kinsman of the Queen. Gloucester 'did not omit or refuse to pay every mark of respect to the King his nephew, in the way of uncovering his head, bending the knee or other posture required of a subject', the Crowland chronicler observes sardonically. It is likely that he told them he had important news which could only be imparted privately and that they went back into their inn, since Mancini says that Edward was separated from his soldiers during the scene which followed. After offering him his condolences on the death of the late King, Richard warned the boy that his father's friends had ruined his health by encouraging him in his vices and would try to do the same with his son—they must be removed. Grey protested indignantly but Buckingham told him to hold his tongue. Gloucester continued that these people were plotting his own death and preparing to attack him on the way to London or in the capital itself—everybody knew they planned to stop him becoming Protector. He also insisted that Rivers and Dorset were scheming to rule young Edward and the realm for themselves and intended to 'destroy the old nobility', and that not only had Dorset seized the Royal Treasury but he had taken money from it.

'What my brother Marquess hath done, I cannot say,' Edward replied with surprising self possession, 'but in good faith, I dare well answer for my uncle Rivers and my brother here that they be innocent of any such matters.' The Duke of Buckingham broke in rudely 'They have kept the dealing of these matters far from the knowledge of your good Grace.' When the boy went on to say that he had complete confidence in the ability of his lords and the Queen to govern his Kingdom, Buckingham again interrupted roughly to say that it was 'not the business of women but of men to rule Kingdoms and if he had any confidence in her he had better relinquish it.' Edward gave in to his uncle of Gloucester—while the Dukes were respectful enough, it was abundantly clear that they were insisting and not merely asking. They then arrested Grey, Vaughan and Haute. They also dismissed all the King's household servants, many of whom he must have known throughout his short life, sending them home and replacing them by reliable men of their own. Even his tutor, John Alcock, Bishop of Worcester was sent away. The boy wept, 'but it booted not.'

Richard and Buckingham returned to Northampton for a triumphant dinner. (This, the main meal of the day, was eaten between 9.00 a.m. and noon.) During it Gloucester was in such a good mood that he sent a dish from his table to Lord Rivers, 'praying him to be of good cheer and all should be well'. As with so many other vivid scenes in his history, More's version of the affair at Northampton and Stony Stratford may not perhaps be completely accurate, but nevertheless it plainly contains many details which can only have been obtained from eye witnesses. Richard's amiable gesture towards Rivers gives us a fascinating glimpse of his almost Italianate combination of courtesy and cynicism—far from all being 'well', with hindsight we know that he must have had every intention of killing Rivers as soon as possible. Two days later he sent the prisoners to his strongholds in the North, where they would soon be beheaded without trial. As soon as he became Protector he at once seized their estates although they had not been found guilty of any crime.

The news reached London a little before midnight on the following day, Thursday 1 May. More says that on hearing it the Queen broke into lamentations, 'in great flutter and heaviness, bewailing her child's ruin, her friends' mischance and her own misfortune', and cursed her mistake in persuading her brother from gathering an army. She at once took sanctuary in the Abbot's Lodging at Westminster, bringing with her the nine-year-old Duke of York and her daughters. Dorset made a feeble attempt to find troops, but quickly despaired and joined his mother at Westminster. She was having all her furniture brought with her; there was 'much heaviness, rumble, haste and business, carriage and conveyance of her stuff into sanctuary, chests, coffers, packs, bundles, trusses, all on men's backs, no man unoccupied, some lading, some going, some discharging, some coming for more.' (Even at this terrifying moment her avarice did not desert her.) However, when the Lord Chancellor, Archbishop Rotherham of York, came in the middle of the night bringing a message which he had received from Lord Hastings, he found Elizabeth Woodville sitting 'alone a-low on the rushes, all desolate and dismayed'. She was not reassured by her old enemy's message that 'all shall be well'—it is ironical that it was exactly what Gloucester had been telling her brother. 'Ah, woe be to him!' she cried, referring to Hastings, 'for he is one of them that labour to destroy me and my blood.' After leaving her the Great Seal—presumably as a kind of placebo since there was little use she could make of it—Rotherham returned to his palace by the Thames. It was already dawn and when he looked out from his window he saw that the river opposite Westminster was crowded by boats manned by the Duke of Gloucester's retainers, who were intent on stopping anyone getting in or out.

Most people in London were horrified. Many gentlemen put on

armour. Mancini reports that 'a sinister rumour' started to circulate that Gloucester intended to seize the throne, and More too says that it was generally believed that the Duke was attacking not just the Woodvilles but the little King himself. Next day a group of peers met anxiously to discuss the situation. However Hastings, whose loyalty was known by everyone to be impeccable, persuaded them that Richard had no designs on the crown but was merely protecting himself against the Woodvilles. The alarm began to die down—what was left of it would be quickly dispelled by the Duke when he arrived in the capital on Sunday 4 May. Even so, Mancini tells us 'Some, however, who realized his ambition and his cunning, always suspected where his enterprise would lead.'

Before Edward V and his escort reached London, they were met at Hornsey Park by the Lord Mayor, Aldermen and Sheriffs of the City on horseback, clad in red, and by 500 members of the twelve great livery companies, also mounted but wearing violet. The long cortège continued to the Bishop of London's palace next to St Paul's Cathedral, where the King was to lodge. Everyone was delighted by the respectful way in which the Duke of Gloucester treated his nephew, a small yet striking fair-haired figure in purple velvet. As they rode to St Paul's, Richard, still in mourner's black, repeatedly bowed low from the saddle and presented him to the cheering crowds—'Behold your Prince and Sovereign Lord!'

At the same time, the Dukes' servants showed the spectators four cartloads of armour they had brought with them, shouting 'Here be the barrels of armour that these traitors had privily conveyed in their baggage to destroy the noble lords!' More comments that any intelligent man was sceptical, while Mancini says the armour was meant for the Scottish war. Nevertheless most people were quite convinced of the Woodvilles' evil designs, muttering it was good enough evidence to hang them.

From being under a cloud, Gloucester now became trusted to the point of adulation. His violence at Northampton and Stony Stratford was explained away as being necessary 'to part the Queen's proud kindred from the Prince' [Edward V]. All too many people were glad to see the Woodvilles go down—the Crowland chronicler says that Lord Hastings was 'bursting with joy at the way events were turning out'. The next Council made Richard Protector of the Realm and of the King, with absolute power. More remarks 'the lamb was betaken to the wolf to keep.' At the same Council the Great Seal was removed from Archbishop Rotherham—who had somehow retrieved it from the Queen—and Dr John Russell, Bishop of Lincoln, was appointed Lord Chancellor in his stead. More informs us that the change was due to Rotherham having made a fool of himself over the seal, but Mancini thought the Archbishop was replaced because he 'would be faithful to Edward IV's heirs, come what may.' The Primate nonetheless remained a member of the Council. Russell was very unwilling to accept his promotion. Although, in More's words, 'a wise man and a good and of much experience and one of the best learned men undoubtedly that England had in his time', the Bishop was plainly not a strong personality. Later, if Dr Hanham is correct, he dealt so briefly in his continuation with the usurpation because he 'felt a personal responsibility' for Edward V's fate. Some members of the Council were dismissed, though naturally Hastings was retained. Among others who remained were Lord Stanley and Dr Morton, Bishop of Ely—as will be seen, the latter was a perculiarly tough and wily prelate.

The general public was further reassured when the Council chose a new date for the King's Coronation. Parliament was summoned to meet three days after. No less soothing, an order was given for coins to be struck in the name of Edward V.

Gloucester emphasised his total supremacy in his letters and proclamations, styling himself grandiloquently 'Brother and Uncle of Kings, Duke of Gloucester, Protector, Defender, Great Chamberlain, Constable and Admiral of England.' Even his nephew's coinage bore as a mint mark Richard's badge of a boar's head. By 14 May he was asserting himself in earnest, sending ships to sea to intercept and arrest Sir Edward Woodville, who only just managed to escape. On the following day the Duke of Buckingham was made Constable, and Steward of all Royal castles in Wales and on the Welsh Borders and also of all those in Wiltshire, Dorset and Somerset; while Lord Howard was given great offices and created a Privy Counsellor. One suspects that these rewards to his closest allies were meant to whet their appetites. Buckingham would never rest content without the Bohun lands.

Nor would Howard without the Dukedom of Norfolk, even though at the moment it might still happen to belong to Edward V's brother. Howard's little cousin Anne Mowbray, Duchess of York and Norfolk, had died in 1481. Through his Mowbray mother he was one of the two co-heirs, certainly to the Earldom and arguably to the Duchy, to whom her inheritance should have reverted. However Edward IV had had no intention of letting it pass from her child 'widower' and early in 1483 had an Act of Parliament passed which confirmed its possession by his younger son; moreover the late King had given lavish compensation to the other co-heir, William Berkeley, but nothing to Howard. The latter and his own very formidable son, Sir Thomas, must have at once realized that the present situation offered a glittering prize. Richard had something to give them which they coveted more than anything else, and he knew it. Old Howard's magnificent gift to him on 15 May of a covered gold cup weighing 65 ounces was not without significance.

It has been suggested that the prospect of Edward's coming of age forced the Lord Protector to seize the throne. The little King was already displaying distinct signs of character—as at Stony Stratford—

and would reach his majority when he was fifteen, which was less than three years away. He might well re-habilitate and re-instate the Woodvilles. As has been seen, the two previous Dukes of Gloucester had perished at the hands of their nephews' men.[3] 'Probably it was fear for his own safety and future which inspired his action, rather than any deeply laid plan,' is Professor Ross's explanation of the ensuing usurpation by Gloucester. But this argument ignores the extreme likelihood of Richard having made contingency plans in case his brother should die. More states, again and again, that this was the impression received by many contemporaries with whom he had spoken, even if the Duke was so secretive that no one ever really knew what was in his mind. It was also Mancini's impression. Certainly the extraordinary smoothness of Richard's seizure of power and then of the crown would seem to indicate the most careful planning.

Up to now Gloucester had been so popular—he was out of London during the uproar which followed his first *coup* at Northampton and Stony Stratford—that he may well have believed that the country could not fail to welcome his ascending the throne. Very probably he had heard vaguely of the events in Milan only three years before, when Ludovico Sforza had seized the Duchy from his half-witted nephew. But it was different in England. Edward V was far from half-witted, a most promising and attractive boy. His youth and good looks aroused English sentiment of the strongest sort.

Some time in the middle of May the young monarch was moved to the Tower of London. In the fifteenth century the Tower was still a palace, a refuge of the court at times of danger, with many luxurious apartments—including a great banqueting hall—which survived until Cromwell's day. There was nothing necessarily sinister about the move. The Protector's ostensible motive may have been to keep the boy as far away as possible from his family at Westminster.

For Edward's mother was still in sanctuary. Much more worrying, so was his brother, the Duke of York. There was no point in deposing Edward V while his heir remained out of reach, to provide a focus for future disaffection. As the days went by Richard grew anxious. He had to strike before the Coronation, which was supposed to take place on 22 June.

On 16 June the Council met at the Tower to discuss the continuing embarrassment of the Duke of York being in sanctuary. The Protector and the Duke of Buckingham produced various disingenuous arguments to persuade the other members that York ought to join his brother. Richard blamed the Queen's 'malice', saying that she was trying to discredit the Council. He added that it was bad for the boy to have no one of his own age to play with and to be entirely in 'the company of old and ancient persons'. He then suggested that the octogenarian Archbishop of Canterbury, Cardinal Bourchier—an acknowledged kinsman of the House of York—should go and remonstrate with the Queen. Bourchier agreed to try, though he told the Council it was possible he might fail because of 'the mother's dread and womanish fear'. Buckingham said angrily that her attitude was due not to womanish fear but to 'womanish forwardness'— perversity. He continued that she knew perfectly well there was nothing of which to be afraid and, in a long and eloquent speech on sanctuaries in general, argued smoothly that they were intended for adult criminals, not little boys. 'But I never heard before of sanctuary children.'

A party at once set off by boat for Westminster up the Thames. It included the Protector himself, Buckingham, Howard, Bourchier and Russell. Someone who was in London at the time, Simon Stallworth, noted on that day 'at Westminster a great plenty of harnessed men' [men in armour]. When the party arrived from the Tower, the two Dukes waited in the Star Chamber while the old Cardinal, accompanied by Howard, went in to the Queen. Bourchier began by telling her that the King was missing his brother, quite apart from everyone else regretting that he was in a sanctuary for criminals. In any case he would have to be let out to take part in the forthcoming Coronation. His mother replied that no one could look after him better than she. The Cardinal then said that all the Council wanted was for her to be with both her sons in suitably regal accommodation. Elizabeth answered that she was not prepared to put herself in the same danger as her kinsmen.

Lord Howard asked why she thought they were in danger. She retorted that she did not know—nor did she know why they were in prison. Bourchier made a sign to the tactless nobleman 'that he should harp no more on that string'.

After further wrangling, during which the Queen began to express openly her fear of the Protector, the Cardinal threatened not just to leave but to refuse to have anything more to do with the matter. Since he was the arbiter in all questions of sanctuary, she realized that her son might be taken away by force. Bourchier, quite unaware of what was at stake, was perfectly sincere in promising that he would be returned as soon as the Coronation was over. At last Elizabeth gave in, weeping. 'Farewell, mine own sweet son', she said to little York, 'God send you good keeping. Let me kiss you once yet ere you go, for God knows when we shall kiss together again!' The Cardinal led the tearful boy to the Star Chamber, where Richard picked him up and kissed him, crying 'Now welcome, my Lord, even with all my heart.' More comments sardonically that Gloucester was undoubtedly speaking the truth on this occasion. The boy was taken to the Tower by boat to join his brother.

One reason for the success of the second *coup d'état* which Richard was about to launch was that very few people understood him, let alone realized his ultimate objective. His secrecy was his greatest asset. We do not know when he told the few men he trusted that he was going to make himself King, though it was almost certainly before he obtained possession of the Duke of York. The strictness of the guard on Westminster—ostensibly to catch Dorset, but above all to stop York getting out or Edward V getting in—may well mean that Gloucester had told both Buckingham and Howard before he reached London. The former had been committed to him from the very beginning, and Vergil states specifically that Richard revealed his plans to the Duke at Northampton. Lord Howard, noticeably active in prising York out of sanctuary, may also have been let into the secret; More says that he 'was one of the priviest of the Lord Protector's counsel and doing.' It was time for Richard to take all his friends into his confidence. He had cunningly divided the Council into two. Those members who supported him absented themselves from its ordinary meetings at Baynard's Castle and instead met privately with the Protector at Crosby Place. The remainder, loyal to Edward V, went on arranging the Coronation and dealing with routine matters.

Nevertheless there was some sort of opposition, though no details survive. Polydore Vergil states that a counter-*coup* was being planned but does not give names. Gairdner and more recent historians believe that Lord Hastings may have been intriguing with, of all people, the Woodvilles. The alleged motive is jealousy of Buckingham, who had taken the place he no doubt expected to occupy in Richard's favour— Howard too was more in favour with the Protector. Hastings, it is suggested, discussed the counter-*coup* with Rotherham, Morton and Lord Stanley during their meetings, their contact with the Woodvilles being his mistress Elizabeth (commonly called Jane) Shore, who was secretly visiting her former lover Dorset in the sanctuary at Westminster. Yet More, the Crowland chronicler and Mancini make no mention of such a plot, even if the latter reports that Hastings, Stanley and the two prelates sometimes met in each other's houses and were known to be faithful to Edward IV's offspring. In addition, More implies that as late as 19 or 20 June Richard still hoped that Hastings would join in helping him seize the throne.

If a counter-*coup* was plotted, it is likely that it was by the Woodvilles alone. Their party was far more broadly based than is generally realized. With its kinsmen by marriage, its clients and retainers, and its friends, it constituted a surprisingly widespread network, which had formidable teeth—to be displayed later that year. The Protector certainly received information during the second week in June which seriously alarmed him. About 12 June Sir Richard Ratcliff, one of Richard's most trusted agents, left London. He was on his way to York with a letter written on 10 June for its Mayor and Corporation, requiring them to send as many armed men as possible to the capital 'to aid and assist us against the Queen, her bloody adherents and affinity, which have intended and daily doth intend to murder and utterly destroy us and our cousin the Duke of Buckingham and the old royal blood of this realm.' In his letter Richard also claimed that

16. (Above) *Edward V,
from a 16th-century panel in
St George's Chapel, Windsor.*

17. (Right, top) *Signature of
Edward V and signatures and
mottoes of the Dukes of
Gloucester and Buckingham.
British Library, London.*

18. (Right, middle) *Garter plate
of Francis, Viscount Lovell in
St George's Chapel, Windsor.
Note his crest of a dog.*

19. (Right, bottom) *Lord
Lovell's signature.*

20.   (Above) *Lord Lovell's house of Minster Lovell in Oxfordshire before its demolition in the eighteenth century.*

21.   *Richard III as King. From a sixteenth-century copy in the National Portrait Gallery, London of a lost original.*

22.   (Opposite, bottom) *Signature of Richard as King.*

23.   (Opposite, left) *The last man known to have seen the Princes in the Tower alive – Edward V's personal physician, Dr John Argentine, later Provost of King's College, Cambridge. Brass in King's College Chapel.*

24.   (Opposite, right) *Bishop Morton's secret agent, who warned Henry Tudor in 1484 that he must escape from Brittany – Dr Christopher Urswick, later Dean of Windsor. Brass in the church of St John, Hackney.*

25. *One of Richard's most formidable opponents – Margaret Beaufort, Henry Tudor's mother. Bronze tomb effigy by Pietro Torrigiano in Westminster Abbey.*

the plotters were bent on destroying and disinheriting all men of property in the North. When Ratcliff reached York on 15 June he told the Corporation that this force should proceed to Pontefract and link up with the Earl of Northumberland (who may have been acting on instructions which Gloucester had given him before going South). Ratcliff had another letter, for the Protector's kinsman Lord Nevill; written on 11 June, it made a similar plea for troops. 'And, my Lord, do me now good service, as ye have always before done, and I trust now so to remember you as shall be the making of you and yours.' Richard's motive in summoning more troops may indeed have been fear of a Woodville rising, though it could also have been a precaution in case his own projected *coup* went wrong.

In the event there was no counter-*coup*. The only man left who might stand in the Protector's way was Lord Hastings, still just capable of rallying magnates to the cause of the young King. His friend Lord Stanley seems to have begun to suspect Richard and warned Hastings to be careful. More's story of Stanley's dream of a boar (Richard) slashing them with his tusks is of course to be discounted as mediaeval superstition, yet may nonetheless preserve some memory of Lord Stanley's uneasiness. A practised intriguer himself, he plainly had a sensitive nose for a plot. He was particularly worried by the division of the Council and the separate meetings. But Hastings was unconcerned, since he thought he knew what was being discussed at Crosby Place; his retainer Catesby was attending the meetings there, and he told Stanley that this man would tell him of anything said against him, practically before it was out of the speaker's mouth. In reality Catesby was a double agent.

The Protector had to discover whether or not Hastings was still unshakeably loyal to the memory of Edward IV, the friend who had asked that he should be buried near his tomb. Mancini tells us that Buckingham sounded him out, but More says that it was Catesby and goes into very convincing detail. William Catesby is one of the most sinister figures in the usurpation. A young lawyer, he was a protégé of Hastings who had given him important administrative posts in Leicestershire and Northamptonshire. Hastings trusted him more than anyone, 'reckoning himself to be beloved of no man more than he'. The trusty Catesby was 'one of the special contrivers of all this horrible treason', his original motive being to obtain some of Hastings's offices in his own counties. Commissioned by Richard to find out discreetly if it was possible to win over his patron, Catesby reported that he spoke 'so terrible words' that his interrogator dared not press him, and also said that some people were beginning to mistrust the Protector. More thinks that Catesby may have exaggerated in order to make sure that Richard would get rid of him.

It seems that Gloucester was genuinely sorry to be forced to destroy Hastings. 'And undoubtedly the Protector loved him well, and loath was he to have lost him.' But Richard was never a man to be deflected by sentiment even if, as will be seen, he may have been uneasy about his prospective victim's soul—after he had murdered him. He struck with the same carefully calculated timing he had employed at Northampton.

More's account of the Council meeting at the Tower on Friday 20 June is almost certainly based on information obtained from Cardinal Morton, who was actually there. He could also have heard something from Rotherham, who did not die until 1500. (The traditional, erroneous, date of Friday 13 June may be an error created by popular superstition—Dr Hanham argues conclusively in favour of the following Friday.)[4] The Council had met to discuss the final details of Edward V's Coronation, and among those present besides Morton and Rotherham were Hastings and Stanley, together with Buckingham and Howard and other supporters of the Protector. Howard's son, Sir Thomas (whom More may also have spoken to, since he was the father of a friend) had accompanied Hastings to the Tower—perhaps to ensure that he arrived. The Lord Chancellor, Russell, presided over a meeting of the remainder of the Council at Westminster.

Richard himself entered the Council chamber at the Tower at about 9.00 a.m., apparently in a most amiable mood. He apologised for being so late, explaining that he had overslept, and then made his famous request to Morton. 'My Lord, you have very good strawberries in your garden at Holborn. I require you, let us have a mess of them'. After setting the discussion in motion again, the Protector left the room. He returned an hour later, at about 10.30 a.m., in a very different temper—'frowning and fretting and gnawing on his lips.' Everyone present was taken aback. For a while he sat in silence. He then asked quietly what did men deserve for having plotted 'the destruction of me, being so near of blood unto the King, and Protector of his royal person and his realm?'

Hastings answered boldly that, whoever they were, they ought to be punished as traitors. At this Richard told him they were 'yonder sorceress, my brother's wife, and others with her'. (Clearly he had not forgotten Clarence's allegations about the Queen.) The Lord Chamberlain, was not particularly disturbed. But then the Protector added 'You shall all see in what wise that sorceress and that other witch of her counsel, Shore's wife, with their affinity have by their sorcery and witchcraft wasted my body.' He pulled up the left sleeve of his doublet to show his withered arm. Everybody there knew that it had been like that since birth and realized immediately that his rage was simulated. Hastings, who was Elizabeth Shore's lover and had spent the previous night with her, began to lose his nerve. He replied that, if it really was true, those who had done it certainly deserved severe punishment.

'What!' exclaimed Richard, 'thou servest me, I ween, with ifs and ands! I tell thee, they have so done! And that, will I make good upon thy body, traitor!' He banged the table with his fist. At once there was a cry outside of 'Treason!' The door burst open and men in armour—including Sir Thomas Howard—rushed into the chamber, filling it almost entirely and brandishing their weapons. One aimed a blow at Lord Stanley, who dived under the table though not before receiving a wound which sent the blood running down over his ears; had he not ducked, 'his head would have been cleft to the teeth.' Amid the confusion the Protector shouted at Hastings 'I arrest thee, traitor.' 'What, me, my Lord?' gasped the astonished nobleman. 'Yea, thee, traitor!' replied Richard. Rotherham and Morton were hauled off to imprisonment in the Tower cells, while Stanley was taken under guard to confinement in his own house. As for Hastings, the Protector told him to find a priest and confess himself at once. 'For by St Paul I will not to dinner till I see thy head off.' (Dr Hanham questions 'this nasty addition to the story' since 'the councillors must have dined about 9.00 a.m. in accordance with the custom at the time', but this was not invariable; the Duchess of York dined at 11.00 a.m. or at noon on fast days while Richard's own household at Sheriff Hutton had to 'go to dinner at the furthest by eleven of the clock on the flesh days'—perhaps later on fast or fish days, and both 13 June and 20 June were Fridays.) Within a very few minutes Hastings was brought to the green outside the Tower chapel and beheaded, a log serving for a block.

'Thus ended this honourable man,' says More, 'a good Knight and a gentle, of great authority with his Prince, of living somewhat dissolute, plain and open to his enemy and secret to his friend, easy to beguile as he that of good heart and courage forestudied no perils. A loving man and passing well beloved. Very faithful, and trusty enough, trusting too much.'[5] His body, reunited to his head, was buried in St George's Chapel at Windsor, close to Edward IV as the latter had asked. It is unlikely that this was due to feelings of remorse on Richard's part—more probably it was from certain fears for the repose of Hastings's soul.

The public disgrace of Mistress Shore which followed was to substantiate the Protector's accusations of sorcery. Charges of witchcraft were a recognised method of discrediting political enemies. Sir Thomas Howard arrested her and after robbing the lady of £1,000— everything she had—dragged her off to prison. Embarrassingly, no evidence of witchcraft could be found so instead she was forced to do penance for being a harlot. The Bishop of London sentenced her to walk barefoot through the City streets, clad only in her kirtle and carrying a taper. She blushed so much and looked so pretty that most spectators—'more amorous of her body than concerned for her soul'—were full of admiration.[6] Indeed 'every man laughed' at the idea of her harlotry being suddenly taken so seriously and thought that Richard had arranged her humiliation 'more of a corrupt intent than any virtuous feeling.' In any case, she was very popular for having persuaded Edward IV to pardon a number of people and for other kindnesses. She was still living, a beggar—'old, lean, withered, and dried up, nothing left but shrivelled skin and hard bone'—when More was writing his history.

Immediately after his triumphant dinner the Protector sent for the leading citizens of London. He and Buckingham met them in ostentatiously rusty armour, as though they had been taken by surprise and had had to put on whatever was available. They told them that Hastings had been planning to murder them at the Council meeting, that they had only acted in the nick of time. By now there were wild rumours all over the City, so to restore calm a herald rode through London reading a proclamation which described Hastings's 'treason'—only two hours had elapsed since his death, but the document was so well phrased and neatly drawn up that it had obviously been prepared long beforehand (no doubt by Catesby).

A reign of terror ensued. There were many arrests. A member of the Lord Chancellor's staff, Simon Stallworth wrote to his friend Sir William Stonor on the following day, 21 June. He speaks of 'much trouble' in London, of Hastings's death and of the imprisonment of Rotherham and Morton and also Elizabeth Shore, of how 20,000 men belonging to the Protector and the Duke of Buckingham were expected to arrive within the week though why he couldn't see, that all Hastings's men were switching their allegiance to Buckingham, and that 'every man doubts the other'. It was the unmistakeable atmosphere of *coup d'état*.

About the same time, it was discovered that the Marquess of Dorset had somehow escaped from sanctuary at Westminster. Richard had the surrounding countryside cordoned off by troops, who searched the standing corn and woodlands with dogs 'after the manner of huntsmen' but without success. Surviving many dangers, the Marquess eventually reached France.

The *Great Chronicle of London* tells us that after Lord Hastings's death 'was the Prince and Duke of York holden more strait and there was privy talk that the Lord Protector should be King.' Now that he had disposed of the Lord Chamberlain and was in possession of both boys, Richard could complete his second *coup*. Edward V's Coronation was again postponed. Buckingham, grown closer than ever, would play the leading part in trying to persuade the populace to accept the Protector in Edward's place. As reward, the Duke's daughter was to marry Richard's son while he himself would receive the Bohun Earldom of Hereford together with large gifts from the Royal Treasury. The strategy on which they decided was to accuse both the late King and his children of being bastards, even if it meant publicly dishonouring the Protector's own mother. More says that Richard was anxious for this last point to be touched on as little as possible—not so much to spare his mother's feelings as to give an impression that he did not want the whole truth to come out. They enlisted the aid of the Mayor, Sir Edmund Sha, of his brother Dr Sha and of Friar Penketh, Provincial of the Augustinians—the two latter being well known preachers, 'of more learning than virtue'—in winning over the Londoners.

On Sunday 22 June—the day when Edward V should have been crowned—Dr Sha preached a sermon at Paul's Cross, outside St Paul's Cathedral, on the text 'Bastard slips shall not take deep root'. He first explained that the late King's marriage to Elizabeth Woodville had been invalid since he was already betrothed to Lady Eleanor Butler, the daughter of the Earl of Shrewsbury, upon whom he had fathered a child; in the then Canon Law the 'troth-plight' was considered no less binding than a marriage if not dissolved by mutual consent. Curiously enough, there may be some truth in Sha's story; Eleanor Butler and the child were dead long ago, but the priest before whom the troth-plight had been sworn, Robert Stillington, now Bishop of Bath and Wells and a former lord Chancellor, came forward to attest it shortly afterwards. Dr Sha had some sort of a case, though scarcely a popular one. He made it still more unpalatable when he went on to speak of the adultery of the Duchess of York, claiming that not only were Edward IV's children bastards but so had been the late King himself and Clarence, that the Duke of York's only legitimate son was the Protector—'This is the father's own figure, this is his own countenance, the very print of his visage, the sure undoubted image, the plain express likeness of that noble Duke!'

Apparently it was intended—if Sir Thomas is to be believed—that at that moment Richard should appear, as though by accident, on a nearby balcony and it was hoped the crowd would shout 'King Richard! King Richard!' Unfortunately the preacher spoke so fast that the Protector arrived too late. (As Gairdner says, Richard had 'a certain Machiavellian cunning which at times overshot the mark'.) When at last he appeared Sha had gone on to talk of other matters—however he abruptly broke off the repeat his high flown comparison of the Protector to the late Duke of York. But instead of shouting 'King Richard!' his hearers 'stood as if they had been turned into stones for wonder of this shameful sermon.' The preacher was so shaken that henceforward he would only go about after dark 'like an owl.'

Dr Hanham finds this scene particularly hard to accept. 'Once again, the authenticity of More's picture is at best unproved.' She discerns a desire to write comedy, to turn the Protector and Buckingham into 'sheer figures of farce'. But she does so in order to strengthen her curious hypothesis that Sir Thomas was writing satire instead of history. None of his contemporaries saw anything satirical or farcical about his account, nor have modern historians, however much irony there may be in it. The most plausible explanation is that More is simply telling the story as he has heard it, even if he tells it rather well.

Elsewhere other preachers delivered similar sermons. They demanded the disinheritance of the children of Edward IV, echoing the allegations at Paul's Cross of adultery and bastardy, and claiming that he had never been a legitimate King and nor could his sons be. But they had no more success with the public than Dr Sha.

The Protector was undeterred. He exchanged his black clothes for the purple mourning worn by Kings of England and began to ride through the London streets with an escort of a thousand men.[7] Every day he entertained vast numbers to dinner at his houses. Yet when he rode past no one cheered—'instead they cursed him with a fate worthy of his crimes, since nobody was in any doubt about his aims,' Mancini tells us. Few rulers have forfeited their popularity so swiftly. The London crowd's reaction was one of horror at 'the madness of Richard the Duke's wicked mind' says Vergil.

Buckingham now took a hand. Indeed he became the instrument of the *coup's* success. On Tuesday 24 June he went to the Guildhall, escorted by a large group of peers and knights. The Mayor, Aldermen and all the leading citizens of London were gathered in the hall to hear what he had to say. Perhaps More has polished the speech for dramatic effect, but as in other speeches he reports, it is full of references which suggest that it is substantially accurate. Moreover it reveals a detestation of Edward IV which is very much what one might expect from Buckingham.

The Duke, 'marvellously well spoken', addressed his audience in a loud, clear voice. 'Friends, for the zeal and hearty favour that we bear you, we come to break unto you a matter right great and weighty' he began. He told them how in recent years they had suffered the most miserable afflictions under the late King's misgovernment. There had been cruel taxation and legalised theft—he cited Edward IV's 'benevolences' and the despoiling of Sir Thomas Cooke. He blamed the King for shedding so much blood in the recent wars, and for killing Clarence—'whom spared he that killed his own brother?' He dwelt at length on Edward's wenching, claiming that no woman in the City had been safe. And yet the late King of all people should have been grateful for the Londoners' loyalty to the House of York.

It is truly extraordinary that such a vicious diatribe against Edward should have been countenanced by the brother whose motto was 'loyalty binds me', who had recently shed 'plenteous tears' at his Requiem.

Then Buckingham went on to refer to the sermon at Paul's Cross on Sunday, repeating all Sha's arguments. 'Woe is that realm that has a child to their King,' declaimed the Duke. 'Wherefore so much the more cause have we to thank God that this noble personage, who is so rightfully entitled thereunto, is of so mature age and thereto of so great wisdom joined with so great experience.' Buckingham continued that though 'this noble personage'—the

Protector—was extremely reluctant to assume the Crown, he might accept if the citizens of London would join with the peers of the realm in petitioning him to do so. He ended by asking his 'dear friends' to speak up and ask for Richard to become their King.

The *Great Chronicle of London* bears out More's report of the speech. It tells us that it lasted a good half hour and was 'so well and eloquently uttered and with so angelic a countenance . . . that such as heard him marvelled.' But it agrees with More that the speech hardly received an enthusiastic reception.

For 'all was hushed and mute.' The citizens remained dumb. Plainly shaken, Buckingham consulted the Mayor who, much embarrassed, suggested they might not have understood. Then the Recorder of London tried, very unwillingly. The assembly remained obstinately silent, 'as if they had been men amazed'. Buckingham made a third attempt, saying that he was offering them a chance to share in the honour of deciding, if 'you be minded, as all the nobles of this realm be, to have this noble Prince, now Protector, to be your King or not?' All that happened was a buzz of whispering—'as it were, the sound of a swarm of bees'.

Finally John Nesfield from Yorkshire—one of Richard's future Esquires of the Body, and a noted thug according to the Crowland chronicler—together with some of the two Dukes' servants and a few apprentices who suddenly appeared at the back of the hall, threw their caps into the air and began to shout 'King Richard! King Richard!' This was enough for Buckingham, who hastily announced that it was quite plain they wanted 'this noble man' for their King. More describes how everybody then left the Guildhall sadly, how even some of the Duke's escort turned their faces away to hide their tears. But they had not dared to protest.

The day after, Buckingham and various peers and gentlemen, together with the Mayor and Corporation, called on the Protector at Baynard's Castle. All were prominent, men of large property, not only anxious to curry favour with an irresistably rising star but aware that their necks and goods were at stake. All knew that a Northern army was expected at any moment. Richard came out on to a balcony, declaring coolly that he did not know why they were there. Buckingham then made an elaborate speech on behalf of the deputation, begging the Protector to take the Crown. After a fine show of reluctance—in which he mentioned the 'entire love he bore unto King Edward and his children'—Richard graciously accepted. 'We be content and agree favourably to incline to your petition and request.' More comments that everyone present was astonished by such a theatrical performance—he says they compared it to 'stage plays'—and realised very well that it had all been arranged beforehand.

Later that day the Lords, Knights and Burgesses who had come to London for the Parliament which could not now meet, drew up a petition, to be recorded by the next Parliament. The Crowland chronicler says it was rumoured that it 'had been conceived in the North, whence such a large force was expected in London. But nobody was ignorant of the sole originator of the great sedition and infamy going on in London.'

The petition echoes Buckingham's speech at the Guildhall. It too dwells on Edward IV's bad government and morals, when 'such as had the rule and governance of this land, delighting in adulation and flattery, and led by sensuality and concupiscence, followed by the counsel of persons insolent, vicious and of inordinate avarice' [i.e., the Woodvilles]. In consequence, 'the prosperity of this land daily decreased, so that felicity was turned into misery, and . . . ruled by self-will and pleasure, fear and dread.' There had been 'murders, extortions and oppressions, namely of poor and impotent people, so that no man was sure of his life, land nor livelihood, ne of his wife, daughter ne servant, every good maiden and woman standing in dread to be ravished and defouled.'

This is not an extract from some much decried 'Tudor propagandist', but a document which was later approved by Richard himself. As Gairdner comments, he 'had resolved to make use of every available prejudice, calumny and scandal, to advance his own pretensions.'

The petition states that the late sovereign's marriage had not only been made out of 'great presumption' but also through witchcraft and sorcery by Elizabeth Woodville and her mother. It was invalid because of Edward's previous troth-plight to Eleanor Butler, so that 'the said King Edward during his life and the said Elizabeth lived together sinfully and damnably in adultery against the law of God and of his Church . . . it appeareth evidently and followeth that all the issue and children of the said King Edward been bastards and unable to inherit or to claim anything by inheritance by the law and custom of England.' The invalidity of the marriage is 'the common opinion of the people' and can be proved 'if and as the case shall require . . . in time and place convenient.'

The petition asserts Richard's claim to the throne in terms which are fulsome even by mediaeval standards. After stating that it was his by right of inheritance, 'We consider also the great wit, prudence, justice, princely courage, and the memorable and laudable acts in divers battles which (as we by experience know) ye heretofore have done for the salvation and defence of the same realm, and also the great noblesse and excellence of your birth and blood.'

On the same day the petition was drawn up, Wednesday 25 June, Earl Rivers, Lord Richard Grey, Sir Thomas Vaughan and Sir Richard Haute were beheaded at Pontefract, after which their naked corpses were thrown into a common grave. They had been brought there from the various castles in which they had been imprisoned—Rivers from Sheriff Hutton, Grey from Middleham. The Earl of Northumberland and some Northern peers apparently set themselves up as a sort of court but the 'trial' had no legality whatsoever. The man in charge of the executions was the brutal Ratcliff. On being taken out to his death, Vaughan spoke of a prophecy current a few years before, how 'G'—popularly believed to be Clarence—would destroy Edward IV's children. Plainly 'G' signified Gloucester, whom 'now I see . . . will accomplish the prophecy and destroy King Edward's children' said the old Welshman, who then declared his innocence, appealing to 'the high tribunal of God.'

'You have appealed well, lay down your head,' replied Ratcliff brusquely.

'I die in right,' answered Sir Thomas, 'beware you die not in wrong.'

It is clear that before leaving London on 12 June Ratcliff had received orders from the Protector to see to the killing of all four prisoners. It was not even judicial murder, but just murder plain and simple. Moreover, we know that the Council in London had refused to agree to their execution. One remembers Richard's amiable message to Rivers, after taking him prisoner at Northampton, 'to be of good cheer and all should be well'.

On Thursday 26 June the Protector went to Westminster Hall with a great retinue and 'obtruded himself'—the phrase is the Crowland writer's—into the monarch's marble throne in the Court of King's Bench.[8] The petition was presented. As a lawyer himself, More, from whom this account is partly taken, must surely have met elderly barristers who had been present. He tells us that Richard announced to the audience that this was the place for him to assume the Crown because he believed that a King's chief duty was to administer the laws, and that he then made an ingratiating speech which was principally addressed to lawyers. In conclusion he dramatically pardoned a kinsman of the Woodvilles, Sir John Fogge—whom he was known to dislike—having him brought out specially from the sanctuary at Westminster and shaking his hand.[9] (Fogge was no 'low intriguer' as Markham calls him, but a very considerable Kentish landowner, a former Member of Parliament for his county, and a former Treasurer of the Royal Household; he was connected with the Woodvilles through having married a relative of that Sir Richard Haute who had just been beheaded at Pontefract.) The more intelligent spectators watched the pardoning of Fogge with some cynicism— 'wise men took it for a vanity.' As he rode home, the new King bowed effusively to everyone whom he met on the way.

Once again Sir Thomas is partly confirmed by an official document. Shortly after 26 June Lord Dynham, Captain of Calais, received instructions dated two days later from royal messengers, which informed him of Richard's accession. They refer to the petition being presented on 26 June and describe how 'the King's said Highness notably assisted by well near all the Lords Spiritual and Temporal of the Realm, went the same day unto his palace of Westminster, and there in such royalty honourably apparelled within the great hall there, took possession and declared his mind that the same day he would begin to reign upon his people.' The document also claims that when he rode to St Paul's Cathedral to give thanks he was loudly cheered and greeted 'with great congratulation and acclamation of all the people in every place'.

The reign of Richard III had indeed begun after 'this mock election' on 26 June. A date was fixed for his Coronation. As More observes, 'Now fell there mischiefs thick.'

CHAPTER NINE

'KING RICHARD THE THIRD'

*'in seizing a state the usurper should carefully examine what injuries
he must do, and then do them all at one blow so that he does not have
to repeat them day after day; and by taking care not to unsettle men
he can reassure them and win them over with gifts. Anyone who fails
to do this, either from cowardice or bad advice, has to keep a knife in
his hand all the time.'*

Machiavelli, Il Principe

*'Where he went abroad, his eyes whirled about, his body secretly
armoured, his hand ever on his dagger.'*

Sir Thomas More The History of King Richard The Third

The reign which now opened was to be the unhappiest in English
history. The black legend had begun before the King even ascended
the throne. For the rest of his short life he was to be a byword,
inspiring more dread and terror than any monarch before or since,
not excepting Henry VIII. More is not exaggerating when he says
that Richard III ruled in an atmosphere of nightmarish insecurity. He
'never had quiet in his mind, he never thought himself sure. Where
he went abroad, his eyes whirled about, his body secretly armoured,
his hand ever on his dagger, his countenance and manner like one
always ready to strike back. He took ill rest a-nights; lay long waking
and musing, sore wearied with care and watch; rather slumbered
than slept, troubled with fearful dreams—suddenly sometimes start
up, leapt out of his bed and ran about his chamber.' Sir Thomas tells
us he heard this 'by credible report of such as were secret with his
chambermen'.

Even before Richard's subjects had reason to suspect that the
Princes had been killed, it is likely that the majority disliked and
mistrusted their new King. He was a scandal, by the lights of his
own violent age. Dr Hanham emphasises that his nephews were
dispossessed 'on grounds which were evidently not thought
adequate by the country at large'; in More's words, 'upon how slip-
pery a ground the Protector builded his pretext, by which he pretended King Edward's children to be bastards.' There had not been
the slightest pretence at legality in taking away the younger Prince's
peerages—the Petition contains no mention of depriving him of
these. Above all, neither could be bastardised, even by Act of Parliament, unless a full canonical investigation by the Church had proved
beyond doubt that their parents' marriage had been invalid.[1] Few
crimes were considered more heinous than swindling heirs out of
their birthright; as that venerable lawyer, Bracton, had written 200
years before, 'God alone can make an heir.'

Moreover, as Mancini attests, many Londoners believed that usurpation would be followed by murder. And, although they lived in a brutal age, fifteenth-century Englishmen could be sentimental enough about children. The Feast of the Holy Innocents—commemorating King Herod's massacre of all the children in Bethlehem—was an enormously popular devotion in the late Middle Ages. Richard would be commemorated as the Wicked Uncle in the ballad of the Babes in the Wood, which may have an origin earlier than the sixteenth century—it was undoubtedly inspired by the fate of the little King and his brother. The capital was stunned by shock and horror.

It may be asked why was there no resistance. The answer is that, as with all successful *coups d' état*, Richard had taken everyone completely by surprise and with overwhelming military superiority. It was common knowledge that thousands of his much feared Northerners were on the way South. No great magnate was available to drum up opposition to the *coup*, and lesser folk were not ready to risk their necks. But, as will be seen, this did not stop bitter and mounting resentment.

Thr Princes seem to have been attractive boys. The Crowland writer says that they were 'sweet and beauteous children', and he must have seen them with his own eyes. Mancini heard glowing reports of Edward V. 'He had such dignity in his whole person, and in his face such charm, that however much they might gaze, he never wearied the eyes of beholders.' Obviously he had inherited the good looks of his magnificent father. 'I have seen many men burst forth into tears and lamentations when mention was made of him after his removal from men's sight.' The Italian scholar adds that Edward showed signs of intellectual ability unusual in one of his age. We know hardly anything about his younger brother, Shakespeare's 'little prating York'. A French chronicler, Jean Molinet—not the most reliable of sources—informs us that he was 'joyous and witty, nimble and ever ready for dances and games'.[2]

For all Richard III's Plantagenet blood, military prowess and proven ability many Englishmen simply could not think of him as the true King of England.[3] They still acknowledged young Edward. But Richard was cursed with a weakness for self delusion, which weakened his political judgment. Being 'blind with covetousness of reigning', he could not believe that he was unacceptable. A Latin poem in the Crowland Chronicle, which plainly refers to him, warns that those who usurp power 'confound themselves and their cause by confusing private desires with public good'. No doubt the new King deluded himself for some time into believing that he was popular; after all, he really was the man best fitted to govern the country. He retained a certain amount of good will in the North, though in the end many Northerners abandoned him—the two key magnates who were to betray him at Bosworth both came from the North. He was unable to identify a whole host of secret enemies until they declared themselves and it was therefore impossible for him to re-

move all opposition at one blow. In consequence he failed to imple-
ment what was to be one of Machiavelli's cardinal tenets for a
successful usurpation.

The mental climate of his age may well have conspired to prevent
Richard from seeing himself as a hypocrite. There was an all too
seldom resolved conflict between emotion and action in fifteenth-
century minds. The King's slightly older contemporary, Sir Thomas
Malory, the author of the exquisitely noble *Morte d'Arthur*, was little
better than a gangster and gaolbird, who stood accused of armed
robbery, sacrilege, and rape on not just one but on several occasions.

The reign began with a forced gaiety. On Friday 4 July Richard and
his wife travelled by state barge along the Thames to the Tower of
London, the royal residence from which by tradition Kings and
Queens of England rode to their Coronation. Anne had come down
from the North early in June, apparently bringing with her the Earl
of Warwick, Clarence's nine-year-old son. (Probably Richard regarded the boy as a potential rival, even though he was excluded
from the succession by his father's attainder.)

'Edward Bastard, late called King Edward V'—as he was now
described officially—was still at the Tower, together with his brother.
The *Great Chronicle of London* refers to the two children being 'seen
shooting and playing in the garden of the Tower by sundry times,'
but gives no precise date. Probably they had been moved out of the
platial apartments by the river long before the arrival of their uncle
and aunt and taken into the fortress itself—Mancini says this happened as soon as Hastings was liquidated. It has been plausibly
suggested that they were moved twice, first to the Garden Tower
(now the Bloody Tower) from where they had access to the garden,
and then into the White Tower in which State prisoners were held
and where they could be kept out of sight—they had disappeared
for good from the public gaze by the time of their uncle's Coronation.
It is unlikely that he visited them, though they cannot have been
entirely absent from his thoughts.

Yet perhaps Richard was too busy exulting over the Kingdom he
had seized. His capital was world famous for its riches and size,
dwarfing even his cherished York. Thanks to Mancini, who left it the
same week and recorded his impressions only a few months later,
we know what it looked like at this very moment. He notes how the
Thames is navigable by large vessels up to London itself, how had
the South Bank been walled it could be described as a city in its own
right. He mentions the 'very famous bridge, built partly of wood,
partly of stone. On it there are houses and several gates with port-
cullises; the houses are built over workshops belonging to various
types of tradesman.' He is impressed by the 'very strong citadel next
to the river, which they call the Tower of London', and by 'enormous
warehouses for imported goods' on the banks of the Thames, and—
a curiously modern note—by 'many cranes of extraordinary size to

unload merchandise off the ships'. He describes the three main streets. The one nearest the river [Thames Street] is full of 'all types of metal, wine, honey, pitch, wax, flax, rope, thread, grain and fish, and other rough goods'. In the central street [comprising Tower Street, East Cheap and Candlewick Street] 'you find nothing for sale but cloth.' The third street, running through the town centre [from Aldgate on the East side to Newgate on the West, and including Cornhill and West Cheap] deals in 'more precious goods, such as gold and silver plate, cloths of rich hue and all sorts of silks, carpets, tapestry and other rich wares from abroad'. He says he simply does not have room to describe 'the citizens' refined ways, the magnificence of their banquets, the lavish decoration and opulence of the churches'. Other foreigners were equally dazzled. Twelve years later a Venetian wrote that he had seen fifty-two goldsmiths' shops in Cheapside alone, that in Milan, Rome, Venice and Florence together he had never seen so much silver plate as in London. This was indeed the 'Flower of Cities all' (even if as many as a third of the population may have been destitute or near destitute). Its proud inhabitants had enough confidence in their private judgement to be deeply disturbed by the usurpation. But it made no difference.

On 5 July the new King and Queen rode from the Tower of London to their Palace of Westminster. He was dressed with breathtaking splendour, in a doublet of blue cloth of gold over which he wore a purple velvet gown trimmed with ermine. He far outshone his wife, who followed him in a litter escorted by five mounted ladies-in-waiting. The royal pair were accompanied by the vast and gorgeously clad procession of the Lords Spiritual and Temporal, which included almost the entire English peerage—three dukes, nine earls and twenty-three barons. The Duke of Buckingham outshone even Richard, in a robe of blue velvet embroidered with blazing golden cartwheels. (According to Rous, the Duke was already boasting that he now had as many men wearing his livery as Warwick the King-maker.) In addition there were nearly eighty knights and countless gentlemen—a surprising number of whom would rise in rebellion within a very few weeks. As he rode through the London streets, the bare-headed King bowed to right and to left.

Richard III and Anne Nevill were crowned in Westminster Abbey by Cardinal Bourchier (despite the old man's unwillingness—he stayed away from the Coronation banquet[4]) on Sunday 6 July 1483. Contemporaries claimed it was the most magnificent Coronation that had ever been seen. The boar badge was much in evidence—13,000 white boars on fustian hangings decorated Westminster—and a new officer-of-arms had been specially created for the occasion, Blanc Sanglier Pursuivant. The King and Queen walked barefoot to the Abbey. Here they submitted to the ancient (but nowadays long since discontinued) annointing with the holy oils on the breast, both standing naked from the waist up. After being crowned they heard High

Mass and took Communion, the King drinking from the Chalice—a privilege then enjoyed by no other English layman. (No doubt he had made a Confession of his sins, in preparation.) The *Te Deum* after the crowning and the anthems during the Mass must have been heard only too easily by the miserable Elizabeth Woodville and her daughters in sanctuary at the Abbot's Lodging. Wearing their crowns, the anointed King and Queen retired briefly. In their absence the Duke of Norfolk and Earl Marshal, mounted on a charger whose cloth-of-gold trappings swept down to the ground, rode up and down to drive out the crowds. At four o'clock they entered Westminster Hall, still wearing their crowns, to preside over the Coronation banquet attended by several thousand people. On bended knee the Mayor of London served them with hypocras (hot spiced wine), wafers, and wine. During the banquet the King's Champion, Sir Robert Dymmock, wearing a white armour and mounted on a charger caparisoned in white and scarlet, rode into the hall and flung down his white steel gauntlet—as a challenge to anyone who disputed Richard III's right to the throne. There were cries of 'King Richard! God save King Richard!' and he rode off with his silver gilt bowl of wine, after drinking the monarch's health. The banquet continued until nine, when it was growing dark and great wax torches were brought in. As soon as these were lit, the lords and ladies went up to the royal dais to renew their homage and say goodnight, and then at last the King and Queen left the hall too.

Coins were at once struck to proclaim that Richard was now a consecrated King. As was customary the silver groats and half groats showed him crowned with a bare, annointed breast; they had the boar's head for their mint mark. Perhaps symbolically, the sole gold denominations issued were the beautiful angel and angelet—these were touch pieces for the 'King's Evil' (scrofula) which only the hand of a consecrated monarch could heal. No act of ostentatious piety was left undone. On 12 July he and Anne processed barefoot around Edward the Confessor's shrine at Westminster.

Foreign rulers were informed with due ceremony of Richard III's accession. The Pursuivant Blanc Sanglier was sent to Plessis-les-Tours to announce it to Louis XI and to ask for his friendship. If Commynes is to be believed, Louis had no wish to answer the usurper. However he sent a curt note of acknowledgement. Even Kendall admits (in his study of Louis XI) that 'so shaky a government could never trouble France'. Richard appears to have been piqued by the Valois's coldness.

While Dymmock's white gauntlet had been left lying on the floor of Westminster Hall, there had nevertheless been a hint of discord during the Coronation. At the moment of crowning it was noticed by some that the Duke of Buckingham—who was enjoying the privilege of carrying his new sovereign's train—'could not abide the sight thereof', but turned the other way to avoid seeing the crown being placed on Richard's head.

Nevertheless, Harry Buckingham had been richly rewarded, as indeed had everyone else who had helped with the usurpation. Already he possessed half the Bohun inheritance and now the King gave him the remainder—estates worth over £700 a year—with the promise that the gift would be ratified by Parliament as soon as it met. He also received Richard's former office of Lord Great Chamberlain, besides being appointed Constable of England—in modern terms, Commander-in-Chief. He was supreme in Wales and the West Country.

John Howard received another of the King's former posts, that of Lord High Admiral. Moreover on 28 June, only two days after his master's seizure of the throne, he had received his real reward and had been made Duke of Norfolk, Earl Marshal and Earl of Surrey— the latter title being borne by his son, Sir Thomas. The new Duke had carried the crown itself at the Coronation. He was also presented with nearly as many manors as Buckingham, besides other revenues. His domain was East Anglia.

The Earl of Northumberland, who had marched into London with some 5,000 Northern troops on 3 July—Richard reviewed and thanked them in Moorfields—received the King's old offices and privileges in the North West, becoming the new Warden of the entire Scots Marches. He was also appointed to many other great Northern offices and likewise received a vast grant of manors. However, most unwisely, he had only been given many of his posts for a limited tenure and his determination to restore Percy dominance in the North remained a dream. Even so, he was nonetheless the most powerful magnate in the North.

Lord Stanley, who had been forgiven, seems to have been allowed to retain his office of Steward of the Household. Presumably this was thought sufficient to secure his friendship—a gross miscalculation. He too controlled large blocks of territory, in the North Midlands.

Buckingham, Norfolk, Northumberland and Stanley, these were the four props of the new régime. They formed an alarmingly narrow power base. All were 'over mighty', with large private armies. The desertion of anyone of them could place Richard in grave peril.

Yet very few people were happy about the new régime. It is likely that, with most Englishmen, the majority of peers regarded the King as an usurper for all his crowning and annointing. Robert Fabyan's chronicle makes this very clear. (The author was fully adult in 1483 and living in London.) Because Richard had stolen the throne, he 'fell in great hatred of the more part of the nobles of his realm, in so much that such as before loved and praised him still as Protector, now murmured and grudged against him, in such wise that few or none favoured his party, except it were for dread or for the great gifts that they received of him; by mean whereof he won divers to

26. *Henry Tudor as a young man. Mid-sixteenth-century drawing by Jacques le Boucq, presumably a copy of a lost contemporary sketch. Bibliothèque Municipale, Arras.*

27. *Early sixteenth-century brass in St George's Chapel, Windsor, of Richard's sister Anne, Duchess of Exeter and her second husband Sir Thomas St Leger.*

28. *Bodiam Castle, Sussex, which was held briefly against Richard in the rebellion of 1483. It soon surrendered.*

29. *Fra John Kendall, Turcopolier (general of light horse) of the Knights of Rhodes, one of Richard's ambassadors to the Pope. Museum of the Order of St John, London.*

mee/And also to be allwey redy to serue/
theyr prynce whan he shalle calle them/ or
haue nede/Thenne late euery man that is
come of noble blood and entendeth to come
to the noble ordre of chyualry/rede this ly
tyl book/and doo therafter/in kepyng the
lore and commaundements therin compry/
sed/And thenne I doubte not he shall at/
tryne to thordre of chyualry/et cetera /
'And thus thys lytyl book I presente to
my redoubted naturel and most dradde so/
uerayne lord kyng Rychard kyng of En/
glond and of Fraunce/to thende / that he
commaunde this book to be had and redde
Vnto other yong lordes knyghtes and gen
tylmen within this royame /that the noble
ordre of chyualrye be herafter better vsed &
honoured than hit hath ben in late dayes
passed / And herin he shalle do a noble &
vertuouse dede/ And I shalle pray almygh/
ty god for his long lyf & prosperous welf
fare/ & that he may haue victory of al his
enemyes/and after this short & transitory
lyf to haue euerlastyng lyf in heuen/whe/
re as is Joye and blysse world without
ende Amen /

30.   *William Caxton prays that Richard will have 'victory of all his enemies'.*
From The Book of the Order of Chivalry, *1484.*

follow his mind, the which after deceived him.' Plainly he sensed an undercurrent of disloyalty; there are indications that he suffered from the paranoia which afflicted his brother Clarence. This might well explain why he was always clutching his dagger and wore a mail shirt.

However Richard had henchmen, household men, upon whom he could rely. They appear to have worked as a team and included, to name only a few, Francis, Viscount Lovell (Lord Chamberlain), Lord Scrope of Bolton, Sir Richard Ratcliff and William Catesby (Chancellor of the Exchequer), together with Sir Robert Brackenbury (Constable of the Tower), Sir Robert Percy (Comptroller of the Household), Sir Ralph Assheton (Vice-Constable), Sir James Tyrell (Master of the Henchmen and Master of the Horse), John Harrington (Clerk of the Council), John Kendall (the King's Secretary), Walter Hopton (Treasurer of the Household), Sir Thomas Burgh, Sir Marmaduke Constable, Sir Humphrey Stafford, Sir Thomas Pilkington, Sir Gervase Clifton, and John Nesfield. Nearly all were Knights or Esquires of the Body. Edward IV had run a similar team—household men and estate managers used in central government or for security purposes—but was never sufficiently isolated to rely on it in the way that his brother did. Richard's team came to constitute a 'mafia', in the modern political sense. It was a general staff, a bodyguard (from whom today's Gentlemen-at-Arms are descended), and an administrative élite. Its military functions were especially important: Dynham was at Calais while Brackenbury as Constable of the Tower, was in control of the chief arsenal and arms depot; Brackenbury was also keeper of castles in Kent, as Tyrell was in Cornwall; Assheton would take over most of Buckingham's military duties; and many other members served as castellans or commissioners of array. The 'mafia' contained some very tough men indeed, as became increasingly evident during their master's short reign.

It is possible that Lord Lovell had been a boyhood companion of Richard at Middleham but there is no proof that he was, as Kendall maintains, the King's 'oldest and dearest friend'. Nor was he a Northerner, even if he possessed estates in the North. His real home was a beautiful Oxfordshire mansion, Minster Lovell, which his master visited on at least one occasion and whose ruins are still elegant. Even so he was plainly close to Richard, who made him Lord Chamberlain (Hastings's old place) and therefore the man responsible for organising and administering his household. At the Coronation he had the honour of carrying one of the Swords of Justice. He was also appointed Chief Butler of England—a position formerly occupied by Rivers—and was later created a Knight of the Garter. Undoubtedly he was deeply committed to the King, which may well be why two years after Bosworth he was one of the leaders of a revolt against Henry VII.

Richard Ratcliff was the team's hit man. A Northerner and one of the King's three principal lieutenants, Ratcliff belonged to a well-established family of minor gentry of Lancashire and Westmorland squires; in London he had lodgings in the suburb of Stepney. He was a younger son and a typical career 'household man'; his maternal grandfather Sir William Parr had been Comptroller to Edward IV, while his Parr uncles may have fought by Richard's side at both Barnet and Tewkesbury, one of them being killed. Ratcliff himself had been knighted after Tewkesbury, and then created a Knight Banneret during the siege of Berwick—no doubt for his services against the Scots at sea, off the Cumberland and Galloway coast. He could even claim distant kinship with the King, through being Lord Scrope of Bolton's son-in-law. Richard had the utmost respect for his opinion, consulting him on matters of special importance. More says specifically that Ratcliff was employed by the King in carrying out 'lawless enterprises', being 'a man that had long been secret with him, having experience of the world and a shrewd wit, short and rude in speech, rough and boisterous of behaviour, bold in mischief, as far from pity as from all fear of God'. Richard heaped honours on him and made him a Knight of the Garter together with Lord Lovell in 1484.[5]

With a certain exaggeration, Catesby may be described as the intellectual of the team. The Crowland chronicler places him among the King's leading advisers, and states that Richard hardly ever dared oppose his views. The same writer comments, with uncharacteristic savagery, that he was executed after Bosworth 'as a final reward for such excellent services'. We know little of his background save that he was a Northamptonshire squire, born about 1450, the son of Sir William Catesby of Ashby St Ledgers (of the same family as the Gunpowder Plot conspirator). His London residence was an apartment in The Harbour, Warwick's former mansion in the City. He also appears to have had country retreats, rooms at Woburn Abbey as well as at Ashby. As for his personality, the betrayal of Hastings indicates ruthless ambition and a total lack of scruples; he was probably no more loyal to his new master—it is likely that before Bosworth he tried to arrange a secret bargain with the Stanleys to save his skin. He may also have had an odd streak of vanity; judging from an inventory of his belongings, he possessed a peacock—and most un-lawyerlike—taste in clothes, wearing garments which included white or green satin doublets, scarlet hose and purple satin gowns. The Crowland chronicler plainly disapproved of him intensely. Yet his will, dictated just after Bosworth, shows that Catesby was deeply religious; it makes obviously sincere requests for prayers from family and friends, besides telling his wife that he has 'ever been true of my body' to her. This curious contrast between unprincipled self-seeking and compulsive piety reflects the dichotomy of Richard's own nature. A lawyer and administrator by profession, he was almost certainly the King's principal legal and financial as well as political adviser. He worked very closely with Ratcliff; together, they are known to have overruled Richard on at least one occasion. Both were identified with their master in the public eye—and were detested with him. Although he served the King so industriously, Catesby never received honours like Ratcliff; he was not knighted, but merely made an Esquire of the Body; perhaps he was too much of a lawyer and too little of a soldier to be thought altogether a gentleman, even if his father-in-law was Lord Zouche. In many ways he was a forerunner of the powerful bureaucrats to whom the Tudor monarchy would owe so much. Beyond question, he, Ratcliff, and Lovell were the three most influential men in the realm.[6]

What was remarkable about Richard's chosen servants is that so, many came from the North, to a quite extraordinary extent. Of the fifteen barons known to have been members of the Council eight were Northerners as were a large proportion of the other members. Only one among seven Garter Knights created by the King was not a Northerner. Of the thirty-two Knights of the Body who have been identified at least fifteen came from Yorkshire, Cumberland, Westmorland or Lancashire, as did at least thirteen of thirty-four Esquires of the Body. This bias in favour of men from the North was no less apparent in his ecclesiastical appointments. It is important to realise that, as Professor Ross reminds us, 'in southern England men from the North were still regarded with fear and mistrust, as wild, warlike, fearless and licentious . . . At best they were aliens, men largely unfamiliar with court and capital.' This Northern predominance is something unique in English history. At the time it caused much bitter feeling in the South.[7]

While Richard ruled largely through his household and professional henchmen, most of whom owed their careers to him, he had of course a Council. Nothing could have been more decorous, even though some of the henchmen belonged to it. Besides Lord Chancellor Russell there were several other churchmen. Among them were Archbishop Rotherham, restored to favour; the invaluable Stillington of Bath and Wells; and Alcock of Worcester, who had been Edward V's tutor. Another was an old friend from the North, Richard Redman, Abbot of the White Canons at Shap in Cumberland and now in addition Bishop of St Asaph's; if a noted pluralist he was devout enough and rebuilt his ruinous Welsh cathedral in the form in which we know it today. Undoubtedly the King consulted these prelates frequently, especially in the drafting of statutes. It helped him, so he hoped, give the impression of being a diligent, conscientious and, in particular, pious ruler.

One may be sure, however, that Richard did not ask their advice about the matter which was most in his mind at the beginning of his reign—the future of his nephews. He must have realized that popular feeling still recognised Edward V as the true King, and York as his heir, that it had not swallowed all the chicanery about Eleanor Butler. While the boys lived he was at risk. During the following reign Henry

VII was to dispose of Warwick, the last surviving Plantagenet male, for much the same reasons, but would use legal murder (after trapping the youth into a technically treasonable plot). It is a measure of Richard's neurotic insecurity that he could not wait for the Princes to reach a more acceptable age and use the same method.

For the deposition of Edward V by the Petition was obviously invalid to those who knew anything about legal matters. If Edward IV's marriage really had been null and void, then it was up to the Church to prove it, an investigation which could easily have been conducted discreetly and thoroughly under the Protectorate. Problems of troth plight, annulment and bastardy were familiar to Englishmen of that time, since they frequently provided an excuse for a tacit divorce (a loophole only tidied up by the Council of Trent). It is quite possible that Richard and his secret advisers were certain that the canon lawyers would discover that Edward IV's children were legitimate after all. The prelates might have protested, but the Archbishop of Canterbury was nearly senile, while, though Russell must have been only too well aware that it was a matter for the Church the usurpation was a *fait accompli*; his embarrassment may perhaps be reflected in the Crowland chronicler's scant treatment of events during these months.

The decision to kill the Princes may even have been taken before Richard seized the throne. Mancini informs us that immediately after Hastings had been eliminated on 20 June all the little King's servants were forbidden to go to him. 'He and his brother were taken into the innermost rooms of the Tower and as the days went by began to be seen more and more rarely behind the bars and windows, until at length they ceased to appear altogether.' More heard of more sinister rumours. As soon as Edward was told that his uncle had seized the throne he was 'sore abashed, began to sigh and said: "Alas, I would my uncle would let me have my life yet, though I lose my Kingdom." ' According to Mancini, his friend Dr Argentine (the royal physician and future physician to Prince Arthur, and who would end his own life as Provost of King's College, Cambridge), who was brought in to attend Edward—probably for toothache, to judge from his skull—seems to have been the last member of his household to visit him.[8] Argentine reported that the boy was going to Confession daily and doing penance 'because he believed that death was facing him'. The French chronicler, Molinet, apparently heard a similar story. This confirms what More has to say. 'But forthwith were the Prince and his brother both shut up and all others removed from them only one; called Black Will or William Slaughter, was set to serve them and see them sure.' More adds that Edward stopped washing and dressing properly and, with his brother, was sunk in listless gloom. Mancini, who left England just after Richard's Coronation on 6 July, says that even then there were already suspicions that the little King had been murdered. 'Whether in fact he has been done away with, and how he was killed, I have so far been unable to discover.'

The Crowland chronicler tells us that by autumn 1483 a rumour was circulating that Edward IV's sons had died a violent death, but it was not known how. It is clear that by early September at latest their mother, with Buckingham, Morton and others, was certain the boys were dead, since by then they were putting forward Henry Tudor as Pretender and hoping to strengthen his cause by marrying him to the sister of the late Edward V.

Commynes may give the earliest dated reference to the Princes' death. While he says confusingly in one passage that Buckingham 'caused the death of the two children',[9] in others he states that Richard killed them,[10] He also makes it clear that Louis XI thought Richard had had them murdered and that he considered him 'extremely cruel and evil'. Louis died on 30 August 1483 after an illness which had struck him speechless for a week. This gives a date of at least before 15 August for the murders. Gairdner does not think that the news could have reached the French King in time, but this is arguable—communications were quicker than he supposed, especially with a spy master like Louis.[11]

The first definitely dated reference is also from a French source. In January 1484 when the Chancellor of France, Guillaume de Rochefort, was warning the Estates General at Tours of the dangers of a minority—Charles VIII was only fourteen—he asked them to remember what had happened in England after Edward IV's death. 'Think of his children, already well grown and promising, being murdered with impunity and of the Crown's passing to their assassin being countenanced by the people.'[12] It is known that in December 1483 Mancini was in the Chancellor's neighbourhood and it has been suggested that the Italian had told Rochefort of his fears for the boys' lives. Yet it nonetheless remains logical to assume that the Chancellor was not announcing the news of Richard III's usurpation and murder of the Princes to the Estates, but simply reminding them of something already known to most reasonably well informed Frenchmen.

The earliest documented English reference is the Act *Titulus Regius* passed after Bosworth by Henry VII's Parliament in January 1486. It charges Richard with 'unnatural, mischievous and great perjuries, treasons, homicides, and murders, *in shedding of infants' blood.*' The next date is April 1486, when the Second Continuation of the Crowland Chronicle was written and specifically accused Richard of killing 'his brother's progeny'. Henry's son, Prince Arthur, was born in September the same year and the court poet, Pietro Carmeliano (who had been Richard's poet too), wrote some verses in celebration—in them he reviles the late King for having murdered both Henry VI and his own nephews.

It is curious that Commynes should think even for a moment that Buckingham might have killed the Princes, though admittedly the

French chronicler, Jean Molinet, says that the Duke was *mistakenly* suspected.[13] Both Buckingham and Norfolk may, just conceivably, have been consulted by Richard about the murders. The two noblemen had a lot to lose if Edward V ever regained the throne—in particular Norfolk who would have forfeited his new Dukedom at the very least. However, it is going too far to suggest that either of them rather than the King were responsible for killing the boys. Kendall investigates, and rejects, the theory that Buckingham contrived their murder in order to increase his own chances of succeeding to the throne. There is absolutely no evidence to support this theory—the Duke may perhaps have urged the need to get rid of the children, yet no contemporary English source accuses him of killing them. Nor does any contemporary source, either English or French, even mention Norfolk in connection with the crime. The theory that it was Norfolk who murdered the Princes was first heard in the nineteenth century and is based on a misinterpretation of his household accounts, together with a totally erroneous impression that he, and not Brackenbury, was Constable of the Tower.[14] Indeed it is hard to believe that anything could have happened to the boys without Richard's personal command.

It was to be many years before anyone learnt what had actually been done with the Princes. This was certainly by deliberate design; Rous emphasises that because they had been in prison 'it was afterwards known to very few by what manner of death they had suffered.' Richard Arnold, a London merchant, wrote vaguely in his commonplace book for the year 1482–3 'the two sons of King Edward were put to silence.' Polydore Vergil believed that Richard had deliberately put about a rumour of their death within a few days of the murder, to make people resigned to his government. The ballad of the *Ladye Bessiye* preserves another contemporary rumour in stating that, like their uncle Clarence, they were both drowned in a pipe of wine.

Nothing really substantial was heard until 1502 when Sir James Tyrell was awaiting execution for conspiring with the then Yorkist Pretender, the Earl of Suffolk. In fear of death and presumably concerned for their salvation, he and his servant John Dighton made confessions-in which they described how the Princes had died. The confessions were not made public, possibly because of the sacramental seal (if they were made to a priest who then broke it) though also perhaps for another reason. Nevertheless various versions seem to have circulated. More therefore attempted to make an approximate reconstruction of the events of 1483 and, it has to be admitted, may well have indulged his sense of the dramatic. Yet the account which he gives, although rejected by many historians, carries considerable conviction.

We know from other sources the details of the new King's progress, which began on 20 July. He set out from Windsor accompanied by a train of magnates and courtiers, though without the Queen or the Duke of Buckingham. He spent a night at Reading Abbey, reaching Oxford on 24 July where he lodged at Magdalen; next day he listened to two learned dissertations on theology and moral philosophy in the great hall of the college—one of the orators was the humanist Grocyn. Richard then stayed a night at the nearby royal palace of Woodstock, returning briefly to the university before going on to Gloucester. Here he presented to the town whose name he had borne for twenty years a charter which gave it a Mayor and Corporation and created it an independent county with special privileges. He gracefully declined a large donation proffered by its townsmen, as he did everywhere else, saying that he wanted their hearts rather than their money. At Gloucester Buckingham caught up with him, *en route* for his Brecon stronghold. It was the last time that the King and the Duke would ever meet, after a friendship of little more than three months; they parted on seemingly amiable terms. Richard went on to Tewkesbury, where Edward of Lancaster and George of Clarence lay buried, giving the Abbot an enormous sum of money—£300—after which he proceeded by way of Worcester to Warwick, which he reached on 8 August. Here he passed a week in his late father-in-law's mighty palace-fortress on its bluff overlooking the river Avon, and here he was joined by Anne. Perhaps it was now that he began his programme of building at Warwick, on his usual grandiose scale; it is known that he planned a great bastion which would be able to withstand the surprisingly effective gunfire of the period—he is also reputed to have built the Bear and Clarence Towers and the Spy Tower and Lodgings, still to be seen today.

More tells us that it was during the stay at Warwick that the King gave orders to dispose of his nephews. Arguably, this seems to be confirmed by what very scant evidence there is. A comparison of the few contemporary sources—the Crowland chronicler, Vergil, Rous, Molinet and Commynes—indicates that they were murdered at the end of July or in early August.

Gairdner believes that Richard gave the command on impulse, in reaction to the growing threat of an attempt to release the Princes. As will be seen, the threat was real enough. Undoubtedly the King's spies had got wind of some sort of plot, but they had not discovered what exactly was being planned or just who was behind it. There was a report that men who wished to restore Edward V wanted some of his sisters to escape overseas in case anything should happen to him and his brother, an illuminating comment on what they expected from their new King. As soon as he heard of it he so ringed Westminster with armed men 'of the toughest sort' under John Nesfield that the Abbey looked like a fortress and no one could get in or out unless they had Nesfield's leave. The report may also have spurred on Richard to take action to solve the problem of his nephews. Yet it is logical to suppose that he had long been contemplating their liquidation.

The trusted household man whom he chose for the task was a Suffolk knight, James Tyrell of Gipping, who had been with him for at least a dozen years. Tyrell had received the accolade after Tewkesbury and with Ratcliff had been promoted to Knight Banneret in 1482 for services during the Scots war. As has been seen, he had already performed at least one secret and dangerous commission for the King; in 1473 he had lured the dowager Countess of Warwick out of her sanctuary in Hampshire and, eluding Clarence's watchful spies, brought her North to life-long imprisonment at Middleham. He was an able administrator, well used to dealing with high officials. More thought him 'a man of right goodly personage . . . and worthy to have served a much better Prince'. He explains that Tyrell 'had a high heart and sore longed upward, not rising yet so fast as he had hoped, being hindered and kept under by means of Sir Richard Ratcliff and William Catesby'—who clearly did not care for competition. However he was recommended to the King as the right man for the unpleasant job in hand by 'a secret page of his'.[15]

According to More, Richard had already sent a messenger from Gloucester, one John Green 'whom he specially trusted', to Brackenbury, Constable of the Tower of London, with a letter ordering him to put the children to death. Robert Brackenbury of Selaby in Co. Durham, near Barnard Castle, was one of the King's Northern protégés and had only just been appointed Constable on 17 July.[16] But he was either too cautious or too squeamish to carry out such terrifying orders and refused saying that he would 'never put them to death therefore'—he was not going to risk his neck. Richard was very angry indeed when he received his answer, sighing 'Ah, whom shall a man trust?' It was then that he asked the 'secret page's' advice. When approached Tyrell was ready and willing. The King thereupon gave him a letter for Brackenbury, which ordered the Constable to hand over the keys of the Tower to Tyrell for one night.[17] It is best to give More's actual words as to what happened:

'Sir James Tyrell devised that they should be murdered in their beds. To the execution whereof he appointed Miles Forest . . . a fellow fleshed in murder beforetime. To him he joined one John Dighton, his own horsekeeper, a big broad strong square knave. Then all the others being removed from them, this Miles Forest and John Dighton about midnight (the innocent children lying in their beds) came into the chamber and suddenly lapped them up among the clothes—so bewrapped them and entangled them, keeping down by force the featherbed and pillows hard unto their mouths, that within a while, smothered and stifled, their breath failing, they gave up to God their innocent souls into the joys of heaven, leaving to the tormentors their bodies dead in the bed. [The *Great Chronicle of London* records, long before More, how 'some said they were murdered atween two feather mattresses'—though it also mentions rumours of other methods.]

'After the wretches perceived them—first by the struggling with the pains of death and after, long lying still—to be thoroughly dead, they laid their bodies naked out upon the bed and fetched Sir James to see them. Who, upon the sight of them, caused those murderers to bury them at the stairfoot, meetly deep in the ground under a great heap of stones.'

More adds that a priest of Brackenbury's later disinterred them and reburied the bodies, since the King did not like to leave them 'in so vile a corner'. However the priest died, and with him the secret of the Princes' burial place.

Sir Thomas's account has been dismissed as a tale of melodramatic invention, full of errors and incongruities. Certainly it contains many mistakes, though this becomes understandable when one realizes that it was at most a very approximate reconstruction of what had happened, much of it based on guesswork. In his *History of the Reign of King Henry VII* Francis Bacon explains why. More gives as his source the reports 'of them that much knew and little cause had to lie', rather than the actual confessions of Tyrell and Dighton. Bacon tells us that though Henry was informed of the confessions, he 'made no use of them in any of his declarations; whereby, as it seems, these examinations left the business somewhat perplexed.' But while Tyrell went to the block, Dighton—who does not even seem to have been arraigned—was set free after which, according to Bacon, he told the story of the Princes' death to anyone who would listen. More had not met Dighton, though he says that he is still alive at the time of writing—he 'yet walketh on alive in good possibility to be hanged ere he die.' (Modern scholarship has traced a number of Dightons and Forests, who may or may not have been the men in question.) He must therefore have had to glean details of the confessions indirectly, perhaps from tavern gossip, and to balance them against other rumours which were circulating.

Many historians are puzzled why Henry VII did not publish the confessions, to discredit Richard III and discourage further spurious pretenders like Lambert Simnel and Perkin Warbeck. But the Tudor King had an excellent reason for not reminding the English people of royal murders; only three years before, he himself had legally murdered the last male Plantagenet—the mentally subnormal Earl of Warwick, whom he had kept in the Tower since Bosworth—by deliberately involving him in a pathetic little plot with Warbeck and then beheading him for treason. In any case Henry was secretive by nature and disliked re-opening unprofitable debates; in Bacon's words, he preferred 'showing things by pieces and by dark lights'. Above all, he cannot have wanted publicity for the House of York, since there was still a Yorkist Pretender in the person of Edmund de la Pole.

Polydore Vergil definitely accepts Tyrell's guilt, but merely says that he killed the boys. He ignores the confessions—'with what kind of death these sely [poor] children were executed is not certainly known.' He also tells us that Tyrell was dispatched not from Warwick, but from York. Much has been made of this by Richard's defenders in order to discredit Sir Thomas's version. However Vergil was an excessively self-conscious stylist, who believed in the elegance of brevity, and who in any case had no experience of criminal investigation. More on the other hand, as cannot be too much emphasised, was a professional lawyer with very considerable experience of investigating crimes, of assessing evidence and weighing probabilities, and of trying to establish what had really happened. He makes it perfectly clear that several conflicting versions of the confessions by Tyrell and Dighton were circulating. 'I shall rehearse you the dolorous end of those babes, not after every way that I have heard, but after that way that I have so heard by such men and such means as methinketh it were hard but it should be true.' What he does not say, but which is obvious from his treatment of other incidents in the *History* is that the version which he had accepted was in part his own reconstruction. Vergil may not make use of Sir Thomas's reconstruction, but that does not mean he rejected it—if, indeed, he even knew of it.

The author of the *Great Chronicle of London* is another contemporary who supports More. He believed that the murderer was either Sir James Tyrell or an un-named 'old servant' of the King. He wrote before the publication of More's *History*. It is surely significant that both he and Vergil as well as Sir Thomas identify Tyrell as the prime murderer.

Kendall tries to demolish More on the most specious grounds. He claims it is inconceivable that King Richard would have sent letters to Brackenbury ordering him to kill the Princes. But the letters were carried by well trusted men and even in the fifteenth century 'sealed dispatches' were far from unknown. He makes great play (as do all Richard's partisans) with Sir Thomas's ignorance of Tyrell's previous employment by the King, yet this is surely irrelevant; a curriculum vitae or an obituary cannot have been exactly easy to come by in the sixteenth century. Tyrell's recommendation by the 'secret page' in particular carries conviction rather than otherwise; for 'secret page' one should read modern 'secret agent', a man employed by Richard to spy on and report on his household—it would obviously make sense to consult him about which of the henchmen was most suitable for such a tricky job.

Beyond question, More's account of the murders is full of errors—one serious—and partly based on sheer surmise, and cannot be accepted in every detail, but as a reconstruction it is a *tour de force*. It is also probably very near the truth. Instead of being criticised for mistakes or too much imagination, Sir Thomas deserves to be congratulated for an inspired piece of detective work.

What gives More's account such conviction are the two skeletons discovered in 1674. A staircase to the White Tower was being demolished when, at a depth of ten feet, the workmen found a wooden chest. (It may have been an arrow chest of the sort in which Anne Boleyn was coffined so hurriedly.) Inside were the bones of two children, the taller on its back, the smaller lying face down on top of it. Some of the bones were stolen by souvenir hunters—and replaced by animal bones—until in 1678 King Charles II ordered the remainder to be interred in a fittingly regal urn in the Henry VII Chapel at Westminster Abbey—near the tomb of their sister, Elizabeth of York. Furious attempts have been made to show that these are not the remains of the Princes. However, when the urn was opened in 1933 and the skeletons were examined, both were found to be male, the larger four feet ten inches tall and the smaller four feet six and a half inches, and each slenderly built; a dental surgeon estimated their ages at about twelve and ten (roughly those of the Princes in 1483) and also deduced that the elder suffered from a painfully diseased jaw which might well have caused melancholy. Twenty years later these findings were submitted by Kendall to a group of anthropologists and dentists, who differed in their opinions; some believed that the conclusions of 1933 were probably more or less correct, others disagreed about the larger skeleton's age and even sex. Richard's partisans have argued that it would have been impossible to dig ten feet down into solid stone in a single night; in fact the murderers need not have dug downward but could have dug from the side, into the rubble which composed the foundations of the staircase since it is known to have been an external stair. This would certainly tally with Sir Thomas's description of the boys being buried 'at the stair-foot, meetly deep in the ground under a great heap of stones'. If these are not the Princes, it is an almost miraculous coincidence that the bones of two mediaeval adolescents should have been buried in this particular place.

More's most serious mistake is his tale of a priest having later reburied them. But perhaps this was the impression of Tyrell and Dighton themselves since 'whither the bodies were removed they could nothing tell.' It might have been the King's original intention but was never carried out. It could also be accounted for by Brackenbury having a priest say the prayers *De Exequis* or even a Mass over the spot where they lay although it was unconsecrated ground—this would undoubtedly be in keeping with Richard's always obsessive anxiety that the souls of the dead should rest in peace.

In the meantime their uncle was basking in the seeming adulation of his new subjects. When he was still at Warwick he received an ambassador bearing letters from Ferdinand and Isabella the Catholic, King and Queen of the Spains. The envoy, Sasiola, made 'by mouth' the barely credible though unquestionably tactful assertion that his sovereign had been 'turned in her heart' against Edward IV because he had refused her hand for that of Elizabeth Woodville; she and Ferdinand wanted Richard to join them in a war against Louis XI of France. The English King was in no position to wage a long and expensive campaign against the French, but he sincerely welcomed the idea of a treaty of amity with the Spaniards. Also at Warwick on this occasion he saw once more his old comrade-in-arms, the egregious Alexander Albany, who had quarelled yet again with his brother. Technically England was still at war with the Scots, but a letter was sent by James III on 16 August in which he asked for an eight-month truce with a view to negotiating lasting peace. Nevertheless the Duke of Albany might well prove useful to Richard III.

The day before King James sent his letter Richard had left Warwick to continue his progress, going by way of Coventry, Leicester and Nottingham. From the last town his secretary, John Kendall, wrote to the Corporation of York asking them to give the King a particularly splendid welcome, 'to receive His Highness and the Queen as laudably as their wisdom can imagine.' Kendall assisted their wisdom's imagination by suggesting that the streets of York should be adorned by hangings and tapestries. He confided to the Corporation that this was to impress the 'many Southern lords and men of worship' who were accompanying Richard. We know from Rous, who had been an eye-witness at Warwick, that the Royal retinue included the Bishops of Worcester, Coventry, Lichfield, Durham and St Asaph's, the Earls of Warwick, Lincoln, Huntingdon and Surrey (Thomas Howard) the Lords Stanley, Dudley, Morley, Lovell and many others together with a multitude of knights and gentlemen. 'And ladies of similar rank with the Queen.' No doubt Kendall's letter to York emanated from the King. Clearly Richard wanted his magnates and his courtiers to appreciate his popularity in the North and the fact that he still had a strong power base there.

At Pontefract near Nottingham the King and Queen were joined by their nine-year-old son, Edward of Middleham, Earl of Salisbury, probably on 24 August. This was the day on which the boy was given the heir apparent's traditional titles of Prince of Wales and Earl of Chester. Clearly he had been too sickly to come South for his parents' Coronation, and he had had to travel from Middleham to Pontefract by 'chariot'—a conveyance used only by delicate women or invalids. Yet he seems to have been a normal enough child. He kept a fool called 'Martyn' and a pack of hounds, besides two running footmen to accompany him during the hunt. And his health was at least good enough for him to visit fairly frequently the local religious houses of Coverham, Fountains and Jervaulx—the latter still famous for its horses. As soon as his father had 'ascended' the throne, the Corporation of York had ridden out to Middleham to pay their respects to the small boy who might one day be their King. As presents the burgesses brought such delicacies as six herons, six cygnets, twenty-four rabbits, a barrel of red wine and a barrel of white wine.[18]

During the family's stay at Pontefract, Richard took the opportunity of making yet another ostentatious display of piety, which at the same time conveniently blackened his late brother's name. Edward IV had appropriated twenty-four acres of land belonging to a local priory. The new King gave it back 'calling to remembrance the dreadful sentence of the Church of God given against all those persons which wilfully attempt to usurp unto themselves, against good conscience, possessions or other things of right belonging to God and his said Church, and the great peril of soul which may ensue by the same.' In all probability it was only a few days since he had ordered the liquidation of his nephews.

York gave the Royal Family the magnificent reception for which Kendall had asked, and much more besides. On Friday 29 August Richard and his cortège were met at Brekles Mills, just outside the city, by its Mayor and Corporation in their furred gowns of scarlet velvet and by an attendant host of leading citizens expensively dressed in red. They escorted their guests through the chief gateway, Micklegate, to be cheered to the echo by a mass of more ordinary citizens, though everyone was in their best clothes. The people of York vied with one another in staging special displays in welcome. As the King and Queen and the Prince passed through the densely thronged and richly bedecked streets, they were greeted by three splendid and elaborate pageants in token of the city's rejoicing. Richard was presented with two great silver-gilt basins filled with gold coins, while Anne received a gold plate piled high with more gold coins, to the value of a hundred pounds.

The 'Southern lords and men of worship' with the King must have been gratifyingly impressed by such solid testimony to his Northern popularity. Richard himself was plainly delighted. He decided, obviously on impulse, to invest his son as Prince of Wales in this rich and friendly city, sending to London in haste for suitable robes and hangings—in particular for 13,000 tapestries bearing the badge of the white boar. (No doubt these were the hangings used at his Coronation; some would have been cloth badges to be worn by royal retainers.) The messenger was none other than Sir James Tyrell, who presumably had speedily rejoined his master with the news that he had successfully accomplished his delicate mission. The three weeks at York which followed were one long celebration, during which the Corporation entertained the King and his court to two memorably extravagant dinners and many other entertainments. These were 'stage plays, tournaments and other triumphal sports'. On 7 September, a Sunday, the Corpus Christi Guild—which Richard and Anne had joined in 1477—put on a special performance of the Creed mystery play for their benefit, in the superb Perpendicular Guildhall with its brilliantly coloured glass windows. He reciprocated by giving 'most gorgeous and sumptuous feasts and banquets, for the purpose of gaining the affection of the people.'

However the visit's highlight was the investiture of the Prince of Wales in York Minster. The King placed a golden circlet on his son's head and put a sceptre into his hand. To enhance the solemnity of the occasion he also knighted the Spanish ambassador, Sasiola. Finally, preceded by forty trumpeters, Richard, Anne and the Prince, still wearing their diadems, walked in procession through the city streets—the Queen holding Edward's hand. (The streets they walked must have been narrow, winding, tall gabled lanes very like today's Shambles.) The King wore a crown of notable richness and magnificence and 'the common people of the North so rejoiced that they extolled him above the stars.' It should of course be borne in mind that as yet probably no whisper of his nephews' murder could have reached Yorkshire. The day's ceremonies were so majestic, Richard's crown so imposing and the crowds so large that some spectators thought a second Coronation had taken place.

The King was intoxicated by such an enthusiastic reception. He remitted more than half a year of York's taxes, a characteristic display of prodigality which probably he later regretted. Then he took the opportunity to re-visit his favourite houses of Sheriff Hutton and Middleham. Anne and Prince Edward remained at Middleham—no doubt the sickly child had been exhausted by the celebrations.

Certainly Dr Thomas Langton—a Westmorland man—Bishop of St David's, who accompanied Richard's progress had no reservations at all about his new sovereign's popularity, as he wrote the same September to the Prior of Canterbury. It would be too cynical to attribute his exuberant approval entirely to the fact that the King had made him a Bishop and appears to have told him to expect further preferment. 'He contents the people where he goes best that ever did Prince', says Langton in his much quoted letter, 'for many a poor man that hath suffered wrong many days have been relieved and helped by him and his commands now in his progress. And in many great cities and towns were great sums of money give to him, which all he hath refused. On my troth, I never liked the conditions of any prince so well as his. God hath sent him to us for the weal of us all.' However the Bishop then breaks into Latin in a sentence which is smudged and faint but appears to read 'I do not take exception to the fact that his sensuality [*voluptas*] seems to be increasing.' This last comment goes quite contrary to the modern theory that Richard was something of a puritan.

One man definitely not delighted by all the junketings at York— celebrations unparalleled in the city's recent history—was Henry Percy, Earl of Northumberland. From his future behaviour one can see that secretly the Earl was angered by Richard's return to the North. He must have resented his presence there during Edward IV's reign and it is very likely that he had helped with the usurpation in the hope of being rewarded by the restoration of Percy dominance. But if the King was to keep visiting the North regularly and continue to use it as a power base, then Northumberland would still be overshadowed—the monarch himself on one's doorstep was even worse than a royal duke. The enthusiasm for Richard shown by York—over which the Earl wished to regain the control exercised by his forefathers—must have irritated him intensely. He would have been further incensed on learning that the King was establishing a permanent Royal Household in the North at Sheriff Hutton. Northumberland may gloomily have suspected, and with justice, that this was going to develop into something more.

Leaving his Queen and his son behind him at Middleham, Richard resumed what appeared to be a triumphant progress. He spent several nights at Pontefract, a favourite residence, and then travelled by way of Gainsborough to Lincoln. Here astounding news reached him on 11 October. A widespread and well planned rebellion had broken out against him—it was led by his dear friend and mightiest subject, the Duke of Buckingham.

Chapter Ten

'HIM THAT HAD BEST CAUSE TO BE TRUE'

'from hostile nobles he has not only to fear desertion, but that they will rise against him; since they are far seeing and astute in matters of state, they always move in time to save themselves and to extract favours from the man they think is going to win.'

Machiavelli, Il Principe

'the malice of him that had best cause to be true, the Duke of Buckingham, the most untrue creature living.'

Richard III, letter of 12 October 1483

Paradoxically, the Duke of Buckingham's revolt inaugurated the seven prosperous months of Richard III's reign—October 1483 to April 1484. He put down with ease what at first sight looked like a very formidable rebellion indeed, and then ruled with a splendour which staggered even Commynes. Parliament met, and proved gratifyingly tractable. Even Elizabeth Woodville agreed to leave sanctuary with her daughters. Yet although the Duke was to be crushed, his revolt spelt Richard's eventual doom. It united all the many strands of opposition.

No one knows what made Buckingham turn against the King. One might have thought he would have been satisfied by such enormous rewards. More says 'a man would marvel why the Duke plotted against the King; and surely the occasion of their variance is by divers men diversely reported.' Sir Thomas may well be right in identifying jealousy as Buckingham's motivation. Some observers detect a long-term plan to bring down the House of York and replace it with himself. This seems to have been the opinion of many contemporaries; Polydore Vergil tell us, even if he reflects their opinion, that 'the multitude said that the Duke did the less dissuade King Richard from usurping the Kingdom, by means of so many mischievous deeds, upon that intent that he afterward, being hated both of God and man, might be expelled from the same, and so himself [Buckingham] called by the commons to that dignity, whereunto he aspired by all means possible . . . ' Certainly the Duke was very much aware of his own descent from Edward III.

However there is another, simpler, more convincing possibility— that Buckingham had very quickly reached the conclusion that a regime so unpopular as that of the new King could not endure. One of Edward IV's greatest strengths had been an ability to win genuinely popular support—it was one of the principal props of his monarchy. It was precisely this quality which Richard III lacked. And without it he could not hope to overcome the widespread indignation at his usurpation. Indignation was turning into hatred as rumours circulated that the boys had been liquidated. An unknown, but undoubtedly contemporary, chronicler writes simply that he had 'put to death the children of King Edward, for which cause he lost the hearts of the people. And thereupon many gentlemen intended his destruction.' The Duke was probably the first man to identify a political loser, and certainly the last to back one. He must have been badly shaken by the rising fury against the new regime. He knew that a serious rebellion was being planned; its leaders must have approached him very early on and as will be seen they were men of substance and position, not just adventurers. More tells us that what finally decided Buckingham on his course of action was the long discussions which he held with Dr John Morton, Bishop of Ely, whom the King had most unwisely placed in his custody—'whose wisdom deceived the Duke's pride, to his own deliverance and the Duke's destruction.'[1]

According to Sir Thomas, Buckingham may have been considering putting forward his own claim to the throne. He shows Morton flattering the Duke about his ability, and how he possessed 'excellent virtues meet for the rule of a realm'. Unfortunately More's *History* ends at this precise point, and we know that, even if it had continued, the author would have been unable to explain the real reasons for Buckingham's astonishing volte-face in the autumn of 1483. But, had the Duke really intended to aim at the crown, it is more than likely that it was the Bishop who—after first convincing him that Richard could not survive—persuaded Buckingham to step down in favour of the senior Beaufort-Lancastrian candidate, an obscure exile called Henry Tudor. His basic motive was self-preservation—he knew now that the King was doomed and he was determined not to go down with him.

Like the Duke of Buckingham, Dr Morton had a Lancastrian background. Indeed, he was now in his sixties, having been born in 1420 when the Lancastrian dynasty was at its zenith under Henry V. A typical prelate politician of the age, he had served Henry VI well and faithfully—in More's words 'He had been steadfast upon the party of King Henry while that party was in prosperity, and nevertheless left it not nor forsook it in woe.' Taken prisoner at Towton in 1461, instead of changing sides like most of his fellow Bishops who recognised the new Yorkish monarch, he had escaped from the Tower of London and gone to France to Margaret of Anjou and her son. This was at a point when their cause seemed quite hopeless and he knew that he would have to live as a penniless exile. He accompanied Queen Margaret on the disastrous road to Tewkesbury in 1471. Only when her son was dead and her cause finally lost, and only then, did he transfer his allegiance to Edward IV, whom he served with equal steadfastness. Sir Thomas makes him tell Buckingham 'if the world would have gone as I would have wished, King Henry's son had had the crown and not King Edward. But after God had ordered him to lose it and King Edward to reign, I was never so mad that I would with a dead man strive against the quick. So was I to King Edward faithful chaplain and glad would have been that his child had succeeded him.'

Thomas More, whose good opinion is not to be dismissed lightly, had a 'pleasant remembrance' of Morton and quite clearly admired and respected him. As a youth he was attached to his household, by which time the former Bishop of Ely—now in his eighties, but still sharp and vigorous—was Cardinal Archbishop of Canterbury and Lord Chancellor of England. In *Utopia* More puts a fascinating and attractive portrait of the old man into Ralph Hythloday's mouth. 'He was not more honourable for his authority than for his prudence. He was of a mean stature, and though stricken in age, yet bare he his body upright. In his face did shine such an amiable reverence as was pleasant to behold, gentle in communication, yet earnest and sage.' In his youth, *Utopia* continues, John Morton was 'taken from school into the court, and there passed his time in much trouble and business, being continually tumbled and tossed in the waves of diverse misfortunes and adversities. And so by any and great dangers he learned the experience of the world.' This estimate of his qualities is confirmed by Mancini, writing over thirty years before—'of great resource and daring' he says of the Bishop of Ely, 'trained in politics since King Henry [VI]'s time.' The Italian also stresses his unshakeable loyalty. There is no need to emphasise that Henry VII, who was nobody's fool, quickly arrived at a very similar estimate.[2]

However Morton has had a bad press in popular history, most unfairly. This is largely because of the merciless taxation he is supposed to have levied when Henry VII's Lord Chancellor. In fact 'Morton's Fork'—a device for crushing any unwilling tax-payers into the ground—should really be called 'Fox's Fork' since according to More it was Bishop Richard Fox who invented it. Furthermore, in spite of worldliness and a reputation for pluralism, he was a devout and responsible churchman, even according to Sir Thomas's demanding standards. Far from being the time-serving politician of tradition, he was something of a hero—which is plainly how More saw him. He has also been accused of being the real author of Sir Thomas's *History* (a theory long since disproved) or of telling a pack of lies about Richard—regardless of More's opportunities of checking his facts. Certainly he does not appear to have given More the impression that he was a liar.

The King may well have entrusted him to Buckingham because of his reputation as a brilliant administrator, with instructions to win him over. If an experienced politician, Morton was obviously by no means a compulsive intriguer, as he had firmly demonstrated by his steady loyalty to both the Houses of Lancaster and York. Despite his fidelity—and perhaps even readiness to fight for—Edward V during the usurpation, he was being treated with what looks like calculated leniency on Richard's part. Had he shown willingness to co-operate with the new régime, like Rotherham, he could no doubt have expected speedy forgiveness and preferment. Either, as with so many contemporary Englishmen, he simply could not stomach the dispossession and murder of the Princes—he may have learnt of the latter from Buckingham—or else his unusually acute political instinct told him that the country would never be at peace under its new King. Some distinguished modern historians have argued that, given time, Richard III's undoubted abilities and the excellent government he would have provided might have made his subjects accept him. Probably most of them were not prepared to give him the time. It was surely the Bishop of Ely's fertile brain which found a solution to unite the entire opposition to the usurper, whether it was Lancastrian, dissident Yorkist or even Woodville. Dr John Morton was going to be the architect of Richard's ruin.

For all the Petition and the Coronation, in strict law the rightful Yorkist claimant—now that Edward V and his brother were dead—was Edward IV's eldest daughter, Elizabeth of York. But she was still in sanctuary at Westminster and in any case at that date a woman, let alone an eighteen-year-old girl, was not acceptable as a candidate for the throne of England. A grown man was needed, who besides possessing a claim to the throne, could lead a political party and—in name at least—command armies in battle. There was such a man.

Despite Richard's alleged boast, when he murdered Henry VI, there were still heirs of Edward III through the female line, and not primarily Buckingham. The children of John of Gaunt (Edward's fifth son) by Catherine Swynford—the Beauforts, so called from the French castle in which they had been born—had entered the world as bastards, but Richard II had legitimated them with a Patent, which was confirmed by Act of Parliament. Their half-brother Henry IV, himself born in legitimate wedlock, had formally acknowledged this Patent though adding the words *excepta dignitate regali* which debarred them from succeeding to the throne; he omitted to make the disqualification law by a further Act of Parliament. Much later, lawyers were to argue with justice that a royal patent could not alter one confirmed by Parliament, and that in consequence the Beauforts were in no way debarred from the succession. Beyond question, during Henry VI's reign they had acted as full Princes of the Blood and had been tacitly accepted as such. The last legitimate Beaufort males had perished at Tewkesbury, but the family survived in the female line. Buckingham's mother had of course been a Beaufort. However, her first cousin, Margaret Beaufort, Countess of Richmond (now wife to Lord Stanley) was the senior representative. By the first of her marriages—to Edmund Tudor, Earl of Richmond, Henry VI's half-brother who had died in 1456—Margaret had begotten a single posthumous child, Henry.

By origin the Tudors were mere North-Welsh hedge squires, from Anglesey.[3] They claimed the legendary King Cadwallader as their ancestor, but in real life had been the smallest sort of Cymric gentry until the scandalous marriage of Henry's grandfather to the widow of Henry V, when he was still her Clerk of the Wardrobe; *his* father, Maredudd ap Tudur, had been a bastard and butler to the Bishop of Bangor. Yet for all the obscurity of his male forebears, Henry Tudor was the Beaufort and therefore the Lancastrian claimant to the throne of England. Edward IV had been very well aware of the existence of 'the only imp now left of Henry VI's brood' and had once or twice tried to get possession of him, presumably with a view to liquidation.'He [Henry] told me on one occasion,' Commynes remembers, 'that since the age of five he had been guarded like a fugitive or kept in prison.' Henry had seen almost nothing of his mother—only fourteen when she bore him—and spent his early childhood in the household of the Yorkist Lord Herbert, who intended to make him his son-in-law. He was not rescued by his own family until the Re-adeption of Henry VI when his uncle, Jasper Tudor, Earl of Pembroke, found him and then after Tewkesbury fled with him to the semi-independent Duchy of Brittany. Here, Commynes informs us, from the age of fifteen 'he had lived the life of a prisoner', although Duke Francis II treated him 'reasonably well'. Probably about 1475 to 1476 King Edward very nearly laid hands on Henry by pretending that he wanted to marry him to one of his daughters; the youth only escaped by falling ill and delaying his departure for England; during his illness a friendly Breton explained the true situation—that he was being sent to his death—to Francis II who relented and kept him in Brittany.

One should not exaggerate Henry Tudor's importance before the usurpation of 1483. He was taken seriously as the Pretender, if at all, by only a handful of Englishmen—either rare die-hard Lancastrian fanatics or else a few exiles who had despaired of a Yorkist pardon. Yet this tiny group would suddenly grow into a court in exile.

Contemplating the horrific visage of the miserly old Welshman painted by Michael Sittow in 1505, with which we are so familiar, one may wonder how such a creature could attract any adherents at all. But in 1483 he was only twenty-seven and an early sketch (admittedly known only from a sixteenth-century copy) shows a surprisingly amiable, even debonair young man. Polydore Vergil, who often met him in later life and who wrote after he was safely dead, tells us that 'His appearance was remarkably attractive and his face was cheerful, particularly when speaking.' Professor Chrimes, the author of his definitive biography, says 'we have to think of a man impressive and outstanding—tall, rather slender, dignified, of sallow complexion, and rather aquiline features, whose most striking characteristic was the vivacity of his expression and the brilliance of his small blue eyes, especially animated in conversation.' His ruthlessness only showed itself after he had won the throne, his excessive avarice and the mad Valois streak only towards the end of his life. Unquestionably, he was quite as unscrupulous as Richard, but he was also far more intelligent, much subtler. However in the mid-1480s optimists no doubt discerned a romantic young royal fugitive who was the last representative of a tragically lost cause. Exiles and opponents of the King must have been delighted to find a leader who was more Beaufort and Valois prince than Welsh adventurer. Thanks to Buckingham and Dr Morton—and, above all, to his mother—he was soon to become an infinitely preferred alternative to Richard III.

As soon as the Duke had been won over by the Bishop, the latter sent a message to Margaret Beaufort's chief steward, Reginald Bray, asking him to visit Brecon discreetly in order to discuss a matter of some delicacy. Clearly Bray was impressed by Morton's plan and the Duke's support, returning to his mistress with a glowing report. But Margaret Beaufort had already concocted her own scheme, which was very similar to the plot being hatched at Brecon.

Although the real Lancastrian and Beaufort claimant to the throne, like Elizabeth of York Margaret was ruled out as a pretender simply because she was a woman. Still only forty, she had had three husbands: Henry's father, Edmund Tudor, Earl of Richmond; Lord Humphrey Stafford, Buckingham's uncle; and, since 1473, Lord Stanley. A remarkable survivor, she had seen the court of Henry VI and Margaret of Anjou and would live to be aware of that of Henry VIII and Catherine of Aragon. Too little is known about her, yet though convention forced her to keep the most discreet of profiles, she was the first great Tudor and the first successful female politician in English history. The bronze tomb effigy by Pietro Torrigiano in Westminster Abbey—that greatest of monuments to Richard's overthrow—shows a strikingly handsome face of austere refinement with strong, if superbly delicate, features; when young she must have been a considerably beauty. Devout, perhaps saintly, she heard six Masses every day and was an ascetic with a taste for mysticism; she personally translated *The Mirror of Souls* from the French, besides initiating the translation and printing of many other devotional works, including the *Imitation of Christ*. Her future confessor was Bishop John Fisher, a canonised Catholic saint. Nevertheless, Margaret was masterful and plainly attracted by power—during her son's reign she would be described by an informed observer as one of the half dozen most influential people in England, and was allowed to sign herself 'Margaret R.' King Richard had no more dangerous opponent than this quiet, pious lady.

To judge from her behaviour in 1483, and from what we may guess about it in 1485, Margaret was an unregenerate Lancastrian and a natural politician, as shrewd as she was courageous and determined. (Sir George Buck describes her, quaintly but accurately, as 'a lady of a politic and contriving bosom'.) Her ambition, both for herself and her son, was surely fuelled by a sense of moral outrage. No doubt she venerated the memory of poor Henry VI and abhorred Richard for having butchered him, let alone for being a usurper. It is clear that by early September at latest, probably very much sooner, she was aware that the Princes in the Tower had been murdered. Someone with no less keen a policital instinct than the Bishop of Ely, she must have realised at once how powerful a candidate for the throne her only child—whom she had not seen for a quarter of a century, when he was still a baby—would become if he married Edward IV's eldest daughter.

By coincidence, Margaret shared the same physician as Elizabeth Woodville, a Welshman from Caerleon called Dr Lewis. She was therefore able to contact the former Queen who was still immured at Westminster, and propose that the Woodvilles should support Henry's claims; in return he would marry Elizabeth of York. 'Dame Elizabeth Grey' accepted the terms with alacrity. (She too must have known that by now her royal sons were dead.) Margaret then told Reginald Bray to enlist supporters among the gentry. When he brought news, probably totally unexpected, from Dr Morton that—of all people—her nephew Buckingham had decided to come out for Henry, she saw a real chance of a successful rising. Immediately she despatched a messenger to her son in Brittany to explain the situation and to tell him to join Buckingham in Wales. In was probably Henry Tudor's first intimation that one day he might be King of England. The messenger also delivered 'a good, great sum of money'.

Elizabeth of York was almost certainly told of the plan and the projected marriage. *The Most Pleasant Song of the Lady Bessy* is a late version of a contemporary ballad in her honour, composed in her lifetime, though written down only afterwards. (The author seems to have been a household man of Lord Stanley, Humphrey Brereton.) It is often pure fantasy and is full of anachronisms. However it may be correct in saying that Elizabeth sent a ring and a letter to Henry— by the hand of the poet himself—together with a large consignment of gold, presumably from the treasure her mother had brought into Westminster.

The conspiracy gathered momentum. Everywhere there were people who welcomed the hitherto almost undreamt of idea of the Earl of Richmond as Pretender. (Which surely indicates that, like Buckingham, Morton, Margaret, and Elizabeth Woodville and her daughters, they were already fairly certain that Edward V and his brother had by now been murdered.) From Kent Sir Richard Guildford sent a messenger, Thomas Romney, to Henry, pledging his support. By late September the Duke of Buckingham himself was in direct communication with the Earl.

It shows a quite extraordinary lack of political acumen on Richard's part that when the news of a revolt arrived he had not yet recognised that Henry Tudor was the most dangerous of his enemies. Apart from a sense of outrage at the Duke's betrayal, the King's chief reaction was probably alarm at the strategic implications. Not only was Buckingham the Constable of England—Commander-in-Chief—but he had been made supreme in Wales, on the Welsh Border and in the West Country, and given control of all fortresses and arsenals throughout these areas largely because they were hotbeds of die-hard Lancastrianism. If in 1471 Margaret of Anjou's Westcountrymen had succeeded in outmarching Edward IV and linked up with their Welsh comrades, Henry VI might still have been on the throne in 1483. The Severn had foiled them. Now the Duke of Buckingham controlled both banks of that vital river. Moreover he also possessed a base in the Home Counties, in Kent; from his father he had inherited Penshurst Place—a tower there is still called 'Buckingham's Tower'—near Tonbridge.[4] The local Kentish landowners would have known his household men and had very likely met the Duke himself.

Probably Richard's government at first found some difficulty in identifying just who was involved with Buckingham. There had been rumours of angry discontent since the usurpation. It seems that as soon as the new King's progress reached the Midlands, 'meetings and confederacies' began among the gentry all over the South and West Country, 'who had begun to murmur greatly', to discuss how to rescue Edward V and York; none of them realized that they were dead. The Crowland Chronicle—if it really was Richard's Lord Chancellor who supplied the basic text—gives us an invaluable summary of the situation as it must have appeared to the King and his Council in the last half of October. 'The people round about London, and throughout Kent, Essex, Sussex, Hampshire, Dorset, Devon, Somerset, Wiltshire and Berkshire, as well as some other Southern counties, decided to set matters right [i.e., restore Edward V]; upon which it was publicly announced that Henry, Duke of Buckingham, who was then at Brecon in Wales, regretted his former conduct and would be a leader of the movement, but then a rumour spread that King Edward [IV]'s sons had died a violent death, though how it was not known. [Dr Hanham thinks that the writer means that Richard actually encouraged the rumour, in order to scotch the rebellion.] Accordingly, the men who had started the revolt, realizing that without a Pretender they were doomed, suddenly thought of Henry, Earl of Richmond. The chronicler continues 'The Duke of Buckingham, acting on the advice of the Lord Bishop of Ely, who was his prisoner at Brecon, sent a message to him which asked him to come to England to marry Elizabeth, the late King's daughter, and take possession of the throne.' As the days went by, Richard was to be made aware that a very large number of his subjects indeed regarded him as 'the wretched, bloody and usurping boar'.

The regions ready to rise against the King are interesting. As has been seen, the West Country was still fiercely anti-Yorkist, while much of Wales was involved—though not very willingly—under Buckingham. Both were traditionally Lancastrian areas, as was Kent. But the districts round London and the central Southern counties had hitherto been Yorkist.

To a certain degree the rising in the Southern counties was the long expected Woodville counter-*coup*. Lord Dorset and his uncle, Bishop Lionel, suddenly appeared in the latter's see of Salisbury, where they busily recruited supporters. In Berkshire Sir Richard Woodville found an ally in Sir William Stonor, an old friend of Dorset. In Devon there was Sir Thomas St Leger, who wanted Dorset's son as a husband for his daughter. Sir George Browne, of Betchworth Castle near Reigate in Surrey, was the stepson of old Sir Thomas Vaughan who had been beheaded at Pontefract. In Kent Sir John Fogge was married to a Haute, a cousin of the man who had perished with Vaughan.

But it is quite wrong to see the Southerners as being restricted to Woodvilles and their kindred. As has been seen, Buckingham possessed a base in Kent which was only a few hours ride from the houses of Browne and Fogge. Moreover there were plenty of Lancastrians, especially in the West. In Devonshire there was Sir Edward Courtenay of Boconnoc (rightful Earl of Devon) with his kinsman Peter Courtenay, Bishop of Exeter, and in Cornwall the Arundells. And some of the plotters even belonged to Richard's household, while he had made Sir Thomas Lewkenor a Knight of the Bath at his Coronation. Primarily, however, the rebels of 1483 were men who remained loyal to the memory of Edward IV. A considerable number had been members of the late King's household. They rose out of furious resentment at Richard's treachery towards the children, his stealing of their inheritance.

What is also striking is that so many of the conspirators—over a dozen at least—had been Members of Parliament, where they may have first become acquainted. Stonor had represented Oxfordshire, Browne Surrey and Canterbury, and Fogge Kent—Stonor's rising in Berkshire was joined by another former MP, John Norris, Browne in Surrey by yet another Sir Thomas Bourchier of Horsley, who had fought at Barnet. (He was a kinsman of the Cardinal Archbishop and thus of the King himself.) In Sussex Sir Thomas Lewkenor of Bodiam Castle had likewise represented his county. In East Anglia there was Sir William Knyvet, once MP for Norfolk. In Wiltshire both Sir John Cheyney and Sir Walter Hungerford of Farley Hungerford had been members for their county, as in Somerset had Sir Giles Daubeny (one of Reginald Bray's recruits). In Devonshire St Leger too had been an MP—for Surrey—and Sir Richard Edgecombe had represented Tavistock. These were persons of standing, with wide lands and valuable offices, rich, middle-aged men, leaders of local society and not hotheaded, penniless adventurers with nothing to lose. They were able to rally many lesser gentry and substantial yeomen to their cause.

Their eventual plan of campaign was not ill conceived. Separate but concerted risings were timed for 18 October, St Luke's Day. The Kentishmen and the men of Surrey, Sussex and Essex would make a feigned attack on London to divert Richard from the real onslaught from Wales and the West Country. The South-Eastern musters were to be at Maidstone, Guildford and Gravesend under Fogge, Browne and Knyvet with the valuable assistance of Sir Richard Guildford and his son (from Rolvenden on the edge of Romney Marsh). More serious would be gatherings in Berkshire and Wiltshire under Stonor and Cheyney since they hope to be speedily reinforced from the West Country; Sir Richard Woodville was with Stonor at Newbury, Bishop Lionel with Cheyney at Salisbury. The South West would be led by Dorset, St Leger and the Courtenays. But the most important blow was to be struck by Buckingham, who intended to cross the Severn with his Welsh levies and link up with the Westcountrymen. (It was Somerset's campaign of 1471 in reverse.) Finally Henry Tudor, with 5,000 Breton mercenaries—hired with money lent by Duke Francis—would land on the South-Western coast.

The King received news of the impending rebellion and of Buckingham's involvement on 11 October. His spies had discovered the plot just in time. It took him so completely by surprise that he was without the Great Seal. On 12 October he wrote from Lincoln to the Lord Chancellor, ordering him to send it with all speed possible. Richard added a postcript, which rings with almost hysterical rage. It contains these words: 'Here, loved be God, is all well and truly determined, and for to resist the malice of him that had best cause to be true, the Duke of Buckingham, the most untrue creature living; whom with God's grace we shall not be long till that we will be in those parts and subdue his malice. We assure you there was never false traitor better purveyed for . . . ' (The phrase 'loved be God' has a personal sound about it, and may often have been on the King's lips with perhaps a Yorkshire accent.) The Great Seal arrived soon enough, being delivered to Richard on 18 October at the Angel and Royal Inn at Grantham. His army—including 300 men from York—assembled at Leicester, in sufficient strength for him to be justified in his savage optimism and to march South on 24 October.

As Lord High Constable of England, Buckingham had been the King's senior military officer. Among his duties was that of presiding over court martials. To replace him Richard therefore appointed a Vice-Constable. He chose Sir Ralph Assheton of Fritton-in-Redesdale. Born in 1420 and consequently well over sixty, Assheton was by origin a Lancashire man, although he lived in Yorkshire and had been a Sheriff of that county. Not only had he served with distinction in the Scottish War, but he came from a family noted for soldiers, his father having been one of Henry V's most trusted senior commanders in France. A long-standing member of the Household, Sir Ralph had ridden in his master's Coronation procession. He appears to have had an extremely unpleasant name, perhaps partly from the fact that his half-brother was a famous alchemist and partly from his affectation of always wearing black armour, though chiefly because of his ferocity. His conduct during the subsequent campaign in 1483 earned him much hatred. The King gave him power to try treason cases 'without formalities or appeal'. A grim jingle ran:

> 'Sweet Jesu for thy mercy's sake
> And for thy bitter Passion,
> Save us from the axe of the Tower
> And from Sir Ralph of Assheton.'

The 'Black Knight', as he was popularly known on account of his armour, is credited—in legend—with rolling prisoners downhill in barrels filled with spikes. Unquestionably he was the best man for stamping out rebellion of any sort, but Richard did not endear himself to his subjects by employing someone with quite so sinister a reputation as the Black Knight.

Luckily for the King the Duke of Norfolk happened to be in London where the news of the rising broke on 10 October. Apparently the rebels in the Home Counties would not wait and rose prematurely. He at once began to assemble troops; he wrote to John Paston, among others, asking him to bring 'six tall fellows in harness' (armour) and explaining that 'the Kentishmen be up in the Weald and say that they will come and rob the City.' One may guess that Norfolk had the fervent support of the Londoners, who remembered other visitations from Kent, such as those by Jack Cade and the Bastard of Fauconberg, only too well. The Duke quickly despatched a small force to occupy Gravesend, and this effectively stopped the Kentishmen from crossing the Thames to join their friends from Essex. He also occupied Reigate, which frightened off the Surrey men at Betchworth Castle, and sent out raiding parties. Shaken, the rebels withdrew to Guildford to await the arrival of their main army from the West Country.[5]

However the Duke of Buckingham raised his standard at Brecon on 18 October, as originally planned. This was the same day that Norfolk was occupying Reigate. Accompanied by the Bishop of Ely and various others—including a certain Thomas Nandike, 'necromancer of Cambridge' as he was to be described in the subsequent Bill of Attainder—Buckingham began his fateful march. The Westcountrymen also rose as planned, and seem to have proclaimed the Earl of Richmond 'King Henry VII' at Bodmin.

Richard, acting 'in no drowsy manner' according to the Crowland chronicler, had already used his agents to stir up the Welsh Yorkists. These raided the Duke's lands as soon as he marched off. The local Welsh had been bullied and oppressed by Buckingham, 'a sore and hard dealing man' and must have caused considerable damage—no doubt news of it was brought to the Duke's levies, who began to desert. In any case few of his 'tenants' felt any obligation to join him. Still more important, one of the henchmen, Sir Humphrey Stafford of Grafton—presumably with the campaign of 1471 in mind— speedily organised breaking down bridges and blockading roads into England. However, it was all unnecessary. The heavens opened and a deluge like Noah's Flood descended. Soon the Severn and the Avon broke their banks and every little stream became a raging torrent; fords vanished and roads turned into quagmires—the Vale of Evesham transformed itself into an inland sea. The 'Duke of Buckingham's Water' was long remembered, with horror. The chronicler Grafton is almost certainly reporting accurate folk memory when he says that 'Men were drowned in their beds, children were carried about the fields, swimming in cradles, beasts were drowned on hills; the rage of water lasted continually for ten days.'

Buckingham never succeeded in even crossing the Severn, and only got as far as the Forest of Dean. Sodden, famished, hopelessly demoralised, his unexpectedly small army simply disintegrated and ran for cover. He himself retreated North, perhaps making for Brecon though by now his stronghold there had been stormed by the King's men. The Duke had already entrusted his son Lord Stafford to the wife of a faithful follower, Lady Delabeare, who shaved the little boy's head, dressed him like a girl and concealed him in a safe place. Buckingham disguised himself as a labourer and took refuge near Wem in Shropshire in the house of a supposedly trustworthy retainer, his servant Humphrey Bannister. Dr Morton, whose instinct for survival was much more strongly developed, made discreetly for East Anglia and, after hiding for a while in the Fens of his diocese, crossed unnoticed to Flanders. (Ludicrously, Richard's latterday partisans have accused the fugitive prelate of finding time, while on the run, to visit Crowland Abbey and falsify its monks' chronicle.)

Meanwhile the furious King, with his undoubted flair for strategy, was marching Southwards—first towards Coventry, and then towards the West Country, which he had correctly identified as the most dangerous region. He had issued an extraordinary proclamation, phrased in his most self-righteous style, against the 'traitors, adulterers and bawds'. Headed 'Proclamation for the Reform of Morals', it alleges that Dorset was a dishonorer of 'sundry maids, widows and wives' and that the rebels were guilty of 'the damnable maintenance of vices and sin as they had in times past, to the great displeasure of God and evil example of all Christian people.' (Ross comments that it 'reads more like a tract against sexual licence than a condemnation of armed treason.')[6] More practically, besides these clumsy attempts at character assassination, he offered huge rewards for their capture; whoever apprehended Buckingham would receive either £1,000 or lands worth £100 a year (the fortune of a substantial squire or even knight) though some rebels rated only £12 a year.

Richard soon learnt how Norfolk had ended any threat to London, then of the disaster which had overtaken Buckingham.

So did the rebels in the West Country and the Home Counties, themselves demoralised by the wretched weather. They dispersed in panic, those who could fleeing abroad, some going into sanctuary, others taking to the woods. When Richard reached Salisbury at the very end of October, he met no opposition whatever. Shortly afterwards the Duke of Buckingham was brought in by the Sheriff of Shropshire, to whom he had been betrayed by Bannister. (The latter was set up as a gentleman in reward, as Lord of the Manor of Yalding in Kent.) Buckingham was immediately tried by a court presided over by Assheton and sentenced to death. He begged frantically for an audience of the King, who refused; perhaps wisely, since years later the Duke's son claimed that his father had meant to kill Richard with a hunting knife. The over mighty, over subtle, Harry Buckingham was beheaded in Salisbury market place on Sunday 2 November, although it was All Souls' as well as the Lord's Day. His vast estates were forfeited to the Crown. The King marched on into the far West Country, right down to Exeter where he had arrived by 8 November; he installed himself in the Bishops' Palace from where Peter Courtenay had fled only a few hours before. He was watching the situation throughout the entire South and sent orders to besiege Bodiam in Sussex—though that mighty fortress put up little resistance, quickly surrendering to the Earl of Surrey.[7]

In the meantime Henry Tudor had sailed from Paimpol in Brittany, apparently in late October. The same storm which ruined the rising inland struck his little fleet at sea and left him with only two ships—he must have had to run before the wind. When he sailed into a West Country port, either Poole or Plymouth, he saw that the harbour was ringed with troops and sent a boat to investigate. The armed men on shore—who were Richard's—shouted that they were a detachment of Buckingham's army. Henry was too wary to be caught, and realized that there had been a disaster. Wisely, he set sail for Brittany. He was forced to land in Normandy, but after three days received French permission to march back to Brittany. Here he was told of Buckingham's death though also that Dorset and others were at Vannes. He summoned them to meet him at Rennes, the Ducal capital.

At Exeter, among others, the King executed Sir Thomas St Leger on 12 November. He was Richard's brother-in-law, having been the second husband of his sister Anne, and offered a large sum of money in return for his life—to no avail. (There was a familiar moralising note in the subsequent Act of Attainder; St Leger had 'by seditious means married Anne, Duchess of Exeter, late wife of the said Duke, he being then living.') We do not know how many conspirators perished. Vergil names several besides St Leger whom the King executed together with 'divers others, even of his own household'.

Some were taken to London to suffer. They included four former Yeomen of the Crown to Edward IV, who were hanged, drawn and quartered at Tyburn. Sir George Browne and another leading rebel were beheaded on Tower Hill in December.

Half a century afterwards Sir Thomas Wyatt—the poet and lover of Anne Boleyn—boasted of the fidelity of his father, Henry Wyatt, to the Earl of Richmond. Richard had imprisoned the elder Wyatt in the Tower for nearly two years, presumably for involvement in the rising of 1483. According to his son, Richard had him racked in his presence. 'Wyatt, why art thou such a fool?' asked the King, 'Henry of Richmond is a beggarly pretender; forsake him and become mine. Thou servest him for moonshine in water.' The tale is supposedly supported by a fanciful Wyatt family legend of later date: 'King Richard, in a rage, had him confined in a low and narrow cell, where he had not clothes sufficient to warm him and was a hungered. A cat came into the cell, he caressed her for company, laid her in his bosom and won her love. And so she came to him every day and brought him a pigeon when she could catch one.' Wyatt, one is told, persuaded the gaoler to cook the birds for him, surviving to be released by Henry VII and given high office. The legend adds that for the rest of his life Henry Wyatt 'would ever make much of cats'. After allowing for poetic exaggeration, there may be a basis of truth in the story of Henry Wyatt's imprisonment. Wyatt had land in Surrey near Camberwell and could have been recruited for Buckingham by the neighbouring Gaisfords of Carshalton. He was extremely able (to judge from his future career under Henry VII) and the King may indeed have thought that he would make a useful servant.[8]

Richard spent mid-November marching from Devon to London. He went by way of Salisbury, Winchester, Farnham and Guildford. He returned to his capital in the last week of November, receiving the customary welcome from leading citizens who rode out to meet him at Kennington.

He had put down an extremely dangerous rebellion without meeting a sword drawn in anger. Yet he was sewing dragons' teeth. First by confiscating Southern estates on a scale which had not been seen for a century; as Machiavelli might have told him, 'men forget the death of their father sooner than the loss of their patrimony.' Moreover he did not wait for such formalities as Acts of Attainder and confiscated them illegally. Second by giving the estates to Northern henchmen like Scrope, Assheton, and Ratcliff—the last picked up manors worth nearly £700 a year, the income of a minor peer—or to the greatest in the land, whose loyalty would always be dubious. At least a hundred other Northerners profited. He should have brought in support from other regions as well instead of alienating them by his obvious preference for the North. He simply did not know how to use the vast patronage which had fallen into his hands.

The King's ineptitude was especially apparent in his treatment of the Stanleys. Although the head of that wily family had first to suffer interrogation by the Council to make quite sure, he had given a show of loyalty which delighted Richard. Lord Stanley received Buckingham's office of Constable of England together with large grants of land, while his brother Sir William—one of fifteenth-century England's shiftiest personalities—obtained key posts in Wales and valuable estates. Lord Stanley's wife Margaret Beaufort, a principal architect of the conspiracy, had the penalties of attainder 'which she deserves' remitted; her lands were merely taken from her and transferred to her husband 'for the good love and trust that the King has in him'.

The Earl of Northumberland, quite as treacherous as any Stanley, was given Buckingham's great office, that of Lord Great Chamberlain of England—which had been held by Richard himself when he was Duke of Gloucester and even when he was Protector. Many of Buckingham's manors also went to the Percy. The régime's four main props had become three and two of them were far from sound— only Norfolk was genuinely loyal.

However much the Duke of Buckingham's rebellion might have failed, it had secured the long term objective of Dr Morton and Margaret Beaufort. The hitherto almost unknown Henry Tudor was transformed into the acknowledged Lancastrian Pretender—a pretender too for those Yorkists who were horrified by the realization that Edward V had been murdered. As Dr Rowse observes, the Earl of Richmond 'would never have been brought forward if Richard had been content to remain Protector and done his duty by his nephews.' Moreover Henry now had something very like a court in exile, which included several extremely experienced and talented soldiers and prelates—besides an incomparable party manager in the Bishop of Ely, even if the latter preferred to remain in Flanders. Astonishingly, the King's proclamation of 23 October against Buckingham, Dorset and all the other 'traitors, adulterers and bawds', had not even bothered to mention Henry Tudor.

Yet at this time Richard must have seemed unassailable. He had demonstrated triumphantly that he could survive a very widespread, very well-supported and very well-organised revolt. He kept Christmas 1483 with notable magnificence at Westminster. Large quantities of silver plate were purchased for the festivities, even though various royal treasures had to be pawned to pay for them. (These treasures included a gold plated helmet which had belonged to Edward IV.) He bought exceptionally rich robes for himself and his Queen— spending the staggering sum of £1,200—as well as buying costly gems from a Genoese dealer. There is a hint of over-dressing here, like that by some insecure *nouveau riche*. Nevertheless Commynes was sufficiently impressed by what he heard to note that Richard was reigning with greater splendour than any King of England 'these last hundred years'.

Such exuberant magnificence befitted a monarch who is sometimes described as a Renaissance Prince. To apply the word Renaissance to a North-Western European at this date may perhaps seem anachronistic; Gothic art and architecture were still flourishing in England. Yet the humanist revolution was crossing the Alps, even if the English Renaissance was a very slow process, which developed at a different pace and in a different way to the Renaissance in Italy. Undoubtedly there was cultural contact—the very presence in London of an Italian man of letters like Mancini indicates an exchange of ideas. In fact Richard's court poet, Pietro Carmeliano, was a humanist from Brescia while the court clerics included men who had studied Greek in Italy and collected manuscripts. Moreover the decline of Christianity into the popular ritual observances and mechanistic superstitions favoured by the King himself produced the same moral vacuum in England as in Italy which was so opportune for the self-conscious rise of Renaissance *Realpolitik*. It is surely significant that a humanist like Sir Thomas More could believe that he understood Richard—who was his near contemporary—so well. In more ways than one the King anticipated his great-nephew, Henry VIII. For the new Yorkist monarchy was no less a manifestation of the Renaissance than the Tudor monarchy which grew out of it. Richard III may have known nothing of Italian statecraft, and was born too early to be acquainted with the works of Machiavelli (his junior by seventeen years), yet in his lack of scruple and ferocity he was very much of a Renaissance tyrant.

When speaking of Richard, Commynes uses the word 'proud' more than once. Plainly he employs it in the sense of vain glory or self delusion. Had he known the word 'hubris' he would have used that too. For the King was defying fate. Despite his ostentatious splendour, his régime was under constant threat, withgrowing opposition everywhere—at home and abroad.

In Rennes Cathedral at dawn on Christmas morning 1483 Henry Tudor, Earl of Richmond, took a solemn oath that he would marry Elizabeth of York. At the same time his fellow exiles, Lancastrian and Yorkist alike, swore loyalty to each other. Then they knelt before the Earl and did him homage, as though he had already been crowned and annointed King Henry VII. They also swore to return to England and overthrow the tyrant.

King Richard nevertheless remained England's all-powerful sovereign. According to the Crowland writer he celebrated Christmas 1483 with great pomp. He had much to celebrate. He also had many immediate worries.

Understandably, relations between the English government and the Duchy of Brittany had become strained. They were made worse by the increasing activities of West-Country pirates. Although it was winter a fleet of Breton privateers harried English shipping in turn, very nearly capturing the precious Calais wool fleet which only escaped by fleeing back to England. In December a squadron of King's Ships commanded by Thomas Wentworth was sent out to destroy the Breton fleet; Wentworth was unsuccessful, though several enemy vessels were captured. Meanwhile the authorities in London and the West Country confiscated all Breton ships and goods they could lay their hands on. Richard saw the futility of such a conflict, which would only infuriate English merchants, and soon tried diplomacy. Yet he did not make a really serious effort to persuade the Bretons to hand over Henry Tudor until summer 1484—he still did not take him seriously enough.

Despite the dreadful winter roads of the period, in January 1484 the King went on progress through that notoriously turbulent and disaffected county, Kent. Mediaeval Kentishmen had a name for pugnacity and lawlessness, besides a lingering loyalty to the House of Lancaster. When Richard visited Canterbury during the progress the Mayor and Corporation offered him a somewhat meagre purse of gold (£33. 6s. 8d.), which he declined. Bishop Langton took it instead. No doubt the King prayed edifyingly at the shrine of St Thomas.

Kent had not been exactly idle during the recent rebellion and Richard clearly expected more trouble. He had already set up a command centre at Buckingham's princely house of Penshurst Place, installing a Northern *Gauleiter*—Sir Marmaduke Constable from Flamborough in Yorkshire. A Knight of the Body, Constable was plainly a key man in the 'mafia', even if he had begun his career as a Percy retainer; probably he transferred his service before Richard became King—he is known to have distinguished himself at the siege of Berwick.[9] On 16 December 1483 Sir Marmaduke had been appointed Steward of the Manors of Penshurst, Tonbridge and Brasted, his job being principally to stop 'livery and retaining'—to put an end in Kent to private armies—and also to see that every Kentishman of substance took a comprehensive oath of allegiance. Since he spent only a few months in the county, it is likely that he had some success; the Kentishmen remained untypically quiet for the rest of the reign. He was soon moved up to the Midlands, to perform the same task there from Tutbury Castle in Staffordshire. Constable received very substantial rewards, in the form of offices, annuities and estates (among the latter was a certain manor in Leicestershire, Market Bosworth). About the same age as Richard he was popularly known as 'little Sir Marmaduke', and perhaps his small size helped recommend him to the King; little men tend to like other little men.

Shortly afterwards the King issued a proclamation which states that 'His Grace is utterly determined that all his subjects shall live in rest and quiet, and peaceably enjoy their lands, livelihoods and goods, according to the laws of this his land.' He was determined to win popularity by an ostentatious display of benevolence and by showing himself to be an efficient ruler concerned with justice before

31. *Tomb and effigy probably that of Richard's son, Edward of Middleham,
Prince of Wales. At Sheriff Hutton Church, Yorkshire.*

32. *Richard and his wife, Anne Neville. Richard had to deny publicly in 1485 that he was 'willing or glad of the death of his Queen.' The Duke of Buccleuch and Queensberry K.T.*

ELIZABETHA · VXOR
HENRICI · VII ·

33. *Richard's niece, Elizabeth of York. In 1485 he was forced to deny publicly that he intended to marry her. National Portrait Gallery, London.*

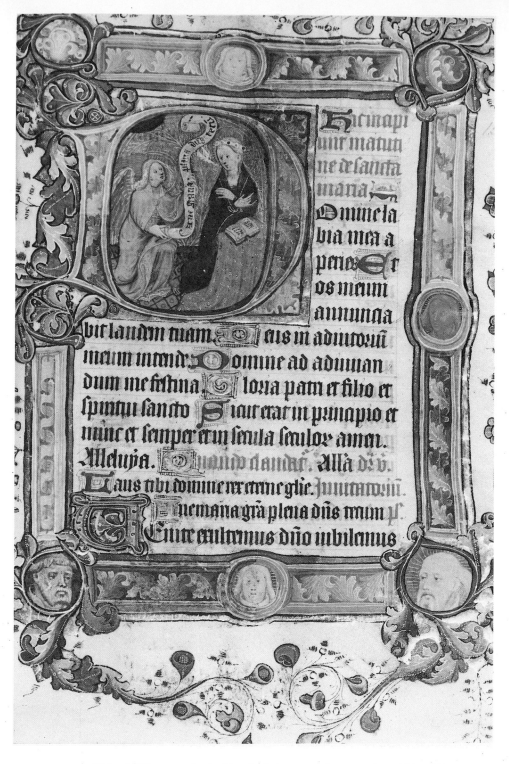

34. *Richard III's prayer book. Illuminated c. 1440 for a member of his wife's family, it eventually passed to the hands of his enemy Margaret Beaufort. Lambeth Palace Library, London.*

all else. Indeed in December he had already deputed some of his Council to sit at Westminster in the White Hall to hear 'the bills, requests and supplications of poor persons'—an innovation which later grew into the Court of Requests.

Richard's obsession with what would nowadays be termed his image was obviously only too apparent to the court poet, Pietro Carmeliano. As a needy sycophant with all his countrymen's talent for insinuating flattery, he knew just what was required. In the introduction to a manuscript copy of his *Life of St. Catherine of Egypt*, produced between 1483 and 1485 and dedicated to Sir Robert Brackenbury, he inserted some Latin lines which refer to Richard. 'If we look for devout religion first and foremost, can any Prince show more piety? If we wish for justice, whom in the entire world may be placed before him? If we contemplate his prudent conduct both in peace and war, whom shall be considered his equal? If we seek for a soul of truth, for highmindedness joined with wisdom, who is there to take precedence of our King?' Brackenbury would certainly have recognised this as his master's ideal picture of himself. (In 1486 Carmeliano, essentially a professional, was to write of Richard as having been an evil and ferocious monster.)

A desperate anxiety to demonstrate that he was a worthy, a devoted King is evident in Richard's conciliatory attitude during his one and only Parliament. It met on 23 January 1484.[10] Summoned for the previous November, it had had to be postponed because of Buckingham's rebellion. Among Members of the House of Commons were William Catesby, Humphrey Stafford, Walter Hopton, Thomas Pilkington and John Harrington, together with at least a dozen others from the Household—probably including Ralph Assheton the Vice-Constable and James Tyrell, by now promoted to Master of the Horse. The King made a conscious attempt to use the Parliament to enlist national support, which may be why its proceedings were recorded in English instead of Law French for the first time. The Lord Chancellor preached an eloquent and learned opening address, skilfully adapted from the one he had prepared for the abortive Parliament of the murdered Edward V. He took as his text the words from Scripture 'We have many members in one body, and all members have not the same office.' Bishop Russell then launched into an appeal for unity, with frequent references to the 'commonweal', claiming that the recent revolt against Richard had violated God's Commandments—he gracefully labelled the late Duke of Buckingham as 'a rotten member'. After this Catesby was elected Speaker of the House of Commons, and spokesman for its Knights and Burgesses.

The first Bill passed confirms the new King's title to the throne, in an attempt to use Parliament to persuade a sceptical England that his claim was valid. It declares Richard III to be the true King of the Realm by inheritance, election, consecration and coronation, and acknowledges his son as heir apparent by settling the succession on the heirs of Richard's body. What in fact was being enacted was the Petition presented to the Protector in the previous June, though now slightly amended. The avowed purpose of the Act (later to be referred to as *Titulus Regius*) is that by 'quieting men's minds' it 'removeth the occasion of all doubts and seditious language.' As Alison Hanham observes, 'When a legal parliament finally gave its authority to this remarkable document, disquiet and sedition had indeed shaken the country.'[11]

The Lords and Commons—the two Houses were meeting together in the Painted Chamber at Westminster—then passed the various Bills of Attainder. A hundred persons are named—among them thirty-three from Wiltshire, twenty-eight from Kent and Surrey, eighteen from Exeter and fourteen from Berkshire. (This was a quarter of all people attainted between 1459 and 1509.) The attainders confirm that their lives are forfeit, save for the Bishops', and that their estates have been confiscated. Richard, behaving with calculated magnanimity, later pardoned over a third of those concerned—this was standard practice during the Wars of the Roses, while many of the others were in any case safe in Brittany. The King even gave a pardon to Sir John Fogge, whom he had pardoned once already; here his motive must surely have been showmanship—a display of unheard of generosity. One again recalls what More says of Richard—'with large gifts he got him unsteadfast friendship.' Gairdner emphasises that these 'concessions granted in the hour of danger to those who had given him the most annoyance, could have done little either to win or strengthen the attachment of the people to his throne.' Indeed, although pardoned, Sir Richard Edgecombe refused to leave Brittany and abandon Henry Tudor.

Certainly the Parliament did nothing to redress the anger caused by the confiscation of so many estates in Southern England, an anger which was not merely confined to their former owners. Most of the henchmen who took them over were Northerners with little time for Southern susceptibilities and, so the Crowland chronicler informs us, their heavy-handed occupation of their new manors aroused bitter resentment. All 'the people of the South . . . daily longed more and more for the . . . return of their ancient rulers rather than the present tyranny of these people.' Professor Ross calls it 'a virtual colonisation of northern barons, knights and esquires'. It continued for the rest of the reign, with a methodical takeover of local administration throughout the Southern counties, Northerners becoming Sheriffs and Justices of the Peace from Kent to Cornwall. Thus, Edward Redmayne from Yorkshire became Sheriff of Dorset and Somerset; Halnath Mauleverer, another Yorkshireman, became Sheriff of Devon; and Thomas Huddleston from Cumberland became Sheriff of Gloucestershire. Sir John Savile, from Thornhill in the West Riding, was appointed Governor of the Isle of Wight.[12]

The Parliament passed some undeniably useful measures. Henceforth it was illegal when selling land to conceal rights, or secret feoffments, held over it by others; this was intended to stop the endless, unjust lawsuits over property, like that which nearly ruined the Pastons. It was made easier to obtain bail and to avoid imprisonment because of unsubstantiated accusations dictated by malice. Plundering the property of persons awaiting trial (as the Earl of Surrey had done so recently with Mistress Shore) was declared illegal. There was some mildly xenophobic legislation against Italian merchants trading in England, though many customs duties were lowered—those on books being abolished altogether. There were statutes on hallmarking silver and against using inferior dyes in the manufacture of wool. Bondsmen, or serfs, on Crown Lands were freed (which probably affected their lives very little). The Parliament's *pièce de résistance*, however, was the abolition of 'benevolences'; these were the contributions to the royal coffers, forced loans in all but name, so common under Edward IV, which had caused 'divers and many worshipful men of this realm . . . by necessity to break up their households and to live in great penury and wretchedness.' The Parliament came to an end on 20 February, after voting the King tonnage and poundage (customs revenues) for life.

In his history of Henry VII Sir Francis Bacon, no admirer of Richard, says that the King was 'a good lawmaker for the ease and solace of the common people'. Needless to say, Kendall claims that the excellent statutes of the Parliament of 1484 were directly sponsored by Richard, while Anthony Cheetham has made much of the King's employment of 'the most able and learned men.' Even Gairdner admits that the statutes were beneficial. Yet, as Dr Hanham stresses, it is highly debatable how far this legislation was initiated by the King. 'So much has been made of Richard's good government that it ought to be said that he was in no position to enact oppressive measures, even if he had wished to do so; that the abolition of benevolences was probably a concession to popular feeling.' Moreover even Kendall has to concede that the legislation of January and February 1484 did not gain Richard any notable good will from his subjects.

During this time the King had also been busy with foreign affairs. Breton privateers were still giving trouble. Early in 1484 Thomas Wentworth had again to take out another squadron to patrol the English coast, reinforced by a second squadron under Lord Scrope of Bolton. Probably their real purpose was as much to guard against another invasion as to fight privateers, even if a few of the latter were captured. Plainly it was expected that Henry Tudor would try again and soon. The much vaunted innovation of a primitive postal service by Richard, a kind of pony express—a single horseman was posted every twenty miles on the main roads so that a letter could be carried 200 miles in two days—was intended solely to give early warning of that dreaded event. Commissions of Muster and Array were constantly issued to keep troops in readiness.

Meanwhile the Scots continued raiding over the Border. In practice the war had never ceased and Dunbar, handed over by Albany the year before, remained in English hands. In February 1484 the King decided to prepare another invasion of Scotland in May. His motive may have been a desire for prestige; perhaps he hoped to recapture some of the popularity which had followed his triumphs of 1482.

In every single one of Richard III's actions one can detect a frantic need to establish his insecure régime as solidly as possible. At some date in February he made the Lords Spiritual and Temporal attending Parliament, together with the Knights and Esquires of his Household, take an oath of allegiance to the Prince of Wales. They swore 'adherence' to him as their supreme lord should anything happen to his father. Although it was 'a new kind of oath', hitherto unknown to the Crowland chronicler who gives us this information, it cannot have been so very different from the one in which Richard himself had sworn allegiance to his brother's son.

In his desperate desire for stability the King was even ready for a rapprochement with the Woodvilles. It was a grave embarrassment that Edward IV's Queen and her daughters were still in sanctuary at Westminster. Moreover the girls were not dangerous in themselves—England was not yet ready for a female sovereign. The Crowland writer tells us how 'after much pleading, and also threats, had been employed Queen Elizabeth, being very strongly entreated, sent her daughters to King Richard.' But she would only do so after he had sworn a solemn and detailed oath on 1 March 1484 before an august assembly composed of the Peers and Bishops who had come up to London for the Parliament, together with the Mayor and Aldermen. In his oath Richard promised that he would see they came to no harm—no 'ravishing or defiling contrary to their wills'—and that he would not 'imprison [them] in the Tower of London.' He also pledged himself to give them dowries and to 'marry such of them as be of marriageable age to gentlemen born . . . And such gentlemen as shall hap to marry with them, I shall straitly charge lovingly to love and entreat them as wives and my kinswomen . . . ' (By 'gentlemen born' the King almost certainly meant Peers.) The clause about the Tower is significant, and so is the absence of any reference to the girls' brothers.[13]

There is no documentary evidence that 'Dame Elizabeth Grey', as the former Queen of England was now officially styled, came out from sanctuary with her daughters. However, it is probable that at about the same time she retired to some obscure refuge in the country, since in his oath of 1 March Richard endowed her with a generous sum for her maintenance. (Her estates had been confiscated and were being administered by a receiver, John Fitzherbert.) The King also appointed that ruffian John Nesfield, 'one of the Esquires of my

Body', to act as her gentleman-in-waiting. He was not taking any chances.

Richard's defenders have cited Elizabeth Woodville's behaviour in March 1484 as 'proof' that the Princes were still alive or else that it was Buckingham who had killed them. No mother, they argue, would have handed over her daughters to the murderer of her sons. They forget that the King had had another of Elizabeth's sons, Richard Grey, killed openly at Pontefract.

Presumably to demonstrate his respectability, on 10 March 1484 Richard sent an extraordinary homily to the clergy in Convocation. He told them 'our principal intent and fervent desire is to see virtue and cleanness of living to be advanced, increased and multiplied, and vices and all other things repugnant to virtue, provoking the high indignation and fearful displeasure of God, to be repressed and annulled.' No doubt the King wished to be the guardian of public morals, yet the members of Convocation cannot have been over-impressed by his official and enthusiastic recognition of two bastards whom he had sired; there are hints—by Bishop Langton and the Crowland writer—that his own private life was still far from impeccable. Thomas More thought him a hypocrite; discussing Richard's futile attempt to discredit Jane Shore, he speaks of him with heavy irony as 'a goodly continent Prince, clean and faultless of himself, sent out of heaven into this vicious world for the amendment of men's manners.' The fangs of malice were all too evident in his moralising.

The King always had a number of priests and prelates in his train. One was the admiring Bishop Langton of St David's, whom Richard employed on diplomatic missions abroad and whom he promoted to Salisbury early in 1485. Bishop Redman was equally in evidence. Another from the North was John Shirwood, a former Archdeacon of Richmond, whom he made Bishop of Durham when that key see fell vacant at the end of 1483. The King had a high regard for Shirwood, who was closely identified with his régime, and tried hard to obtain a Cardinal's hat for him. He was a humanist who had studied at Rome under Byzantine tutors and who could speak Greek as well as read it. Other humanist clerics at court were the Keeper of the Privy Seal, John Gunthorpe, Dean of Wells, who had studied at Ferrara; and the Royal Chaplain John Dogget, Cardinal Bourchier's nephew, who had studied at both Padua and Bologna—as indeed had Langton. Conceivably they may have made their master aware that something very important was taking place in Italy; rather touchingly, Richard's letter to the Pope about Shirwood's red hat mentions his good Greek—he himself could barely read Latin.

Another cosmopolitan English religious whom the King employed was Fra John Kendall, a Knight of Rhodes. The Knights played a considerable role in public life. The Grand Prior of England—'My Lord of St John's'—ranked as premier baron of the realm, and in

London the great hall of the vast priory at Clerkenwell was frequently borrowed for important assemblies. As 'monks of war', they could scarcely be expected to be humanist scholars, but they knew Rome and how to handle curia officials—since they usually travelled through Italy before taking ship to their island stronghold. Kendall, who was the Order's Turcopolier (general of light horse), had been active all over Europe raising funds for the defence of Rhodes against the Turks during the famous siege of 1480. On 16 December 1484 the King commissioned Fra John, together with Bishops Langton and Shirwood, to go to the Eternal City and offer the royal obedience to the new Pope, Innocent VIII. Kendall, who incidentally was a cousin of the Pastons, may have been related to the King's Secretary. What makes him unique among Richard's courtiers is that we have a very good idea of what he looked like, from a contemporary Italian portrait medal.

There is, however, a contemporary representation, if not a likeness, of a member of the 'mafia'. The King's predilection for Northerners was not restricted to men from Yorkshire or the Border counties. It extended to anyone originating from north of the River Trent. One example is Sir Gervase Clifton of Clifton in Nottinghamshire. Born in 1438 and a nephew of Archbishop Booth of York, he belonged to an old established family of the upper gentry. A former Esquire of the Body to Edward IV, he was created a Knight of the Bath at Richard's Coronation. Perhaps significantly, his wife was a Constable of Flamborough so he was a close kinsman of 'little Sir Marmaduke'—that key member of the Household. Clifton seems to have done good service during Buckingham's rebellion, since on 24 April 1484 he was given extensive lands in Derbyshire, Leicestershire, and Huntingdon which had once belonged to the Duke. He was to fight for his master the following year. The ballad of *Bosworth Feilde* tells us how among those that 'came that day to serve their King' was 'Sir Gervase Clifton in rich array'. He was badly wounded and very nearly killed. Nevertheless he survived, dying in 1491. What is particularly interesting is his funeral brass at Clifton which may portray the sort of armour he had worn at Bosworth.[14]

At the beginning of March 1484 the King and Queen set out on a further progress, through the Midlands. On the way they visited Cambridge, where they stayed for some days. Many of Richard's favourite clerics were Cambridge men, for whom he had an agreeable if unexplained preference. He was a great benefactor of the university even by royal standards. On this occasion he founded a number of scholarships, bestowed many privileges, and gave £300 towards the completion of King's College Chapel—begun by Henry VI—while Anne presented Queen's College, once so favoured by Elizabeth Woodville, with valuable endowments. After pausing at Buckden Manor, near Huntingdon, a stone and red brick country house of

Lord Chancellor Russell, and also at Stamford, they proceeded to Nottingham which they reached by 20 March.

Richard's decision to spend several weeks at Nottingham was dictated by strategic reasons. Here news of trouble on the Scots Border could reach him in half the time it would take to get to London; the Moss troopers were out and if they began to do real damage he would have to go North even before the spring. Above all, the news which he considered most serious of any, that of a landing by Henry Tudor, could arrive almost at once, enabling him to muster his army as quickly as possible.

However it is unlikely that the King expected to hear anything unpleasant just yet, and could find time for interests other than affairs of state. Some of his modern defenders suggest that he was a patron of the arts, but while we know that he enjoyed magnificent residences and liked impressive music in church there is nothing to indicate any marked taste for literature or painting. Yet Richard was undoubtedly interested in one, somewhat exotic, art form—heraldry. Even before taking the Crown he had appointed his own pursuivants, displaying his armorial insignia and badges on every possible occasion. The day after he arrived at Nottingham he issued a charter which incorporated the heralds of the Royal Household into a College of Arms under the Earl Marshal (another emolument for Norfolk). The heralds were given Pulteney's Inn in Coldharbour in London for their headquarters. Their business was not entirely confined to blazonry since they also performed diplomatic functions, carrying messages—in particular declarations of war—from one sovereign to another.

The King's interest in heraldry may explain why in 1484 William Caxton dedicated *The Book of the Order of Chivalry* to his 'redoubted, natural and most dread Sovereign Lord, King Richard'. In the book, of which he was the author as well as the printer, Caxton laments the decay of knighthood. 'What do ye now but go to the baths and play at dice?' he rebukes contemporary English knights. He appeals to the King to order Justices of the Peace to ensure that every knight in the realm should possess horse and armour 'so as to be always ready to serve their Prince.' It is perhaps not without irony that Caxton promises his sovereign 'I shall pray almighty God for his long life, and prosperous welfare, that he may have victory of all his enemies and after this short and transitory life to have everlasting life in Heaven.' We do not know whether Richard received a copy.

Important news did indeed come to Nottingham though not from the Scots Border or from the coast. It was far worse than Moss trooper raids, far worse than any landing by the Tudor. On 9 April Edward, Prince of Wales, had died at Middleham.

CHAPTER ELEVEN

THE DEATH OF RICHARD'S SON

'You might have seen his father and mother in a state bordering almost on madness, by reason of their sudden grief'.

The *'Second Continuation' of the* Crowland Chronicle

'a Prince should reckon conspiracies of little account when his people hold him in esteem; but when it is hostile to him and bears hatred towards him, he ought to fear everything and everybody'.

Machiavelli, Il Principe

No one records how Edward of Middleham died. It was clearly a sudden and unexpected death. The Crowland chronicler merely says that it took place after only a very short illness, while Rous calls it 'a tragic death'. Since his mother was apparently consumptive, the ten-year-old Prince may well have suffered a lung haemorrhage, which could have been both messy and painful. Richard and his Queen were crushed by this cruellest, most hideously ironical of blows. He had been their only son, 'in whom all the hopes of the royal succession, fortified with so many oaths, were centred', the Crowland writer tells us. An eye-witness, he adds that 'You might have seen his father and mother in a state bordering almost on madness by reason of their sudden grief.' The boy expired on 9 April, a year to the day after Edward IV, and in an age of omens it seems that many Englishmen saw his death as God's judgement on Richard—it is quite possible the King did so himself. The chronicler at Crowland observes gloomily, 'it was fully seen how vain are the thoughts of a man who desires to establish his interests without the aid of God.' The last Plantagenet Prince of Wales was buried in the parish church at Sheriff Hutton, where his battered, pathetically small, alabaster effigy may still be seen.[1] There was now a succession problem, since there was no obvious heir presumptive to the throne. So shaken was Richard that it took his several months to come to a decision.

It may not be over fanciful to detect a certain deterioration in the King after his son's death. Admittedly, he still tried to be efficient and popular. He negotiated sensible peaces with Scotland and Brittany and found time to deal with Irish affairs. His precautions against Henry Tudor continued to be excellently organised, while he employed a very professional intelligence service—with 'the aid of spies beyond sea, at whatever price they could be secured, from whom he learned nearly all the movements of the enemy.' But plainly he felt crippled by his lack of an heir, as he would show by his sinister treatment of his unfortunate wife. He was increasingly worried about his unpopularity and 'seditious rumours'. There are signs of vacillation, errors of judgement. Growing short of money, he returned to Edward IV's forced loans—the 'benevolences' so ostentatiously foregone in his Parliament. The threat of invasion became an obsession.

When Richard had usurped the throne, Henry Tudor had not even been a cloud on the horizon—simply a Welsh exile from a lost cause, saved only from obscurity by a dash of questionably royal blood. The *Great Chronicle of London* preserves the memory of how little he was known to ordinary people, but how soon they became interested in him—'word sprang quickly of a gentleman being in the parts of Brittany named Henry and son of the Earl of Richmond.' Thanks to the usurpation and to his mother and John Morton his star was clearly rising. By 1484 men were following the fugitives of 1483 across the sea to join him, from motives which varied from sheer opportunism to hatred of the present King of England. It was no longer a fight between Yorkist and Lancastrian but simply a struggle between two claimants. Despite his Coronation, his most royal blood and purity of Plantagenet descent, Richard remained unaccepted by his people. It did not matter that his rival was part Welsh squire, part Valois prince, with a dash of Beaufort in him. Henry Tudor was the sole alternative.

For—as contemporaries, including the King himself, must have realized with bewilderment—the once invincible Yorkist party had broken in pieces. The loyalties which had triumphed at Towton, at Barnet and at Tewkesbury, which had eventually made Edward IV impregnable, no longer existed. The members of Edward's Order of Our Lady of the White Rose may still have worn their insignia, yet they were ready to abandon their rose. Some former Yorkists had joined Henry Tudor, more would do so, while many who did neither nevertheless detested Richard and were not going to risk their necks for him in battle. In place of the old Yorkist party the King had only his henchmen and three overmighty subjects—two of them treacherous.

Henry's supporters were an increasingly formidable band.[2] What was beginning to look like a court in exile included Lords Dorset, Pembroke (Jasper Tudor), Rivers (Edward Woodville), Devon (Edward Courtenay) and Welles, and many knights and gentlemen. There was also a briefless barrister from Lincoln's Inn, Thomas Lovell, who would end his life as Treasurer of the Royal Household. Clerics too were joining the cause, not just the Bishops of Ely and Exeter, but men like Richard Fox, a future Bishop of Winchester. Morton who for some reason preferred to stay in Flanders, communicated with Henry through Christopher Urswick, Rector of Puttenham in Hertfordshire, Margaret Beaufort's confessor and one day to be Dean of Windsor. (Perhaps ironically this thirty-six-year-old 'honest, approved and serviceable priest' was a Northcountryman, from Furness in Lancashire.)[3] Henry of Richmond may eventually have had as many as 500 followers with him in Brittany and France. They were certainly not a revived Lancastrian party, whatever Henry may have claimed, but simply an anti-Richard III party—as the King himself must have recognised with some bitterness.

Plainly Richard was by now only too well aware that the Welshman whom he had not even bothered to name in his proclamation against Buckingham the previous year was a danger to be eliminated at all costs. Once Henry Tudor was out of the way Richard would be perfectly secure. There was no other possible Pretender capable of challenging the King with any hope of success. Buckingham was dead; admittedly he had left a son—later to be executed by Henry VIII precisely because of his royal descent—but in 1484 he was only six. Otherwise there was Clarence's son Warwick aged eight (and perhaps mentally retarded though there is no firm evidence), Warwick's sister—also to be executed by Henry VIII—and the bastardised daughters of Edward IV. The 'Old Royal Blood of England' had run very thin indeed.

Since the summer of 1483 Richard had had an envoy at the court of Duke Francis, one Dr Thomas Hutton—'a man of pregnant wit' and presumably of unusual diplomatic skill—and a member of his own Council. Hutton's first instructions make no mention of Henry, and his main business seems to have been to negotiate a friendly alliance, Brittany standing in relation to France much as Scotland did to England. He was sharp enough to pick up news of Henry's first expedition and rush back to warn Richard. The difficulty with Francis II of Brittany was the Duke's fear, admittedly quite understandable, of Louis XI of France—the English King's refusal to supply troops to defend the Duchy against the French threat explains why Francis had helped the Tudor. The situation was further complicated by the fact that the Duke was suffering from what appears to have been fits of premature senility, and that control over Breton affairs was passing into the hands of his unusually venal minister Pierre Landois.

Landois realized the financial possibilities of the situation. Some time in May 1484 his agents arrived in England and negotiated what was meant to be a lasting peace. At considerable expense Richard signed a treaty at Pontefract on 8 June, a treaty with secret clauses. He would supply a thousand archers, pay the Duke the revenues of the Earldom of Richmond—which had once belong to the House of Brittany—and pay other large sums. In return Landois, who would be the real pecuniary beneficiary, would ensure that Henry Tudor was kept under strict confinement—probably he had every intention of handing Henry over.

Once again, Morton thwarted the King. Somehow he heard of the negotiations with Landois and sent Urswick to warn Henry. Also acting under Morton's instructions, Urswick—having delivered his message to Henry at Vannes—went on to the French court to beg an asylum in France. The Tudor would plainly be of use to the French as a stick with which to threaten England if necessary, especially in any conflict over Brittany. The actual ruler of France was not of course the boy Charles VIII, but his elder sister Anne de Beaujeu. Although only twenty-two, she was extremely formidable, a true daughter of Louis XI, who controlled the French Council through her husband, the future Duke of Bourbon. Francis II had no male heir and it was more likely that when he died both Richard and the new Habsburg rulers of Flanders would do their best to stop France from taking over Brittany—the last of the semi-independent *appenages* within the French Kingdom.

Urswick found the French court at Angers and had no difficulty in obtaining a passport for Henry. The Tudor then sent a large deputation of his followers from Vannes to plead his cause with Duke Francis, who at that moment was most conveniently in residence near the Anjou border. This was a feint; his uncle Jasper had orders to take the party into France by side roads and bridle paths, which they did successfully. Meanwhile Henry stayed behind at Vannes with a considerable group, to avoid causing any suspicion. However two days after Jasper's departure, escorted by only five servants, he himself left Vannes on the pretext of visiting a friend at a nearby manor. Five miles on, the little group disappeared into a wood where the Tudor changed clothes with one of his servants. They then rode as hard as possible by a secret route for Anjou, deliberately changing direction several times. So careful was he that his followers in Vannes had no idea that he had left them. All went well and Henry crossed the frontier, rejoining his uncle Jasper's party at Angers as planned. It was in the nick of time. Troops sent by Landois with instructions to arrest him reached the border only an hour after he had crossed it.

The exact date of this sensational escape is not known, but Henry Tudor undoubtedly received a friendly welcome at the French court. The Council gave instructions on 11 October that he and his supporters were to be treated with honour; it also made financial provision for them. Then Duke Francis suddenly and unexpectedly recovered his wits and was furious with Landois for having harried this useful refugee into escaping. He summoned Sir Edward Woodville and Edward Poynings, the chief among the Tudor followers left behind at Vannes, and gave them and their friends permission, together with travelling expenses, to rejoin their master in France for over a year. Henry and his by now very substantial following were to accompany the peripatetic French court on progress, from Angers to Montargis and then to Paris.

Richard finally decided that he had no hope of repeating the glories of 1482 in Scotland. That summer the Duke of Albany and his fellow exile, the Earl of Douglas, led what may have been a fairly considerable attack into Dumfriesshire; but on 22 July their English troops were cut to pieces at Lochmaben; Douglas was captured and though Albany succeeded in fleeing back across the Border he was plainly of little future value. It was clear that there would be no more military promenades to an undefended Edinburgh and that Albany would never be 'Alexander IV'; he died in France the following year, accidentally killed in a joust by the Duke of Orleans (the future Louis XII). The raiding and counter-raiding went on and it is likely that the Scots had the best of it.

At sea it was a different matter. We know that Richard had already had experience of directing naval operations. He returned to his familiar base of Scarborough in June and again in July, staying with Anne in the castle. (Though a house in the town is traditionally called 'King Richard's House'.) The first occasion was to organise the large fleet which he had gathered there. To begin with the English ships met with reverses at the hands of the Scots, who were probably reinforced by French privateers since none other than John Nesfield, Esquire of the Body, was captured by a French vessel—though apparently he was soon ransomed by the King. Nevertheless it seems that Richard quickly inflicted a crushing defeat on the Scots fleet, after successfully bringing it to battle; it is not impossible that he himself was in command as the Crowland chronicler attributes the victory to 'his skill in naval warfare'. Certainly his second visit to Scarborough was of comparatively long duration since he was there from 30 June to 11 July. At York shortly afterwards he signed a warrant for 'victualling the King's Ships at Scarborough'. Plainly he had good reason to be grateful to the men of Scarborough since he erected the town into an independent county of its own.[4]

But by now Richard knew that it was a futile war. He took advantage of his victory over James III to suggest they make peace. The King of Scots, who had clearly reached the same conclusion, nominated ambassadors to come to Nottingham in September and negotiate. When they came they agreed a three years' truce without difficulty, to be cemented by the marriage of Richard's niece—Anne de la Pole, daughter of the Duchess of Suffolk and sister of the Earl of Lincoln—to the Duke of Rothesay, James's heir. From the personal point of view, the most notable aspect of the Scots embassy to Nottingham was the Latin oration delivered before Richard by its leader Archibald Whitelaw, Archdeacon of Lothian. During it the Archdeacon quoted and applied to the English King 'what was said by the poet of a most renowned Prince of the Thebans, that nature never enclosed within a *smaller frame* [italics mine] so great a mind or such remarkable powers.'[5]

Whitelaw's polite compliment confirms yet again every other contemporary source as to Richard's size. In addition to Rous, Vergil, and More, the Elizabethan antiquary John Stow (born in 1525) had spoken to men who remembered him and who agreed that he was of short stature. There is one exception, however. A certain Nicolas von Poppelau from Silesia visited England as the Ambassador of the Holy Roman Emperor Frederick III. It is likely that he was both boastful and an oddity; in his travel diary he says he carried a huge lance with him everywhere, which no one but he could lift—even if they managed to pick it up for a moment, its weight quickly dragged them to the ground. He was given an audience by the King at Pontefract on 1 May and spent ten days at his court. After the customary oration, Richard shook Poppelau's hand and told an attendant to give him good accommodation. Next day he was present at the King's Mass (was it yet another Mass for the Dead?) where he was impressed by superb music. Afterwards he watched Richard dine—Kings then dined alone or with their consort, served on bended knee—amid a crowd of courtiers. Richard singled him out, asking him many questions about the Emperor and the Princess of the Empire. He was delighted by Poppelau's account of the Hungarian King's victory over the Turks the previous year, exclaiming 'I wish my kingdom was on the Turkish border; with my own people alone and without being helped by other Princes, I would so much like to drive out not only Turks but all my other enemies.'

Richard may well have had the fashionable, if impracticable, enthusiasm for the crusade shared by many contemporary noblemen. He expressed more than once a wish to fight the infidel. The ballad of *Bosworth Field*, most convincingly in view of Poppelau's report, makes the King say 'I would I had the great Turk against me to fight.'

The Silesian was fed at the same table as the greatest courtiers for the remainder of his visit, and Richard gave him a gold collar which he 'took from the neck of a certain lord.' What is so interesting is Poppelau's description of his host. 'King Richard [was] three fingers taller than I, but a little thinner being not so thickset and much leaner; he also had very thin arms and legs, though a great heart.'[6]

Poppelau's fascinating account of his meeting with the King is—in modern terms—the only personal interview which has survived, even though it has to be treated with some caution. Clearly Richard flattered the Silesian; he may well have been much more open with a foreigner than he would have with any Englishman. The overall impression made on Poppelau (who, it must be remembered, had met other monarchs) is undeniably that of a formidable, dignified and intelligent ruler, but it is also that of one with a Sword of Damocles hanging over him. The only puzzling detail is the Silesian's claim that Richard was three fingers taller, but no doubt Poppelau was a barrel-chested dwarf.

Even if the King could not persuade his English subjects to approve of him, he was much more successful with the Irish lords, as the House of York had never lost the esteem earned by his father's reign in Dublin as Lord Lieutenant. What authority there was in that turbulent country—or in the part of it supposedly subject to English rule—was exercised by the mighty FitzGerald family, Earls of Kildare and of Desmond. Richard left the Earl of Kildare undisturbed as Lord Deputy, though he seems to have had an excessive estimate of the Earl's powers; hearing that Kildare's sister had married The O'Neil, he somewhat optimistically asked the Earl to persuade that peculiarly intractable chieftain to return something of the royal Earldom of Ulster. The King was equally amiable to the Earl of Desmond, declaring he had 'always had inward compassion of the death of his said father' (who may indeed have been killed to please the Woodvilles). If certain reports had travelled across St George's Channel, the Earl would no doubt have been surprised by this sympathy for his parent's fate, especially when described by Richard as 'atrociously murdered by colour of the law, against all manhood, reason and sound conscience', though such moralising was becoming familiar enough to his English subjects. The 'Lord of Ireland'—Richard's official title—apparently feared that Desmond might go native among 'the wild Iresshe' and succumb to Gaelic culture; he asked him to wear English dress—presumably instead of trews and saffron mantle—and presented him with English doublets and hose, together with a robe of velvet and cloth of gold bearing a collar of golden suns and roses and a white boar.[7] Polite messages were sent to other Irish magnates, thanking them for their loyalty. He secured it by leaving them alone.

Richard's most important and lasting work was at home in England. In July 1484 he set up a permanent Council of the North, to be presided over from Sheriff Hutton by John de la Pole, Earl of Lincoln. It was to meet quarterly at York. This body replaced the unofficial condominium exercised by Gloucester and the Earl of Northumberland prior to 1483. A genuine administrative achievement, it was to endure for 150 years. But nothing could have been better calculated to anger Henry Percy, one of those three principal props of Richard's throne. Northumberland must have been still more incensed when, that autumn, Lord Dacre of Gilsland was appointed Warden of the Western Marches.

In August Richard at last brought himself to settle the succession. This too must have irritated Northumberland, since the new heir to the throne was none other than the Earl of Lincoln, President of that most unwelcome Council. Lincoln was the eldest son and heir of Richard's brother-in-law, the Duke of Suffolk. He was nineteen, already married, vigorous and intelligent. He received the titular Lord Lieutenancy of Ireland, held by all Yorkist heirs apparent. Rous says that the young Earl of Warwick had previously been acknowledged as heir, and 'in ceremonies at table and chamber was served first after the King and Queen', but this is unlikely; if his father's attainder were reversed he would have a better claim to the throne than Richard. Rous adds that then 'the Earl of Lincoln was preferred'.

Few people took Lincoln seriously as a future King of England. Richard confided in Archbishop Warham that he was worried by his lack of children. He compensated by advancing his bastards. Although still a minor, John of Gloucester, referred to in household documents as 'My Lord Bastard', was made titular Captain of Calais. The patent of his appointment, surely dictated by his father, refers to 'our dear son, our bastard John of Gloucester, whose quickness of mind, agility of body and inclination to all good customs give us great hope of his good service for the future'. 'Dame Katherine Plantagenet' was married to the Earl of Huntingdon—Great Chamberlain to her half-brother, the Prince of Wales—in 1484 and given a notably splendid dowry. (She died young like her brother, bearing no heirs.) But the King never contemplated legitimising them, although he and his wife must have known that they would have no more children by each other.

His bewilderment, possibly remorse and fear, is evident during the time he spent in the North from May to July 1484. The Grey Friars of Richmond were engaged to say a thousand Masses for the repose of Edward IV's soul. The Austin Friars of Tickhill were given an annuity and the Trinitarian Friars of Knaresborough also had a benefaction. His gift to his old acquaintance Prior Bell and the Austin Canons of Carlisle Cathedral was an undeniably agreeable way of asking them to drink the King and Queen's spiritual health—two tuns of claret annually in return for saying Mass for their well being. Yet, curiously enough, there is no evidence that Richard ever visited or endowed the Carthusian hermits of Mount Grace, whose charterhouse was within easy reach of Sheriff Hutton. This is most surprising in view of their widespread reputation for extraordinary holiness. It may be that he was afraid of them.

His grim side was again in evidence in the autumn of 1484 when Mr William Colyngbourne was caught at last. Colyngbourne had immortalised himself the previous summer by posting his famous couplet on the door of St Paul's:

'The Cat, the Rat, and Lovell our Dog,
Ruleth all England under a Hog.'

The Cat was of course *Cat*esby, the Rat was *Rat*cliff, and the Dog referred to Lovell's crest,[8] while Hog expressed what all too many Englishmen thought of Richard and his boar. A gentleman from Wiltshire of handsome and impressive appearance, once Sergeant of the Pantry to Edward IV, Colyngbourne had been active in raising his county for Buckingham. Moreover there had been some sort of trouble in the West Country during the summer of 1484—armed disturbances, rumours that men were waiting eagerly for a second invasion by Henry Tudor. Colyngbourne's real crime—one which deprived him of any hope of mercy—was to have offered a certain Thomas Yate £8 to go to Brittany and persuade the Earl of Richmond to invade England; he had also suggested that Henry should tell the French government that the King was about to attack France. He was

tried at Guildhall in the City by an imposing tribunal which com-
prised two dukes and seven other peers, besides five Justices of the
King's Bench, so seriously were his offences regarded. Found guilty
of high treason, after a new pair of gallows had been specially built,
he was half hanged, then castrated, disembowelled, and quartered
on Tower Hill; during the torments which followed the formal pretence at strangulation he showed remarkable fortitude, but, when his
testicles and entrails had been burnt before him and the executioner
began to pluck out his heart, he screamed 'O lord Jesu, yet more
trouble!' The London draper Robert Fabyan says that Colyngbourne
was 'cast for sundry treasons and for a rhyme which was laid to his
charge', adding that he died 'to the great compassion of many
people'. Despite all the battles, the statutory penalty for treason had
been witnessed comparatively rarely in recent years. Early Tudor
London had reason to remember the reign of Richard III.

Another to suffer for his opposition to the King was Sir Roger
Clifford. A member of the great Lancastrian family, he too had been
implicated in Buckingham's rebellion. He was caught outside
Southampton, probably while trying to find a ship to take him abroad
to safety, and brought back to London to be tried and executed.
Fabyan, perhaps an eye-witness, tells us that as he was being
dragged on the customary hurdle to Tower Hill through the City, the
priest attending him untied his bonds and when he passed the
church of St Martin's-le-Grand his servants tried to pull him into the
sanctuary. But the Sheriff's officers threw themselves on him and
held him down till he could be secured again. Clifford was at least
spared the agonies of Colyngbourne and died by the axe.

Colyngbourne had been a household man of the old Duchess of
York. His replacement, probably long before his execution, was the
occasion of Richard's one surviving letter to his mother. The King
wrote.

Madam, I recommend me to you as heartily as is to me possible.
Beseeching you in my most humble and effectuous wise of your daily
blessing, to my singular comfort and defence in my need. And,
Madam, I heartily beseech you that I may often hear from you to my
comfort. And such news as be here my servant Thomas Bryan, this
bearer, shall show you; to whom please it you to give credence unto.
And Madam, I beseech you to be good and gracious Lady to my
Lord my Chamberlain, to be your officer in Wiltshire in such as
Colyngbourne had. I trust he shall therein do you service. And that
it please you that by this bearer I may understand your pleasure in
this behalf. And I pray God to send you the accomplishment of your
noble desires. Written at Pontefract the 3rd day of June with the
hand of your most humble son,
Ricardus Rex.[9]

One can only wonder what the pious dowager thought of a son
who had directed his usurpation from her own house, who had

35.   *Richard's command centre, Nottingham Castle.*

Howe a man schaff be armyd at his ese whten he schal fighte on foote

He schal haue noo schurte vp on him but a dowbelet of ffustean lynyd with satene cutte full of hoolis. the dowbelet muste be strongeli bounde there the poyntis muste be sette aboute the greet of the arme. and the b ste before and behynde and the gusse tis of mayle muste be sowid vn to the dowbelet in the bought of the arme. and vndir the arme the ar mynge poyntis muste be made of fyne twyne suche as men make stryngis for crossebowes and they

36.   A gentleman arming himself for battle. From a manuscript of c. 1480.
Pierpont Morgan Library, New York. MS 775, folio 122 verso.

37.   *A King of England rides forth to war, c. 1480. Note the open helmet and crown. City of Bristol Record Office reference 0472B (1).*

38.   (Left) *Sir Gervase Clifton, one of Richard's Knights of the Bath. He rode
with the King in his last charge at Bosworth but survived. Brass in the church of
St Mary The Virgin, Clifton, Nottinghamshire.*

39.   (Right) *Brass of the sinister William Catesby, one of Richard's principal
advisers and Speaker of the House of Commons. He was executed after Bosworth.
Church of St Leodegorius, Ashby St Ledgers.*

murdered her grandsons, after branding them as bastards together with her grand-daughters, who had reviled her triumphant Edward's memory, and who had had her accused publicly of being an adulteress. Since 1480 Cicily Nevill had been living the life of a Benedictine nun—or rather of a Benedictine abbess—at her castle of Berkhamsted, which she had transformed into something very like a convent. She was to survive all her sons, dying in 1494, only a few years before Vergil's arrival in England. He tells us that the Duchess 'being falsely accused of adultery, complained afterwards in sundry places to right many noble men, whereof some yet live of that great injury which her son, Richard, had done her.'

In August 1484 Richard briefly abandoned his central command post at Nottingham, to return to London for what he obviously regarded as a very important occasion indeed. This was the ostentatiously magnificent reburial of one of his earliest victims, Henry VI. During the thirteen years that the Lancastrian King's remains had lain at Chertsey Abbey his grave had become a place of popular pilgrimage, multitudes flocking to it to pray for his intercession—some claiming that not only had their prayers been answered but that miracles were performed. Even his murderer may have visited Chertsey,

'And wet his grave with my repentant tears.'

No one was more credulously superstitious than Richard, more anxious to placate a saint. According to Rous—who is clearly reporting widely believed gossip of the time—'That holy body was pleasantly scented [a certain sign of a corpse's sanctity to mediaeval man] and surely not from spices, since he had been buried by enemies and butchers. And for the most part it was uncorrupted, the hair and beard in place, and the face much as it had been, except a little more sunken, with a more emaciated appearance.' If the King himself credited these edifying reports, as seems extremely likely, he must have been seriously alarmed at being reminded of killing anyone quite so holy. It cannot be too much emphasised that by then all England considered Henry VI a saint. Richard saw that Henry's body was re-interred in St George's Chapel, Windsor, on the south side of the high altar in a place of the utmost honour, which at once became a shrine; the fan vaulting above was painted with his personal emblems and badges, and his helmet was hung over his grave; relics were displayed next to it, such as sheets from his death bed and his red velvet cap (which, if worn, cured headaches). Rous tells us how immediately after the re-interrment, which had been accompanied by solemn and splendid ceremonies, 'at once miracles abundantly attested the King's sanctity.' He appeared to a wounded sailor dressed as a pilgrim, in a vision, to reassure him; stemmed the flow from some poor carters' broken wine casks; and healed a hernia caused by a misdirected kick during a football match. No doubt such manifestations, widely reported, made Richard still more uneasy.

The King went back to Nottingham—his 'castle of care', and he is supposed to have named it—the same month, after only a few days in the South. However, early in November he returned to his capital, going first to a long forgotten palace—the Wardrobe on Ludgate Hill, so called because all monarchs from Edward III to James I kept their clothes there. The Scots question had been settled and there was no danger on the Border, while a lasting peace had been concluded with Brittany. It was scarcely likely that Henry Tudor would invade so late in the year. But then, just after Richard's return to London, news came from Calais of an unexpected and damaging blow to his prestige.

John de Vere, Earl of Oxford, the most distinguished Lancastrian commander to survive, had escaped from Hammes after ten years' imprisonment. (He had tried to escape before, unsuccessfully, jumping into the moat where he would have drowned but for the water coming only up to his chin.) He was not merely Premier Earl of England and a former Lord High Constable, but a very brave man and a very fine soldier—the Crowland chroncler calls him 'miles valentissimus'. He had personal reasons for hating the King: in 1473 Richard had reduced his mother to beggary, forcing her to hand over her entire estate to him—'by heinous menace of loss of life and imprisonment' her son afterwards complained. He had at once gone to the French court, then at Montargis, to join the English exiles. Nor did he come alone, bringing with him his gaoler James Blount, the Captain of Hammes, and Sir John Fortescue, the Gentleman Porter of Calais. Vergil says that Henry was 'ravished with joy'.

Moreover Blount had given the garrison at Hammes (one of the fortresses defending Calais) orders to hold it against Richard. He had also left his wife in command of the men, probably about thirty. Lord Dynham the Captain of Calais, immediately moved up troops to retake the castle. But Mistress Blount resisted stoutly, sending to Henry for help. He despatched Thomas Brandon with thirty more men-at-arms, who entered Hammes by a secret path through a marsh and prolonged the siege into the New Year. The King only recovered the fortress at the end of January 1485, at the cost of a free pardon to the Blounts, Brandon, and the entire garrison—the Blounts and Brandon joining Henry at the French court. Richard hastily replaced Lord Mountjoy, Blount's brother, as Captain of Guisnes (the other castle defending Calais) by Sir James Tyrell.

In November Brackenbury was reappointed Sheriff of Kent. The King's agitation during the Hammes affair is very evident. On 6 December the Mayor of Windsor was ordered to take action against anyone found spreading rumours intended to cause unrest, which were being circulated by 'our ancient enemies of France'; such persons were to be imprisoned and severely punished. Next day Richard issued his first proclamation against his rival. It lists various rebels, who have 'chosen to be their Captain one, Henry Tydder'; from 'insatiable covetousness' the latter 'usurpeth upon him the name and title of royal estate of this realm', and has promised his supporters all the possessions of the King's subjects, even bishoprics. On 8 December Commissions of Array were issued on a very large scale indeed. On 18 December commissioners in counties immediately adjacent to London were ordered to report how many reliable men-at-arms they could produce at twelve hours notice. Richard took very seriously a report that Harwich was threatened by attack from the sea. A rising in Essex and Hertfordshire was forestalled just in time; it was connected in some way with the trouble at Calais and was apparently waiting for an invasion to land on the East coast. What made it so alarming was the involvement of two members of the household, John Fortescue and John Risley, both Esquires of the Body.[10]

The atmosphere at court that Christmas, which the King kept at Westminster, cannot have been pleasant. The dancing and revelry during the Twelve Days were noticeably frenetic, the splendour excessive. No doubt there were all the entertainments we hear of in the Paston letters—singing, lute playing, cards, dicing and back-gammon—with fools, jugglers and tumblers and blind man's buff. Surrounded as he was by hidden disaffection, Richard can be compared with the blind man. For the spectres of invasion and renewed civil war would have been in his courtiers' minds, making them forget momentarily the terrible cold, dampness, and darkness of a mediaeval English winter; in the dimly lit palace all too many noblemen were asking themselves whether they would succeed in choosing the winning side. This overcast, doom-laden mood was scarcely dispelled by the fact that Queen Anne was obviously dying; no doubt she had the hectic flush and glittering eyes symptomatic of tuberculosis of the lungs. She was very much in evidence throughout the celebrations and with the King when he presided over the Twelfth Night revels in Westminster Hall. He wore the Crown of St Edward, just as he had on the day of his Coronation. In the midst of the revels, so the Crowland chronicler tells us, 'his spies from beyond sea' brought him an urgent despatch—'notwithstanding the potency and splendour of his royal state, his adversaries would without doubt invade the Kingdom during the following summer.' Richard commented that nothing could give him greater pleasure, a response which perhaps indicates not so much confidence as self command at breaking point. Moreover there were sinister whispers not only of impending battles but of incest.

What shocked the court, if the Crowland writer is to be believed, were the peculiarly personal attentions which the King paid his niece, Elizabeth of York, during that grim winter. In the circumstances she was the last person one might have expected to see there. Although officially a bastard, his brother's eldest daughter had been given dresses of exactly the same fashion and rich material as those of the Queen; indeed they seem to have worn them in turn, 'exchanging apparel'. (These dresses would have been very narrow-waisted, full-skirted gowns with remarkably low necks—a small bosom was fashionable—with tight sleeves down to the knuckles, under great 'butterfly' head-dresses of wired veils which swept back from the forehead.) Plainly Elizabeth gave the impression of being a second consort. The chronicler refers to 'many other matters as well, which are not written down here for shame'; taken in conjunction with Bishop Langton's discreet mention of 'sensual pleasure' increasingly apparent in Richard's behaviour, this hints that some courtiers had little respect for his morals despite his pious exhortations. The prominence of the former Princess Elizabeth 'horrified' prelates. 'It became common gossip that the King was bent on marrying Elizabeth, whatever the cost, either because he expected the Queen would soon die or that he would obtain a divorce for which he thought he could find adequate grounds.'

Shortly after the exertions of Christmas, Anne Nevill fell very ill. Probably she had never recovered from her son's death—perhaps it was he who infected her. It took her a month to die. If her illness was a galloping consumption, as seems likely, the symptoms would have been terrifying; drenching sweats, a constant racking cough and copious vomits of blood. One shudders at the medicine her age prescribed for the disease—potions of arsenic, garlic and mercury. Richard 'shunned his wife's bed entirely. He declared that it was on his doctors' advice.' This may well have been the case and quite justified, since tuberculosis of the lungs can be virulently contagious. However, he appears to have used their advice with a deliberate callousness to hasten the poor woman's end, if one is to credit the Crowland chronicler who comments 'need one say more?' His absence in itself was bad enough; in the fifteenth century the marital bed was an object of symbolical fidelity, as with European peasants until the early 1900s—it was shared regardless of illness. But the Queen had reason to suspect that he wanted her to die.

The King had complained to Archbishop Rotherham and various noblemen of Anne's barrenness and inability to give him children. Dynastically she was an encumbrance. Several days before her death a rumour circulated that she was already dead—allegedly put about by Richard to frighten her and make her condition worse. She was terrified when she heard it and went to her husband in tears, asking if she had done anything which made him think she deserved to die. Both Polydore Vergil and the Crowland writer are convinced that the King tried to finish her off by psychological methods.[11]

There were also tales that Richard was poisoning the Queen. It is possible that, what with her spouse's obvious desire to be rid of her, and the miseries of her medicine and a Lenten diet—no meat, game or poultry, only salt fish—Anne may really have feared this was happening. Alison Hanham is inclined to attribute Rous's changed attitude towards Richard III not so much to a desire to curry favour with the new régime as to a genuine conviction that the King had murdered a member of the beloved family to whose patronage he owed his career—his words are 'And Lady Anne, his Queen, daughter to the Earl of Warwick, he poisoned.' Dr Hanham also cites Rous as evidence that rumours of the Queen having been poisoned were circulating soon after she died, and were not invented by 'Tudor chroniclers'. As will be seen, even firmer evidence of such rumours exists—given by no less a witness than Richard himself. [12]

Anne Nevill died on 16 March 1485 and was buried in Westminster Abbey, in the King's presence, with all the pomp fitting for one of her rank. She cannot have been more than twenty-seven years old. Apart from the bare fact of her existence, she had made little impression on history—though the *Great Chronicle of London* does at least call her 'a woman of gracious fame'. Her death took place on a day when there was a total eclipse of the sun. In that superstitious age such a coincidence did not help her husband's reputation.

CHAPTER TWELVE

'OUR GREAT HEAVINESS'

'evil disposed persons (both in our City of London and elsewhere within this our realm) enforce themselves daily to sow seed of noise and dislander against our person . . . to our great heaviness and pity.'
Richard III, letter of March 1485

'nor willing or glad of the death of his Queen, but as sorry and in heart as heavy as man might be.'
Richard III, speech on 30 March 1485

The final months of Richard III's reign were the unhappiest of all. He was very much aware of his unpopularity, of the sinister tales about him circulating among his unloving subjects.[1] It is hard to imagine a lonelier figure. He had lost his family, he would not be able to find a new wife and beget an heir, and he does not seem to have taken a mistress. Lord Lovell is said to have been 'his best friend' but this is mere surmise, while if Norfolk—thirty years his senior—was a trusted ally, he was usually far away. There were of course 'Mr Ratcliff and Mr Catesby' (as the *Great Chronicle* calls them) yet they scarcely sound people to inspire affection. In any case the King was not a man to have a male favourite. Nor, for all his vaunted piety, was a confessor or priest particularly close to him.

Moreover, 'trusting few of such as were about him', he would surely have sensed the uneasiness of his courtiers, the latent treachery everywhere. Sir Francis Bacon, who could conceivably have met people who had known survivors from Richard's court, writes 'suspicions amongst thoughts are like bats among birds, they ever fly by twilight . . . They dispose Kings to tyranny.' In addition, contemporaries tell us that Richard suffered from a terrifying sense of guilt and was a haunted man, sometimes on the edge of hysteria. Perhaps he awaited Henry Tudor's invasion as a trial by battle before God. As Gairdner surmises the King was leading 'a life of great agony and doubt'. Bosworth may have come as a welcome relief.

There seems to have been something like a standard official portrait of King Richard. The best known version is that in the Royal Collection at Windsor, of which there are several copies. Itself a mid-sixteenth-century copy, it depicts a most unusual face which has made a curious impression on many people. It put Dr Parr, the famous eighteenth-century scholar, in mind of Lorenzo de' Medici. Josephine Tey, the novelist, sees 'Someone used to great responsibility, and responsible in his authority. Someone too conscientious. A worrier; perhaps a perfectionist . . . Someone, too, who had suffered ill-health as a child. He had that incommunicable, that indescribable look that childhood suffering leaves behind it; less positive than the look on a cripple's face, but as inescapable.' G. K. Chesterton discerns 'a remarkable intellectual beauty'. Paul Murray Kendall, who clearly idolised his subject, finds 'a rather thin face of strongly marked but harmonious features; eyes direct and earnest, shadowed by care; a forthright nose; a chin remarkable for the contrast of its bold structure with its delicate moulding. The face suggests the whole man, a frail body compelled to the service of a powerful will.'

The Crowland chronicler casts an interesting light on the clothes the King is wearing. He says that at Christmas 1482 Edward IV had appeared in 'garments of a completely different fashion to those which had been seen hitherto in our land. The sleeves of the robes were very full and hanging, much resembling a monk's cowl [over tunic] and were . . . lined with costly furs and rolled over the shoulders.' This suggests that the only other contemporary portrait of Richard, in which his brocade doublet resembles those in his brother's pictures, may date from before 1483 and would therefore have been painted when he was still Duke of Gloucester. (The inscription, *Richards. Rex Tertius,* could be a later addition.)

This other portrait of Richard is in the possession of the Society of Antiquaries. It is an early sixteenth-century copy of a lost original and undoubtedly the earliest surviving likeness. He looks in the opposite direction to that of the better known portrait, though here too he fiddles nervously with a ring—obviously a characteristic gesture. There is no sign of deformity in the shoulders, though this may be due to a good tailor. It is the hard-favoured, warlike, visage of which More heard, an alarmingly forceful and indeed a merciless face. In the present writer's view, here is the most convincing likeness of him.[2]

There is no question that the King had every intention of marrying his niece. Elizabeth was more than nubile—she was twenty in February 1485—a tall intelligent beauty with the same fair complexion and golden hair as her mother. (The Crowland writer describes all Edward IV's daughters as 'beauteous maidens'.) Richard's sensuality may well have been aroused, and heightened by the gloomy atmosphere of Lent; in the next century Grafton imagined him as having 'fancied apace Lady Elizabeth'. But, above all, the Crowland chronicler stresses, such a marriage made both political and dynastic sense even though the girl had been legally bastardised. Like his great nephew Henry VIII, Richard III was in a dynastic impasse—the Earl of Lincoln was no substitute for a Prince of Wales. The King 'saw no other way of confirming himself as King, nor of crushing the ambitions of his rival [Henry].' Shakespeare is at his most intriguing, and entirely convincing, when he makes an anxious Richard say:

'I must be married to my brother's daughter
Or else my Kingdom stands on brittle glass.'

Significantly, Henry Tudor is known to have been very alarmed when rumours of the projected marriage reached him in France; in the vivid phrase of Vergil's sixteenth-century translator, 'it pinched him to the very stomach.' Furthermore the King was also rumoured to be trying to marry off Elizabeth's only other sister of marriageable age, Cecily, to someone of obscure rank, to end the Earl of Richmond's last hope of a bride from the House of York. In desperation Henry considered marrying a Welsh lady, a Herbert—scarcely an adequate substitute, even if she was Northumberland's sister-in-law.

Predictably, *The Song of the Lady Bessy* claims that the girl was revolted by the thought of becoming Richard's wife. No less predictably, Polydore Vergil declares that she would have preferred 'martyrdom to marrying a man who is the enemy of my family'. Nevertheless, it is not impossible that she accepted the situation. There was nothing against such a marriage in Canon Law; before and since then, the Church has given dispensations for uncle-niece marriages. A gentle soul, Elizabeth of York may very likely have been under pressure from her mother to take the King. The former Queen had lost faith in Henry Tudor and, with her combination of opportunism and political ineptitude, had decided to make the best of a bad job and compromise with Richard.

In early 1485 Elizabeth Woodville was writing to her son Dorset in Paris, telling him to come home and make his peace. After all his perils—hunted with hounds like an animal when escaping from Westminster, then having to flee again for his life after Buckingham's débacle—Thomas Grey, Marquess of Dorset, must have been badly shaken. In any case he was a weak and unstable character. The third senior peer of England, he was living in penurious exile; his vast wealth had been confiscated, and he had had to leave many children behind him. He knew Henry Tudor's plans; plainly he saw little hope for them—without Elizabeth of York Henry's chances were very slim indeed. It looked as though the present régime was going to last. The Marquess accepted Richard's offer. One night in February or March 1485, Dorset left Paris suddenly and secretly. This defection by someone so important and so well informed about them horrified the exiles. A warrant for his arrest was obtained from the French government and a hard-riding Humphrey Cheyney caught up with the Marquess at Compiègne and persuaded him to return to Paris, perhaps unwillingly. We know that Henry would not trust Dorset for a long time. His distrust reflects deep pessimism about his prospects. Richard III was still very much King of England.

Sir George Buck, one of Richard's earliest would-be re-habilitators, compiled a strange book in the 1620s, made even stranger by being re-written by an erratic and over-imaginative kinsman. However, Buck saw documents now lost. He claims to have seen a letter, long since vanished, at Arundel House, which throws an extraordinary light on Elizabeth of York's response to her uncle's amorous intentions. Addressed to the Duke of Norfolk, the letter—according to Buck—asks him to intercede with the King about her marriage to him, swearing that Richard is 'her only joy and maker in this world, and that she was in his heart and thought.' She adds that she fears the Queen will never die. What gives Buck's story some conviction is that he is using the letter to try to show that the King did not want the marriage.

Undoubtedly Richard consulted theologians. (Again, there is an uncanny parallel with Henry VIII.) But, whatever they and the canon lawyers might say, there was no English precedent for such a match. The Crowland writer informs us that 'the King's determination to marry his niece Elizabeth reached the ears of his people, who wanted no such thing.' (If Malory is representative, fifteenth-century Englishmen were revolted by incest; when Mordred wishes to marry Queen Guinevere 'and said plainly that he would wed her, which was his uncle's wife and his father's wife', the Archbishop of Canterbury curses him with bell, book and candle for making 'a foul work in this land'.) What finally decided Richard against the marriage was Catesby and Ratcliff telling him 'to his face' that if he did not abandon the idea and deny it publicly, even the Northerners would rise against him. They would accuse him of killing the Queen—daughter and heiress to the Earl of Warwick through whom he had first won their loyalty—in order to be able to indulge his incestuous lust for his brother's daughter, something abominable before God.' The Crowland chronicler goes on to explain that though Catesby and Ratcliff then produced theologians and canon lawyers of their own way of thinking, their real motive was fear that if she became Queen she might try to avenge her Woodville kindred—after all everyone knew that Ratcliff had personally superintended the murders at Pontefract. This may well be true, though unquestionably Richard would have earned even more damaging unpopularity if he had made the girl his consort, merely because of such a marriage.

The Crowland writer says that 'even the King himself seldom dared oppose' the views of these two. 'And so, a little before Easter, in the great hall of St John's and before the Mayor and citizens of London, the King totally repudiated the whole idea, in a loud, clear voice. Though people thought it was more because of his advisers' wishes than his own.' On the other hand Polydore Vergil says that the marriage was the brain-child of Catesby and Ratcliff—we will never know whether the chronicler or Vergil was better informed. What we do know however, from the records of the London Mercers' Company (first printed and published in 1936) corroborates the chronicler as to the public denial. On 30 March 1485 the Mayor and

Corporation were summoned to the Priory of the Knights of Rhodes at Clerkenwell, together with many lords and citizens, to listen to an extraordinary announcement by Richard. He told them 'It never came in his thought or mind to marry in such manner-wise [i.e., his niece], nor willing or glad of the death of his Queen, but as sorry and in heart as heavy as man might be.' He complained furiously of rumours—presumably about his poisoning Anne. It says volumes for the King's sinister reputation among his subjects that he had to descend to such a humiliation.[3]

During the Clerkenwell address Richard also threatened anyone caught repeating such calumnies with imprisonment until they told the authorities where they had heard them. The Mercers' records are confirmed in their turn, by a letter which the King wrote to the citizens of York very shortly afterwards. He informs them that he is aware that 'divers seditious and evil disposed persons (both in our city of London and elsewhere within this our realm) enforce themselves daily to sew seed of noise and dislander against our person, and against many of the lords and estates of this our land, to abuse the multitude of our subjects and avert their minds from us.' He grumbled that the slanders were being spread by means of posting bills or by 'bold and presumptuous open speech', ordering the arrest of those who were spreading the rumours.

Elizabeth was packed off to Sheriff Hutton, which Richard clearly regarded as the safest place for her. He kept little Warwick there, as he had Lord Rivers during the usurpation. He was not going to risk any attempts at abduction by the Tudor's supporters. The future mother of Henry VIII stayed in Yorkshire all spring and summer, until after the King had fought and lost Bosworth. However at Sheriff Hutton, even if probably under surveillance, Elizabeth of York would have found herself among reassuringly distinguished company. Besides Warwick and his eleven-year-old sister Margaret (who, as the very last Plantagenet, would be executed in 1541), there were John de la Pole, Earl of Lincoln—Heir Presumptive and President of the Council of the North—and his brother-in-law, Lord Morley. Some of Elizabeth's sisters may have been staying there as well. A special scale of allowances of food and drink was laid down for this resident house-party, the largest measures of ale and wine being reserved 'to My Lord [of Lincoln] and the children.' Sir Clements Markham argues speciously that these 'children' of high rank were in fact the former Edward V and his brother, a claim which does not merit serious consideration.

Dynastically Richard was in a complete impasse. He had not dared marry Elizabeth Plantagenet himself; nor did he dare to marry her or her sisters to anyone else, for fear their sons might eventually claim the throne. It had quickly become clear that Lincoln was unacceptable as heir presumptive. Little Warwick, the only other surviving male of the House of York, was the King's obvious successor, but the

Attainder of 1478 would have to be reversed; if that were done, in theory at least, he would then possess a better title to the throne than his uncle. And without an assured succession Richard's régime could not appear secure, as he must have known all too well. Everything and everyone was conspiring against the King.

At the same time there were other, more material, and new reasons for Richard's unpopularity. Although when he had usurped the throne he found 'ample resources' he was soon overspent, despite the bonus of so many forfeited estates after Buckingham's rebellion. It has long been a cliché that the Yorkist monarchy evolved many of the financial methods employed by the Tudors, thought at the same time it is recognised that Henry VII used them much more efficiently. Edward IV gave generous rewards to his followers in order to establish himself on the throne and only managed to balance his books towards the end of his reign. In his desperate need to buy friends Richard III handed out confiscated lands on a truly prodigal scale. The expenses of his ostentatious court, of the Breton and Scots wars and, above all, of costly precautions against invasion or revolt quickly exhausted his funds. There is also some slight indication that Richard had always lacked financial expertise; in 1482 the Council of the Duchy of Lancaster had stated bluntly that his neglect and inefficiency over a period of years had seriously reduced the Duchy's revenues—selling timber to raise ready cash and not re-planting was one example.[4]

According to the Crowland writer the King was now forced to go back to Edward IV's compulsory loans 'which he had openly condemned in Parliament, though he was very careful to avoid using the word "benevolence". He sent out officials to scrape up huge sums out of all records relating to almost any sort of property holding in the realm.' In reality Richard was probably only trying to raise a comparatively small sum, perhaps as low as £10,000; it has been calculated that in the event he obtained less than half that sum. Moreover while Edward IV's benevolences were extorted with no guarantee of repayment, Richard gave 'good and sufficient pledges' the money would be reimbursed. Between February and April 1485 a number of men of substance—prelates, landowners, merchants— seem to have been approached because of 'such great and excessive costs and charges as we hastily must bear and sustain, as well for the keeping of the sea as otherwise for the defence of this our realm.' It is reasonable to suspect that all too many of those approached were sceptical about his ability to repay. Politically, it would surely have been much wiser for the King to borrow from other sources rather than lose face in this way—as Gairdner emphasises 'Commercial credit is a thing without which even tyrants cannot succeed.'

He was growing unpopular in York, of all places. It is true that when the news of Bosworth came the Mayor and Corporation would record how 'King Richard late mercifully reigning over us . . . was piteously slain and murdered, to the great heaviness of this city.' Yet even before his reign some citizens of York were sceptical about the value of his friendship—one asked publicly in 1482 'What may My Lord of Gloucester doe for us of the city? Nothing but grin of us!' The *Great Chronicle of London* speaks of otherwise unrecorded troubles in the North during the summer of 1483 which the King had to repress in the course of his progress. In autumn 1484 there was a nasty riot at York when Richard consented to the enclosure of certain common lands; despite a stern warning from the King, who sent no less a personage than the Comptroller of his Household (Sir Robert Percy) to deliver it, armed rioting broke out again in January 1485 and there were several casualties. Nor, whatever a Mayor might say, did the city remember him with universal affection. During a drunken brawl at Christmas 1490 a local schoolmaster accused Richard of having been 'an hypocrite, a crouchback and buried in a dike like a dog'. It is interesting that an ordinary Yorkshireman should bear witness to the King's crooked shoulders long before 'Tudor chroniclers' are supposed to have invented the deformity—Richard had been a familiar sight in York. The Crowland writer tells us that there were many Northerners among the deserters at Bosworth.

Considerable sums were spent on building up a large arsenal of field artillery and hand guns at the Tower. Much of it consisted of 'serpentines'. These were long, light cannon, which were mounted on pivots and fired a four-pound ball, and were the latest thing in the period's weaponry. The King imported Flemish gunsmiths to manufacture them, presumably at great expense.

All the indications are that Richard was obsessed by the Pretender threatening his throne. Henry's anonymity may have made him seem more formidable than he really was. During the 1939–45 War Field Marshal Montgomery had photographs of the Germany army commanders confronting him hung in his battle caravan to help him guess what was in their minds. The King can have had no idea of what the Tudor even looked like. At Barnet he had known Warwick, Montagu and Exeter very well, and it is likely that at Tewkesbury he could say he had at least met the Beauforts. But if Richard had even heard the name Henry Tudor before 1483, it was merely as that of an obscure by-blow of the Beauforts; indeed he was not even a Beaufort, let alone a Plantagenet of the 'Old Royal Blood of England'. The name is mis-spelt 'Tydder' in all proclamations against him. The proclamations also describe his parentage and descent, pointing to some sort of official investigation. Although the 'spies across the seas' were almost certainly at Henry's little court—not so little now— to judge from his secrecy and reserve after he had become King, they would scarcely have been able to tell Richard much about the man himself or about what he was thinking. The sixteenth-century chronicler may have been using his imagination when he makes Richard tell his captains, before Bosworth, that the Tudor was a 'Welsh milksop', but he is certainly near the truth in making the King say additionally that 'the Devil, the disturber of concord and sower of sedition, hath entered into the heart of an unknown Welshman whose father I never knew, nor him personally saw.' One is tempted to wonder whether Richard thought it was a vengeful God rather than the Devil. Devoured by guilt and superstition as he was, the King may sometimes have suspected, like Commynes, that 'God had raised up an enemy against him.'

Throughout his reign Richard III seems to have taken refuge in the undeniable fact that although a usurper he was nonetheless the legal, annointed and crowned—and therefore divinely appointed—King of England. Hence his excessive wearing of the royal diadem, like some sort of talisman. Hence too his constant, and emphatic, references to treason—plainly a word which obsessed him. 'Treason' was embodied by one man, Henry. The Welshman's use of the royal style, 'Henricus Rex', must have infuriated him.

Both the Crowland writer and Polydore Vergil tell us that on the night before Bosworth Richard had nightmares. Vergil says that this was a frequent occurrence. As has been already said, More claims to have heard from the King's attendants that almost every night of his reign he was troubled by 'fearsome dreams'. This is the origin of the lines which Shakespeare gives Queen Anne:

> 'For never yet one hour in his bed
> Did I enjoy the golden dew of sleep,
> But with his timorous dreams was still awak'd.'

That Richard suffered from remorse, or at least from an uneasy conscience, seems to be indicated by his quite remarkably intense care for the repose of the souls of dead kindred. It is of course true that, before and after his usurpation, his foundations for chantry priests were to celebrate Masses for all members of his family and not just his victims. He could scarcely single out Edward V and little York (which may lend substance to Sir Thomas's stories about a secret reburial, or perhaps a secret Requiem).

In the fifteenth-century Requiems and prayers for the dead were considered a duty to an exaggerated degree. All over Western Europe countless chantries—or endowments to say Masses for them—were being founded. But Richard set up chantries on a truly extraordinary scale. Even Rous praises him for it. It is likely that only a handful, such as the collegiate chapels at Middleham, Barnard Castle and Barking or the thousand Masses for Edward IV by the friars of Richmond have been identified. He must have presented York Minster with many vestments, a common practice by the great at that time because of the high cost of silk and velvet, yet it is curiously fitting that the only one of which the Minster archives give us any detail was black.

Most peculiar of all was the King's projected chantry of six altars and a hundred priests to be attached to York Minster. Such a ratio of priests to altars meant that a Mass for the Dead could have been celebrated incessantly, without any break. The scheme was as massive as it was strange. A vast new chapel would have had to be built, furnished with countless vestments and sacred vessels, while all the priests there would have to have been supporting clerks and choristers, not to mention servants; an enormous endowment was necessary to pay for this staff of several hundred and its maintenance. Probably no one in Christendom has ever contemplated praying for the dead on so exaggerated a scale. Basically his motive must have been the same as that stated in his foundation charter for Middleham—'in part of satisfaction of such things as at the dreadful day of judgement I shall answer for.' He also wanted to make quite sure that the souls of the dead should rest in peace.

An urge for atonement and propitiation is also evident in Richard's treatment of his enemies' wives and children. His partisans ascribe it to unusual magnanimity, but he was no more merciful than Edward IV in providing such casualties with pensions. Both Kings seem to have set store by an ostentatious show of mercy. In the case of Hastings's family, Richard was undeniably lavish in allowing the son to inherit his father's estate, as though there had been no charge of treason, and the widow to have the wardship. Yet again, one discerns an uncomfortable conscience.

The King's personal spiritual life, in so far as we know anything about it, conveys an even stronger sense of desolation. His Book of Hours—his principal prayer book—has fortunately survived. Illuminated between 1430 and 1450, it had at least one previous owner—probably a member of the Warwick family. What makes it so interesting is the addition in a different hand of a long prayer for the King's use. It is in Latin, headed 'De beato Juliano'. 'As you wish to relieve those burdened with sore affliction' it opens, 'release me from the affliction, temptation, grief, infirmity, poverty and peril in which I am trapped and give me aid.' Appeals for protection are repeated over and over again. It begs 'make peace between me and my enemies . . . lessen, turn aside, extinguish, bring to nothing, the hatred they bear me.' After citing the mercies of the Old Testament and the Passion of Christ, it pleads 'Son of the living God, deign to free me, thy servant King Richard, from all the tribulation, sorrow and anguish in which I am and from all my enemies' snares, and deign to send Blessed Michael the Archangel to aid me against them and the evil they are planning.' Undeniably, the prayer is deeply moving. Yet it is not over-fanciful to detect a note of almost hysterical fear, of paranoia. It gives a unique glimpse of the King's innermost feelings.

Professor Lander stresses that one simply cannot write off as propaganda a highly personal and specially composed prayer which reads 'like the incantation of a litany, fraught with notes of the deepest gloom, oppression and danger, in which the highly charged reference to Susannah, *de falso criminere et testimonio*, so prominently stands out.' Lander continues 'Considering the accusations against him, the knowledge that he slandered his brother's memory, the probability that he impugned his mother's chastity, that he authorised judicial murder, that he was prepared to contemplate incest, that he cheated his nephews out of their inheritance if not far worse, the prayer must indicate that either Richard thought he was innocent of the charges or that towards the end of his life he had become in the highest degree schizophrenic, a criminal self-righteously invoking the protection of the Almighty.'

The words *'De beato Juliano'*, overlooked even by Lander, are the key to the prayer. They indicate that it was intended to invoke the intercession of this obscure saint, who enjoyed a widespread popular cult during the later Middle Ages. Little is known of Julian the Hospitaller save that according to mediaeval hagiographers he killed his own father and mother, and that after doing penance for many years it was revealed to him that God had pardoned him. It is almost certain that Richard was familiar with the tale since it appears in the version of *The Golden Legend*, which Caxton printed at Westminster towards the end of 1483. A parricide was a fitting intercessor for an infanticide, let alone a man who had murdered another saint.[5]

Richard would have become still more uneasy about his enemies if a certain letter from Henry Tudor had fallen into his hands. Dating from the first months of 1485, it probably circulated widely. Addressed to Henry's 'Right trusty, worshipful and honourable good friends', it reads:

Being given to understand your good devoir and entreaty to advance me to the furtherance of my rightful claim, due and lineal inheritance of that Crown, and for the just depriving of that homicide and unnatural tyrant which now unjustly bears dominion over you, I give you to understand that no Christian heart can be more full of joy and gladness than the heart of me, your poor exiled friend, who will, upon the instant of your sure advertising what power you will make ready and what captains and leaders you get to conduct, be prepared to pass over the sea with such force as my friends here are preparing for me. And if I have such good speed and success as I wish, according to your desire, I shall ever be most forward to remember and wholly to requite this your great and most loving kindness in my just quarrel. Given under our signet. H.R.

It is likely that Northumberland and the Stanleys, among others, received such letters.[6]

By the spring Henry was at Rouen, looking for ships. No doubt Richard's spies reported his activities to their master, who may not have been unduly alarmed. For the French seem to have been in two minds about the Earl of Richmond. They must have remembered the English King's opposition to the treaty of Picquigny—Commynes certainly did—and may also have seen copies of his proclamations against Henry, in which the Tudor was accused of promising the French King to 'dissever the arms of France from the arms of England for ever', and to abandon all claims to Normandy, Anjou, Maine, Gascony and Guyenne. Obviously if ever Richard felt strong enough he would invade France and try to reconquer the territories once governed by his father. There was therefore a good case for sending Henry to topple him while he was still weak. There was also a case for keeping Henry in reserve, as a threat. Both options would cost money, but especially the first. It is likely that the King understood this and felt that there was a reasonable chance of his enemy being unable to raise sufficient funds for a proper invasion fleet.

Nevertheless Richard was not taking any chances. In April 1485 Sir George Nevill was given a flotilla to patrol the Kentish coast and in May Lovell was ordered to keep a fleet in readiness at Southampton. The King expected Henry would try to land in Southern England, the most disaffected part of the country. His agents had learnt that the Tudor intended to make for 'Milford', and there was a tiny port of that name in Hampshire which would be excellent for a secret landing, and apparently a soothsayer confirmed that this was the danger spot. No one realized that Richmond's 'Milford' was Milford Haven in Wales. Sir Ralph Assheton and Lord Scrope of Bolton, now Constable of Exeter Castle, were guarding the West Country. Assheton was reappointed Vice-Constable of England and given a deputy. In June Richard returned to his command centre at Nottingham.

Meanwhile the Earl of Richmond had not been idle. Fortunately for him, he was not a procrastinator. The French government were still alarmed that the English King might support Breton separatists should Duke Francis die; indeed, by his encouragement of them, he had given the impression that he intended to invade France as soon as possible—by a more placatory attitude he could easily have won French friendship. As it was, French policy suddenly altered in the autumn and Henry would then have received no help. In any case what he did receive was very inadequate. Commynes says it consisted only of a 'little money from the King [Charles VIII] and some 3,000 of the most unruly men that could be found and enlisted in Normandy.'[7] However Commynes says elsewhere that it was 'a large' sum and adds that Charles lent him some cannon as well.[8] We do not even know the precise number of mercenaries he recruited— Vergil contradicts Commynes, giving a figure of 2,000.

However, we can safely guess that Henry Tudor made the most of what was available. King Charles's loan was undoubtedly supplemented by contributions from supporters in England, while Henry also borrowed from Parisian goldsmiths—he was not without humour, leaving the untrustworthy Dorset behind him as security. Moreover historians have accepted Commynes too uncritically and tend to underestimate the fighting potential of Henry's expedition. No doubt some of the rank and file were gaol birds (Hall calls them 'beggarly Bretons and faint-hearted Frenchmen'), but they were stiffened by 1,500 professional troops and by several hundred English exiles—what might be termed the officer-men ratio was extraordinarily high. And when it landed, the little army would be reinforced by some formidable recruits.

Furthermore, while Richmond had never even seen a full-scale battle—he himself called Bosworth 'our first field'—he possessed superlative commanders. The Earl of Oxford had smashed the Yorkist left at Barnet in 1471 (just as he would destroy the last Yorkist army at Stoke in 1487), while the Savoyard Philibert de Chandée who commanded the French troops clearly knew how to handle them, however 'meschantz'. Jasper Tudor's experience of campaigning in Wales would be very useful in the early stages—he understood the management of that valiant but touchy race. And the expedition included an even greater warrior than Oxford. This was Bernard Stewart, Seigneur d'Aubigny, one of the French King's Scots Archers. Although nearly forty his real triumphs lay ahead; he was to be Captain of the Archers and a Marshal of France and a hero of the French invasions of Italy; in 1508 James IV would proudly refer to him as 'the Father of War'. Aubigny had been French Ambassador to Scotland in 1484 and may well have helped persuade the French to aid Henry, perhaps to avenge that humiliating occupation of Edinburgh. Undoubtedly he brought a small Scots contingent; it is improbable that many came from the French King's indispensable bodyguard, though one or two may have been spared—a laird present, possibly an archer, whose name we do know was Sir Alexander Bruce of Earlshall.[9]

Henry assembled his men and his few ships, perhaps at Rouen, and sailed up the Seine. No doubt with unhappy memories of his stormy journey of two years before, he seems to have waited for fine weather at Harfleur on the Norman coast before putting out to sea. His little fleet had a longer voyage ahead than the vast majority of those on board realized. On Monday 1 August a soft wind was blowing from the South, which was what the shipmasters wanted. The Earl of Richmond set sail.

As soon as Richard had reached Nottingham in June his spies brought him reliable information that the long awaited invasion was about to begin. On 22 June he re-issued his proclamation of the previous December against 'Henry Tydder' and his band of rebels and traitors 'of whom many be known for open murderers, adulterers and extortioners', who had been chased out of Brittany for making proposals 'too greatly unnatural and abominable'; they intended to commit 'the most cruel murders, slaughters and robberies and disherisons that ever were seen in any Christian realm' and to steal everyone's estates and offices, even the bishoprics. Either Richard dictated this proclamation himself or it was someone who knew the workings of his mind. The following day he sent out Commissions of Array, ordering the commissioners 'upon peril of losing their lives, lands and goods' to ensure that their men were properly 'horsed and harnessed' and ready to march at an hour's notice.

Lord Stanley came to the King and asked permission to return to his estates in the North West to raise his tenantry. Richard plainly distrusted the man but dared not antagonise a subject whom he had made one of the three principal props of his régime. He compromised, insisting that Stanley leave his son, the twenty-five-year-old Lord Strange, in his place. Stanley, according to Vergil, did not leave Nottingham until Strange had come, to be in fact if not name an unofficial hostage for his wily father's good behaviour.

In July the King received confirmation that Henry's fleet was about to sail. On the 24th of the month he sent for the Great Seal. Five days after sending for the seal, in yet another outburst of suspicion, Richard dismissed Bishop Russell from his post as its Keeper. Without the seal it was impossible to issue Commissions of Array, and raise an army. Predictably, Russell was replaced by a Northerner— or at least a man whom the King had known in the North—Dr Thomas Barowe, Master of the Rolls. A product of Cambridge, he had been the King's Chancellor when he was Duke of Gloucester and was obviously a reassuringly familiar figure. (On Barowe's appointment to the Rolls two years before, Richard had sent him two pipes of wine.)

The Great Seal was delivered to the King at Nottingham on 11 August. That very same day he received news that the Earl of Richmond had already landed, in a place where he had been least expected, and was marching towards him with his army.

CHAPTER THIRTEEN

'THE KING'S ENEMIES
BE A-LAND'

*'for the just depriving of that homicide and unnatural tyrant which
now unjustly bears dominion over you.'*
                    Henry Tudor, Earl of Richmond, letter of early 1485

*'How like you the killing of my brethren dear? Welcome, gentle uncle,
home.'*
    Humphrey Brereton, The Most Pleasant Song of the Lady Bessy

Some time during the third week of August 1485 John Paston
received a hasty note from his great neighbour, the Duke of Norfolk.
It was almost certainly written on Saturday the 13th.

Well beloved friend, I commend me to you, letting you understand
that the King's enemies be a-land and that the King would have set
forth as upon Monday but only for Our Lady Day [Feast of the
Assumption], but for certain he goeth forth as upon Tuesday, for a
servant of mine brought to me the certainty. Wherefore I pray you
that ye meet with me at Bury [St Edmunds] for by the grace of God
I purpose to lie at Bury as upon Tuesday night, and that ye bring
with you such company of tall men as ye may goodly make at my
cost and charge, beside that ye have promised the King. And I pray
you ordain them jackets of my livery, and I shall content you at your
meeting with me. Your lover. J. Norfolk.

Similar summonses were going out all over England, sent by the
henchmen. They were also being sent by the Stanleys and
Northumberland. Richard was taken completely by surprise at the
enemy's choice of landing place—despite all his precautions he had
not received news of the invasion for four days, when the Earl of
Richmond was already approaching Shrewsbury. Nevertheless, on
hearing of it, the King rejoiced 'or at least seemed to rejoice' says the
Crowland chronicler, who may have watched him with his own eyes.

The little Tudor fleet had made land on the north side of Milford
Haven in South West Wales, just before sunset on Sunday 7 August.
As soon as he set foot on Welsh soil, Henry knelt, kissed the ground,
crossed himself and then recited the Psalm *'Judica me, Deus, et discerna
causam meam'*—'O God, sustain my cause . . . ' Then he knighted
several of his supporters. From the start he acted as though he were
a rightful King come to claim his own.

Henry had chosen Pembrokeshire as the invasion point for a
variety of reasons. His uncle Jasper knew the area well and still had
influence there, while his agent John Morgan of Tredegar had sent

a message assuring him that he would be joined by Rhys ap Thomas and Sir John Savage whose mother was a sister of the Stanleys. The former commanded immense respect among the South Welsh because of his descent from one of their greatest Princes, and his castle of Dynevor in Carmarthenshire was only a short distance away. Not only was Sir John Savage (of Clifton in Cheshire) one of Richard's Knights of the Body and a trusted official—very much a member of the 'mafia', he had received rich rewards—but he possessed influence all over Wales. In addition Sir Gilbert Talbot, on the South Welsh Border, had contacted Henry to say that he would come out with him. High Sheriff of Shropshire, Talbot was the uncle and guardian of the young Earl of Shrewsbury.

Yet, to begin with, the little expedition appeared to be in some danger. Henry was told that enemies had been waiting for him for months. There was no sign that Rhys ap Thomas and Savage, let alone Talbot, really were going to risk their necks. Admittedly lesser men such as Evan Morgan and William ap Griffith came in very quickly, bringing a handful of troops, as did a small band from the town of Pembroke who had always stayed loyal to Jasper Tudor. Nevertheless, men of position reacted to news of Henry's arrival with the utmost caution. He had to move as carefully and discreetly as possible. Although a rumour that a large force of troops loyal to Richard was about to intercept him proved false, it seemed that South Wales was firmly controlled by the King's son-in-law, the Earl of Huntingdon (Katharine's husband). Henry therefore marched north until he reached central Wales and then turned east through Powys to enter England. At any moment he might have been overwhelmed by the Stanleys—had they been faithful to Richard. Then the gates of Shrewsbury opened. Suddenly the Tudor army began to grow dramatically.

As it approached Newport in Shropshire Rhys ap Thomas joined Henry with a thousand men. Sir Gilbert Talbot then arrived with every Talbot retainer capable of bearing arms, another 500. Significantly he was a neighbour and friend of the Stanley brothers. Hitherto the Tudor's recruits had been mainly Welshmen, no doubt flattered by his marching under the 'family' banner of the red dragon of Cadwallader; many of them would have responded to the Celtic combination of flattery and threats he was sending out, as in his letter to his distant cousin John ap Meredith, which promised to restore the people of Wales to their 'erst liberties' while commanding John to come and fight for him 'as ye will avoid our grievous displeasure and answer it unto your peril.' However Talbot's troops were Shropshiremen, and as Henry marched further into England, he was joined by still more English knights and gentry.

Nonetheless it was reasonable for Richard to anticipate no difficulty in crushing 'so contemptible a faction'. On Thursday 17 August he went hunting in Sherwood Forest, spending the night at a convenient lodge—a good way of displaying confidence and dispelling tension. He was the King and he had a mighty army—Henry was an adventurer with forces which seemed hopelessly inadequate. One should also take into account the Boar's inflated reputation as a military commander, and the sheer dread and terror which he inspired, 'such great fierceness and such huge force of mind he had.'[1] So far no English peer who was not in exile had come out for the Tudor. Yet, as news of defections by apparently reliable officials began to arrive, Richard grew steadily more suspicious. His nervousness showed when he sent orders for Sir Robert Brackenbury to bring with him to Leicester two of Buckingham's former supporters about whom he was doubtful—Sir Walter Hungerford and Sir Thomas Bourchier.

Then the King was given real cause for alarm. George, Lord Strange, who had come to Nottingham to be a hostage for the Stanleys' good behaviour, was caught trying to escape from the castle. Only a day or two before, his father, Lord Stanley, had written to say that he was suffering from the current outbreak of the sweating sickness and would not be able to join the royal army at Leicester. Obviously Strange was interrogated with savage efficiency; if he was not tortured he was almost certainly threatened with the 'question'. He broke quickly, making an abject confession and begging for mercy. He admitted that he and his uncle Sir William, together with Sir Gilbert Talbot and Sir John Savage, had been planning to join the Earl of Richmond. However Lord Strange insisted that his father was nevertheless unshakeably loyal to Richard; this may have been a deliberate lie, a shrewdly calculated attempt at self preservation. Presumably under strict direction, he wrote to Lord Stanley, explaining the peril in which he stood and beseeching him to come to Leicester and save his life. While Strange remained a hostage in imminent danger of death, the King had some chance of controlling the Stanleys, though Sir William and Savage were at once proclaimed as traitors. It is very likely that the wily Catesby had a good deal to do with fending off Strange's beheading; in the revealing will, which he dictated just before his own execution, he says 'My Lords Stanley, Strange and all that blood, help and pray for my soul, for ye have not for my body as I trusted in you.'

As so often before, Richard's fatal incapacity to judge other men had betrayed him. The key mover in the Stanley conspiracy, Sir William was even more treacherous than his brother and had a long record of changing sides. It had been extremely profitable, William Stanley having done very well for a younger son. He was fifty, the same age as the head of the family whose twin he may have been. In his case the 'second son' complex expressed inself in greed and ruthlessness and was richly rewarded. He had also made a wealthy marriage with 'Butcher' Tiptoft's widow. Half a century afterwards Leland referred admiringly to the mansion William built himself at Ridley in Cheshire as 'The fairest gentleman's house in all Chestershire'. The King had had quite enough opportunity to observe him since he worked closely with William Stanley, too closely for his comfort; declining an invitation to a hunting party, Stanley wrote that he was 'so busy with old Dick that I can have no leave.' This clever and daring intriguer was more than a match for his master.[2]

Every day Richard had increasing reason to suspect treachery all around him. News of more and more defections arrived. Sir Thomas Bourchier and Sir Walter Hungerford gave Brackenbury the slip, to join Richmond near Stony Stratford. Sir John Savage—who, it will be remembered, was one of the henchmen—would join Henry at Tamworth with men-at-arms in white hoods and jerkins. Even so, the Tudor's army was still too small to face Richard with any chance of success in a straightforward battle. However much they may have disaproved of their ruler, too few noblemen and gentry, let alone burgesses and common folk, were prepared to risk their lives and fortunes after nearly thirty years of dynastic warfare.

It is astonishing how many English gentlemen preferred to 'stay a-bed' and thought themselves in no way accursed at missing what would not exactly be another Crispin's Day. And it was they who provided the troops; in consequence whereas perhaps as many as 75,000 men, on both sides, had fought at Towton in 1461, no more than 25,000 were to fight in 1485. Thirty-three noblemen—almost the entire English peerage who were not minors or under attainder— had attended Richard's Coronation, yet only a dozen would be with him at Bosworth, and two of them were traitors.[3] A magnate like the third Lord Stourton, whose family had become briefly pre-eminent in the West Country because of the Courtenays' eclipse, was not going to gamble on the outcome of the present campaign even though the King's defeat would mean the return of his rivals.[4]

Neither would Stourton's brother and eventual heir, despite being married to Richard's niece, Catherine de la Pole. Lesser people, Knights and gentlemen, simply disregarded the King's summons and ignored the threat in his Commissions of Array that they would do so 'on peril of their lives, lands and goods'. The city of York too was growing tired of Richard's incessant demands for its inhabitants to risk their lives for him. It sent a force of only eighty men, who did not arrive in time.

Even so, one should not underestimate the terror inspired by the King's threats and menaces. It is vividly preserved in the ballad of *Bosworth Feilde*, which makes Richard promise

> 'Ladies "well-aday!" shall cry,
> Widows shall weep and their hands wring;
> Many a man shall regret that day
> That ever they rose against their King.'

Apparently the Earl of Richmond's strategy was simply to advance on London and hope for the best, like Bonny Prince Charlie in 1745.

The fact that Shrewsbury opened its gates to him was encouraging—they had stayed firmly shut during Buckingham's campaign, when the Duke tried to enter. Henry had sent messages to the Stanleys—and almost certainly to Northumberland as well, though there is no firm proof—begging for support. He knew very well that if they did not give it, he was lost. The Stanleys were willing enough, as Richard himself now appreciated, but were held back by the perilous situation of Lord Strange. The King hoped to neutralise them and did not want to drive them into the arms of the Earl of Richmond; it was better to have them on the sidelines rather than as open enemies.

What Richard did not suspect for one moment was that he had another, more secret enemy—the Earl of Northumberland. His inability to judge other men was to prove his final undoing. It is likely (despite Gairdner's belief that the Tudor's agents failed to reach him) that the Earl had been in touch with Richmond. On the other hand, he was not Henry's step-father. There are some slight indications that Northumberland contemplated a totally different outcome. First, he would let the Stanley-Richmond faction and the King do each other as much damaged as possible, and with luck ensure that Richard was killed. Then he would proclaim the young Earl of Warwick as King and become the power behind the throne.[5]

If Richard was to survive, he had to intercept and destroy Henry Tudor's army. On Friday 19 August the King marched down the hill from Nottingham Castle and set out for Leicester where his levies were assembling. He rode warily, he and his household men in the van, which was flanked on both sides by mounted men-at-arms who scouted far and wide; suspicious as ever, he did not discount the possibility of ambush. It was an impressive sight, yet Vergil—if he is not indulging in poetic licence—says that its effect was marred by the worried frown on Richard's grim face. Behind their terrifying little leader, his captains must have been equally uneasy. He arrived at Leicester just before sunset the same day, having covered twenty-five miles, entering through one of the north gates and riding down what is now High Cross Street. The town's cannon roared out a salute. Ignoring the ruinous castle, he installed himself at the reassuringly named White Boar Inn, a large, cantilevered, half-timbered building. Servants at once furbished his apartments with his furniture and hangings—as was the custom for great lords, he had even brought his own bed with him. (The bed had a false bottom containing about £300 in gold coin, which was not discovered for a century, until Elizabeth I's reign.) The Duke of Norfolk and his troops were also billeted in the town, soon to be joined by the Earl of Northumberland and his contingent.

The Earl of Richmond was in a far from enviable state of mind. It seems that Sir William Stanley had met him briefly at Stafford and had arranged for him to meet Lord Stanley secretly at Atherstone, between Coventry and Leicester, to discuss the situation. Henry then lost contact with his army on the night of 19 August, while marching from Lichfield to Tamworth. He found himself with only twenty men. They hid in a small village, fearful of being caught by Richard's men. However at daybreak they discovered that they were only three miles from Tamworth and were able to rejoin their friends without incident. The Tudor told his army that he had been on a discreet expedition to receive a message from some allies who were not yet ready to come out openly for him; in reality, as he seems to have confided in Vergil many years later, he had probably been terrified by the danger and by what lay ahead. The same day he again made contact with Sir William at Atherstone. His step-father was not there. Beyond question the Stanleys were well disposed towards him yet, despite their assurances of help, they knew—and he surely guessed—that with Strange in the King's hands they were powerless. They dared not move, even though fully aware that if Richard won the forthcoming battle he was likely to wreak a merciless revenge; but someone so cruel and so ruthless, with so much at stake, would not hesitate to execute the young man, and would give orders for him to be killed instantly if they joined his rival. No one dreamed that the King would present Henry with the one tactical situation which would enable them to act.

Henry Tudor can have had little hope of success. But he could not now avoid a battle. For their part the Stanleys decided that their only course was to take their troops to the battlefield. If Henry looked like winning they could support him—if Richard swept all before him, they would join his side instead, and pretend that they had always been loyal. This is certainly the most plausible explanation of their conduct.

Richard marched out of Leicester on Sunday 21 August. He did so with great pomp, wearing a crown so that all might see that the King of England was going forth to battle. With him were the Duke of Norfolk, the Earls of Northumberland, Lincoln, Nottingham, and Surrey, Viscount Lovell, Lords Scrope of Bolton, Scrope of Masham, Dacre, Greystoke, Zouche and Ferrers of Chartley, and most of the henchmen—including Sir Robert Brackenbury, who had only just arrived. As they rode forth the King's spur scraped the brickwork of the narrow old Bow Bridge over the River Soar—a hag prophesied that very soon his head would bang against the very same bridge.

Richard and his army, flanked by a wide screen of scouts, proceeded along the Roman Road in the direction of Atherstone. At Sutton Cheney the scouts reported that the enemy was near. It was evening and for his camp that night he selected a position near the summit of some rising ground called Ambion Hill. Although only about 400 feet above sea level, it gave an excellent field of vision over the low lying Redmore Plain beneath and was protected by a marsh at its foot. It also commanded the road below between the villages of Shenton to the west and Sutton Cheney to the east. (Market Bosworth was two miles north.)

Henry's army was three miles down the Roman Road below, about three miles south west. He had perhaps 5,000 men, compared with the King's 12,000. He still hoped that he would be reinforced by the Stanleys. Indeed, he knew that he was doomed without them.

It is clear that Lord Stanley and Sir William had not made up their minds. Accordingly they camped to the north of Ambion Hill, Sir William's force in front of his brother's, so that they could await the outcome of the battle and join the winning side. In consequence, as Gairdner points out, there were in fact four armies 'placed, as regards each other, not unlike whist-players'. They still claimed that they had come to fight for Richard. The thought which must surely have been uppermost in the minds of both the King and the Earl of Richmond was: how would the Stanleys and their 8,000 troops act next day?

If a romantic and undocumented tradition handed down among the family of the Earls of Winchilsea is true, Richard had a moving encounter on the day before the battle. About 1530 a Kentish landowner (and ancestor of the Earls of Winchilsea), Sir Thomas Moyle of Eastwell, met an old stonemason who told him that, as a child knowing nothing of his parents, he had been expensively educated in London. On one occasion, the boy was taken to a magnificent house where a gentleman with 'a star and garter' questioned him and gave him money. Later he was brought to a place which he afterwards realised was Bosworth and in the royal pavilion the same gentleman embraced him. It was the King who informed the boy that he was his father, promising to acknowledge him publicly as his son. 'But, child,' added Richard, 'if I should be so unfortunate as to lose the battle, take care to let nobody know that I am your father, for no mercy will be shown to anyone so nearly related.' Richard then said goodbye, giving him a purse of gold. After the battle the boy fled and apprenticed himself to a mason. Moyle, at any rate, believed the story. He gave the old man a cottage at Eastwell and had recorded in the parish register that a 'Rychard Plantagenet' was buried there in 1550.[6]

Professor Ross emphasises that 'There have been as many different accounts of Bosworth as there have been historians, and even today it is hard to produce a reconstruction of the battle which will command general acceptance.' In particular, he writes that 'Kendall's account of the battle remains an astonishing mixture of imagination, speculation and purple prose, and his description of Richard's last moments seems to suggest that he was perched on the crupper of the king's horse.'[7]

No proper eye witness report has survived. A Spanish soldier of fortune, who was actually present, Juan de Salazar, recounts his experiences in a letter but is too brief and confused to be of much value, though he confirms how Richard met his end and gives some useful details. Nevertheless, careful analysis of the information supplied by the Crowland writer, by Vergil, by the compiler of the *Great Chronicle of London*, and by the authors of the ballad of *Bosworth Feilde* and of *The Song of the Lady Bessy* (one of the two ballads about Lady Bessy) make possible an approximate recreation of one of the most dramatic conflicts in English history.

Both contemporary sources and tradition suggest that the King was unable to sleep. There is a fantastic legend of considerably later date that he went round the camp in the dark and catching a sentry dozing at his post stabbed him to death—with the comment 'I find him asleep and I leave him asleep.' It is certainly in character, or at least in character with what his subjects thought of him.

Richard and his men rose in the dark before dawn, towards 4.00 a.m. One can reconstruct the scene in the royal pavilion where the King was being armed by his pages in a ritual with which he was very well acquainted. Various sections of his steel 'harness' would have been laid out on a trestle table together with his weapons; no exact description has survived, but it is possible to guess what they included with a fair degree of accuracy. The armour, which he had worn at Tewkesbury, is likely to have been a German one, perhaps from Nuremberg, since German armours were then the best in Europe. (Those from Italy were made for elegance and show rather than for fighting.) First he put on a satin-lined fustian doublet, cut full of holes for coolness and worn next to the skin, worsted hose with padded kneecaps, and thick leather shoes. The pages began with his feet on which they placed pointed, articulated 'sollerets' to which gold spurs were attached. His legs and thighs were similarly covered in plate, his loins by a mail apron over which was a short skirt of horizontal, overlapping plate 'tonlets'. His torso was protected by breast and back plates, the former reinforced by an extra thickness. His arms were guarded by 'vambraces' and 'rerebraces', though they were probably without the huge butterfly elbow 'cops' so popular until recently, his shoulders by deep, laminated 'pauldrons'. Then came gauntlets of articulated steel. A loose belt was girded round his waist, from one side of which hung a triangular-bladed dagger and from the other a naked, double-edged sword thrust through a round ring so that it could be easily drawn. We know (from Salazar) that overall he donned a short-sleeved red-and-blue-silk surcoat, slit at the sides, embroidered with the golden leopards and lilies of England and France. At last, after many minutes of buckling and strapping, his helmet was put on—to judge from his Great Seal this would have been a sallet rather than a closed bascinet and could be pushed back off the face. Almost certainly it was of gold-plated steel, and surmounted by a crown. The latter was not the massive diadem which he wore on state occasions, but nonetheless an unmistakeably regal coronet of fabulous splendour and price; Salazar valued it at 120,000 crowns—£20,000 in the money of 1485.

When the King emerged from his pavilion into darkness dimly lit by guttering torches, the captains waiting outside started back at the weirdly pale and haggard face and staring eyes beneath the crown. In response to their unconcealed alarm Richard explained, perhaps unwisely, that during the night he had had terrible dreams in which demons had tormented him. (It was an age which took such dreaming very seriously indeed; just before Arthur's last battle the dead Sir Gawain appeared while he slept and warned him 'For an ye fight as to-morrow, doubt ye not ye must be slain.') Still more ominous, no chaplains could be found in the camp to say Mass; considerable importance was attached to hearing it daily, as often as three times, and above all before such dangerous events as a battle. Yet the King, normally so conventional and punctilious in religious observance, did not send for a priest from a neighbouring village. Nor had anybody prepared breakfast for him.

Having given his commands, he mounted a tall grey war horse. He may not have uttered Shakespeare's superb line 'Saddle White Surrey', but we know that an animal with this name was in the royal stables, and according to tradition if not eye-witness testimony, the King rode a white charger at Bosworth. He was handed his principal weapons, a battleaxe and a lance. The former was probably of the type sometimes known as a battle hammer; basically a hatchet with a spike above the small but very heavy blade or hammer, and with a long steel shaft; it was used as a bludgeon rather than an axe, to smash in an enemy's armour and inflict lethal bruising. His lance would have been a much thicker and heavier weapon than the early twentieth-century cavalry lance since it was intended to knock an opponent out of the saddle instead of skewering him, but for obvious reasons was only effective at the first impact.

Even the hostile *Song of the Lady Bessy* admits that Richard III arrayed himself for battle like a true monarch

> 'Give me my battle axe in my hand
> And set my crown on my head so high!
> For, by Him that made both Sun and Moon,
> King of England this day I will die.'

His captains remonstrated with him for wearing the crown—it made him immediately identifiable as well as offering a glittering booty—but he would not listen.

Standing on a small hillock, Richard addressed his men in the cold dawn twilight. He prophesied wildly that, whoever won the battle, its outcome would destroy England—if victorious he would exterminate every rebel, just as Henry Tudor was going to slaughter all opponents should he win. The King had already threatened that 'whoever should be found in any part of the Kingdom after the victory should have been gained, to have omitted appearing in his presence on the field, was to expect no other fate than the loss of all his goods and possessions as well as his life.' The speech may have been an attempt to inspire ferocity in his troops but, in view of the mood which his captains noted with such alarm, it is more likely to have been dictated by rage. It could well be that the last Plantagenet King was on the verge of hysteria when he rode out to his last battle on Monday 22 August 1485.

Nevertheless he disposed his forces in a most elaborate formation on top of Ambion Hill. In front, just on the brow, was the van under the Duke of Norfolk; it consisted of billmen and gunners whose cannon, 140 light serpentines and as many bombards, were joined by chains to stop enemy horse riding through them, with lines of archers before and on the flanks. Canoneers and archers would have been reinforced by several hundred sooty-faced handgunners, of the sort employed at Tewkesbury, whose primitive match-locks were now recognisable as arquebuses and increasingly effective. Richard was behind the van, with a small but picked force of men-at-arms—heavy cavalry—supported by more infantry. Behind him was the 3,000 strong contingent of the Earl of Northumberland. Vergil comments that the van was 'of a wonderful length, so full replenished both with footmen and horsemen that to the beholders afar off it gave a terror for the multitude.' So unusual a formation has been attributed to a knowledge of the new Swiss tactics which had annihilated the King's late brother-in-law, Charles of Burgundy, only a few years before. Richard's military studies went further than merely reading Vegetius. But, as will be seen, his application of what he had learnt, was more ingenious than practical.

Even at this very last moment the King does not seem to have distrusted Northumberland, although he must have known that some sort of treachery was being planned. During the night a jingle had been nailed to Norfolk's tent:

> 'Jack of Norfolk, be not too bold,
> For Dickon, thy master, is bought and sold.'

No doubt all the King's suspicions were centred on the Stanleys. He sent an order to Lord Stanley to join him at once, if he wanted Strange to stay alive. The reply came that Lord Stanley did not feel like joining him and had other sons. Richard at once ordered that Lord Strange be beheaded. But his captains refused to obey the order, so instead he gave instructions for the young man to be kept under close arrest until he could deal with him after the battle. He realised that not only the Stanleys but some of those closest to him were of questionable loyalty.

As the King pondered his strategy he was looking on a forest of banners. On both sides peers and knights banneret (such as Ratcliff and over a hundred others) had their personal standards borne before them as rallying points for their men. Banners were still the best—indeed the only—method of grouping combatants into semi-coherent formations.

Henry Tudor's forces were so inferior that he had only the sketchiest of centres. It was commanded by the Earl of Oxford, who was in charge of the little army's tactics. Sir Gilbert Talbot had the right and Sir John Savage the left. Henry was behind them, with a pitiful reserve which consisted of a single troop of horse and a few foot soldiers. A frantic plea to Lord Stanley to join him received an alarmingly evasive answer. Even Vergil admits that the Tudor was 'no little vexed and began to be somewhat appalled.' He was in what seemed to be a hopeless situation.

Looking up, he could see the dread King's mighty host on the hill, poised to hurtle down and destroy him and his outnumbered troops. A vivid eyewitness memory of the terror on Mount Ambion above is preserved by *The Song of the Lady Bessy*; the challengers saw how the Plantagenet Satan 'hoveth upon the mountain'. Since the Stanleys appeared to have deserted them, Henry's followers had only two choices. They could run for it—and no doubt many wanted to—but everyone knew that their merciless enemy would pursue them to the death. The sole alternative was an attack uphill despite all the odds. There was just a chance that Richard's narrow front would prevent him from making full use of his overwhelming military superiority; it would be impossible for Northumberland to march down and round to take them in flank in time. Furthermore, firing downhill may have made the royal army's serpentines even less accurate than usual. Oxford, a brilliant commander, took what in the circumstances was the only possible decision. If those with him could not match his bravery, they had at least the courage of despair.

Oxford skirted the marsh at the bottom of Ambion Hill, and then began to lead his troops up the slope. Richard's archers shot flight after flight at them. The King, determined to smash them while they were deploying and before they could launch a proper attack, ordered the Duke of Norfolk to advance. The old warrior and the front ranks of the van charged downhill. In all logic he should have annihilated so puny an enemy. But he was faced by Oxford, who knew just what to do. Knowing the poor quality of many of his rank and file, the Earl ordered his men to group round his banners—i.e., around their officers—and not to move more than ten feet away from them, bunching the troops into a tight wedge which cut Norfolk's attack in two. The royal soldiers were taken aback by this manoeuvre and, fearing a trap, withdrew to regroup. There was a brief lull in the fighting. Then the opposing centres came to grips again in a savage hand-to-hand struggle. Tradition says that the Duke engaged Oxford in personal combat and wounded him slightly, but that the Earl hacked off his chinpiece whereupon a stray arrow hit the old man in the throat. Surrey was surrounded and gave up his sword to

Gilbert Talbot. The murderous slogging match continued, though it is clear that the King's troops were astonished by such a reception.

Looking down, Richard must have been badly shaken by Norfolk's death. Plainly, he was already pessimistic enough about the way the battle might go. He had had his cannon roped together to stop them being overrun by a more formidable force than that of his rival—it was the Stanleys whom he feared. But so far they had shown no sign of moving.

Below, Henry was still waiting forlornly. He had taken up a position where the Stanleys could join him, but they had not done so. Without them, despite Oxford's heroic performance, he knew that his defeat was inevitable. Henry decided that his last hope lay in throwing himself on their mercy; if they would not come to him, he would go to them. With his small bodyguard and his Red Dragon banner, carried by William Brandon, he began to ride towards their lines. He was taking a desperate risk. Had he reached the Stanleys, he might well have been seized and handed over to the King as a proof of their loyalty.

On the hill above, Richard was further alarmed by the Earl of Northumberland's totally unexpected refusal to try to bring his troops into action. The Earl might not have been able to take Oxford in flank, but he could probably have prevented the Stanleys from joining the enemy by placing his force between them. In any case the King must have been worried by his own men's increasingly poor morale; there was the possibility of large-scale desertion. As it was, he himself was over excited.

Then Richard identified his rival's party behind the unmistakeable dragon banner cantering over the plain beneath on its way to the Stanley lines. 'Now tide me death, betide me life,' he may well have exclaimed like Arthur on beholding Mordred at the last battle, 'now I see him yonder alone he shall never escape mine hand.' If he could intercept Henry he might win the battle and the entire campaign at one blow. Yet in doing so he would place himself at the mercy of the Stanleys. It was not a brilliant tactical manoeuvre as is sometimes claimed, but an insane gamble—his father had thrown away his life in exactly the same foolhardy gesture a quarter of a century ago. After a quick drink from 'Dickon's Well' (as it is still known) Richard 'all inflamed with ire' ordered his Household to charge. The heavily armoured horsemen couched their massive lances.

There is an almost oriental even Japanese, quality in the magnificent, suicidal, death ride which ensued. The Knights and Esquires of the Body thundered down the hill with their master, under the banner of the White Boar. The two little forces—the King had no more than a hundred men with him, Henry perhaps fifty—collided on Redmore Plain. At the first shock of impact Richard killed William Brandon with his lance, sending the banner of Cadwallader crashing to the ground. He then struck down the gigantic Sir John Cheyney out of the saddle with his axe. The Household did equally lethal execution, they and the King 'Making way with weapon on every side' as Vergil was informed long after. Richard personally slew more of his rival's party in the melee—he may even have exchanged blows with the Tudor himself. The latter's men began to despair though the inexperienced Henry, who had never been in battle before, was fighting better than they had expected. But in a matter of minutes he too would have been cut down.

Only a short distance away, barely more than half a mile off, Sir William Stanley could see what was about to happen. If Henry died, he himself would be doomed. (Ironically, the new Tudor King was to behead him ten years later.) With his 3,000 men in their red jerkins shouting 'Stanley! Stanley!', he charged to the rescue—just in time.

The Royal Household was overwhelmed. Robert Brackenbury had already been slain by his old friend Walter Hungerford, one of the Tudor's escort. Others of the henchmen fell—Richard Ratcliff, John Kendall, Robert Percy, Walter Hopton—and the King was told that he must flee. He refused. 'I will die King of England,' he replied fiercely, 'I will not budge a foot!' His horse was killed under him and somehow a fresh horse was brought to him but he would not mount it. With wolfish courage he went on swinging that murderous axe on foot. The far from uncritical Crowland writer says that at last 'pierced with numerous and deadly wounds, he fell in the field like a brave and valiant Prince.' Even the violently hostile Rous tells us 'he bore himself like a noble soldier and, despite his little body and feeble strength, honourably defended himself to his last breath, shouting, again and again that he was betrayed and crying 'Treason! Treason! Treason!' Vergil too admits that 'King Richard alone was killed fighting manfully in the thickest press of his enemies.'[8]

The royal army fled immediately after Richard's death. Oxford pursued, killing many. In all nearly a thousand men died in the battle. Lovell escaped, but Catesby was captured—to be executed shortly afterwards. One of the Stanleys placed the King's coronet on Henry VII's head. Northumberland rode down from the hill to kneel and pay homage, and to be put under arrest. The battle of Bosworth (as it was later named) had lasted only two hours. Perhaps it was over by as early as 8 o'clock in the morning.

The Crowland chronicler was revolted by the bestial way in which Richard's corpse was treated—after it had been stripped insults were heaped on it 'not exactly in accordance with the laws of humanity'. More speaks of it being 'hacked and hewed of his enemies' hands, harried on horseback dead, his hair in despite torn and tugged like a cur dog.'

A halter was strung round the dead monarch's neck. Finally the mangled remains, covered in blood and mud, were taken back to Leicester for a pauper's burial on the crupper of Blanche Sanglier's horse, the pursuivant being made to carry his late master's banner of the White Boar in mockery.[9]

The *Great Chronicle of London* records wonderingly 'Richard late King, as gloriously as he was by the morning departed from that town so as irreverently was he that afternoon brought into that town, for, his body despoiled to the skin and nought being left about him so much as would cover his privy member, he was trussed behind a pursuivant . . . as an hog or other vile beast. And so, all too bestrung with mire and filth, was brought to a church [that of the Grey Friars] in Leicester for all men to wonder upon. And there lastly indifferently buried. And thus ended this man with dishonour as he that sought it, for had he continued still Protector and have suffered the childer to have prospered according to his allegiance and fidelity, he should have been honourably lauded over all . . . '

The author of *The Most Pleasant Song of the Lady Bessy* imagines Elizabeth of York waiting for her uncle at Leicester and taunting his corpse:

> 'How like you the killing of my brethren dear?
> Welcome, gentle uncle, home.'[10]

The scene is of course pure fantasy, yet the sentiment surely expresses the feelings of most contemporary Englishmen. The reign of Richard III had been a nightmare, not least for the King himself.

40. *The commander of Henry Tudor's small Scots contingent at Bosworth,*
Bernard Stewart, Seigneur d'Aubigny. Bibliothèque Municipale, Arras.

41.   *The Garter Plate in St George's Chapel, Windsor, of Richard's betrayer, Thomas, Lord Stanley.*

42. *John Sacheverell, killed at Bosworth fighting for Richard. From a brass laid down forty years later at the church of St Matthew, Morley, Derbyshire.*

43. *Sir John Cheyney, unhorsed by Richard during the last charge at Bosworth. Tomb in Salisbury Cathedral.*

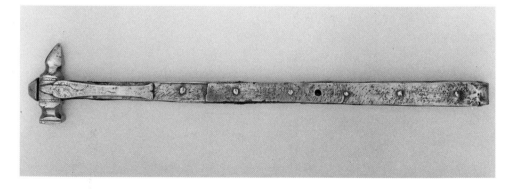

44. *Battleaxe – or 'battle hammer' – of the type probably used so effectively by Richard at Bosworth. Note the belt hook at top. Glasgow Museum and Art Gallery, registered number '39 – 65 ov.*

EPILOGUE

'God never gave this world a more notable example, neither in what unsurety stands this worldly state, or what mischief works the proud enterprise of a high heart, or finally what wretched end ensues from such pitiless cruelty.'

Sir Thomas More, The History of King Richard the Third

'One should avoid being despised and hated.'

Machiavelli, Il Principe

Henry VII later erected a very modest tombstone over his rival in the Grey Friars' church at Leicester. Made of coloured stone, it cost a mere £10. 1s. 0d. This disappeared during the Dissolution of the Monasteries, when Richard's bones were dug up and thrown into the River Soar. For many years a coffin said to have been his was used as a horses' drinking trough.

Much has been made of the dismay shown by the Mayor and Corporation of York at the news of Bosworth. Yet there is no other record whatever of any regret throughout the entire Kingdom. Everywhere King Henry was accepted without demur. So marked a lack of opposition is surely significant.

Some of the Household were attainted, and a few were executed. Most made their peace with Henry, like Sir Ralph Assheton who lived until 1489 when—according to tradition—he was murdered by his tenantry. Another who did so was Sir James Tyrell. Sir Marmaduke Constable survived to command the left wing at Flodden and contribute to the terrible defeat of the Scots in 1513. (A lengthy and somewhat boastful list of Little Sir Marmaduke's military exploits, on a brass plate over his tomb, tactfully omits his campaigns with Richard.)

After allowing a decent interval to elapse, emphasising that he owed nothing to her claims, the new King married Elizabeth of York. Bacon, Henry Tudor's first biographer, says that 'he shewed himself no very indulgent husband towards her, though she was beautiful, gentle and fruitful. But his aversion towards the House of York was so predominant in him, as it found place not only in his wars and councils, but in his chamber and bed.' She bore him several sons, of whom the future Henry VIII alone survived her, and died in childbirth in 1503. Her mother, Elizabeth Woodville, had quickly fallen out with her son-in-law; deprived of her briefly restored estates, she led 'a wretched and miserable life' in poverty at Bermondsey Abbey until her death in 1492.

Richard's sister, Margaret of York—the dowager Duchess of Burgundy—lived on in the Low Countries as a childless widow till 1503. King Henry confiscated her English lands. However, she possessed rich estates abroad from where 'mine old lady of Burgundy' plotted ceaselessly if unavailingly against her brothers' supplanter until her dying day.

However, some of the dead King's men refused to accept the new régime. In 1486 Sir Humphrey Stafford tried to raise Worcestershire, but failed and was beheaded. Yet it was a long time before the Yorkist cause was finally extinguished, although crippled by a lack of acceptable Pretenders. In 1487 an Oxford baker's boy, Lambert Simnel, was transformed into Clarence's son, Warwick—although the Earl was still alive, a prisoner in the Tower of London—with Margaret of York's money and the support of the Earl of Lincoln, of Francis Lovell and of various Irish magnates; he was crowned in Dublin as 'Edward VI'. An army of Yorkist die-hards, of Irish kerne and German mercenaries then invaded England. The battle of Stoke ended this extremely dangerous challenge the same year, Henry being once again indebted to Oxford's superlative generalship.

The new dynasty was then menaced by a young Flemish adventurer, Perkin Warbeck, who posed as the Duke of York, Edward V's brother, and styled himself 'Richard IV'. Perhaps fittingly, in 1495 the arch-traitor Sir William Stanley was executed for intriguing with Warbeck; as Bacon puts it, Henry had recalled 'that Stanley at Bosworth-field, though he came time enough to save his life, yet he stayed long enough to endanger it.' The wretched Warwick was later to be another casualty of Warbeck's ambition.

Lincoln's brothers took up the claim, and it was for harbouring one of them that Tyrell lost his life. In 1525 Henry VIII was beside himself with joy when Richard de la Pole, Duke of Suffolk—the 'White Rose', briefly recognised by the French as King of England— was killed at Pavia. In 1541 Henry beheaded the last living Plantagenet, Clarence's daughter, the aged Countess of Salisbury together with many of her kinsmen, largely because of their Yorkist blood. The ultimate Yorkist victim was Edward Courtenay, Earl of Devon, who suffered a long imprisonment on account of his descent from Edward IV; he died in 1557 as a result of debauchery after his release.

'Neo-Yorkism', and attempts to rehabilitate Richard III, began with the eccentric antiquarianism of the early seventeenth century. It was made fashionable in the eighteenth by Horace Walpole and his taste for perversity and Gothick fantasy. Fuelled by Victorian romanticism, it reached its apogee in 1906 with the publication of Sir Clements Markham's classic defence of the King—a wildly romantic book— whose very special pleading has since been increasingly refuted by the publication in 1936 of Mancini's eyewitness account of the *coups d'état* of 1483, and by the near certain identification of the Crowland writer as Bishop John Russell.

Nevertheless, the White Legend continues to appeal to every Anglo-Saxon lover of a lost cause and, in particular, to lady novelists. All these latter-day champions of Richard share a marked characteristic of their hero, an invincible reluctance to face facts. They cannot accept the stark reality, the tragic grandeur, of the Black Legend.

NOTES

INTRODUCTION

1 'A recent estimate suggested that something has been written about him in every single generation since his death almost five hundred years ago.' Ross, *Richard III*, p. xix. Smetana even composed a peculiarly dreary tone poem about him.

2 This sinister parallel was noted by at least one contemporary, the Crowland writer—'a similar death of a King of England, slain in a pitched battle in his own kingdom, has never been heard of since the time of King Harold, who was an usurper.'

3 In *History Today*, IV (1954).

4 Kendall, *Richard III: The Great Debate*, London 1965, p. 27.

5 Nevertheless Professor Lander acknowledges that More 'is more careful in sifting a rumour from truth than is generally admitted.' *Community and Government*, p. 371.

6 e.g., Mancini's eyewitness account of Richard's usurpation; the entry in the records of the Mercers' company noting Richard's extraordinary public denial of being glad at his wife's death and of intending to marry his niece; and the almost certain identification of the Crowland writer with Richard's Lord Chancellor.

7 '*car estant en plus grand orgueil que ne, fut cent ans avoit, roy d'Angleterre.*' Commynes, *Mémoires*, II, p. 233.

8 *See* Hanham, Ch. 4, 'The "Second Continuation" of the *Crowland Chronicle*: a Monastic Mystery.'

9 As Gairdner observes, 'More is not a writer who would have glossed over a fact to please the court.' *History of the Life and Reign of Richard the Third*, p. 124.

CHAPTER ONE: THE DIFFICULT BIRTH

1 Ross cites the possibility of 'Sprengel's Deformity', a condition arising from an under-developed scapula (shoulder-blade) which results in insufficiently flexible muscles in the shoulder. *See* Philip Rhodes, 'The Physical Deformity of Richard III' in *British Medical Journal*, 2, 1977.

2 *See* Lander 'Marriage and politics in the fifteenth century: the Nevilles and the Wydevilles' in *Crown and Nobility*.

3 Wolffe, *Henry VI* (1981).

4 Storey, *The End of the House of Lancaster*, p. 136.

5 *See* Leland, *Itinerary in England and Wales*.

6 *See* Bonney, *Historic Notices in reference to Fotheringay*.

7 For Fastolf Place *see* M Carlin in *The Ricardian*, vol. V, no. 72, p.311.

CHAPTER TWO: OUR BROTHER OF GLOUCESTER

1 In contrast to Kendall, who believes that Richard joined Warwick's household in 1461, Ross shows convincingly that he did not do so until late in 1465 at earliest. *Richard III*, p. 7.
2 For Middleham *see* Peers, *Middleham Castle*.
3 'Another prolific family which greatly improved its hitherto very modest fortunes in Richard's employ was that of Metcalfe of Nappa, five miles up the dale from Middleham.' Ross, *Richard III*, pp. 50, 51.
4 The most extensive study of the Earl is Kendall's *Warwick the Kingmaker* but like his *Richard III* it relies too much on a vivid and romantic imagination.
5 *See* Armstrong, 'The Piety of Cecily, Duchess of York.'
6 For Lord Lovell *see* 'Francis Lovell, Viscount Lovell' in *Dictionary of National Biography* and *Complete Peerage*, VIII, pp. 223–6.
7 For the Nevill feast, *see* Scofield, I, pp. 399–400.
8 Mancini, writing in 1483, says that Edward tried to force Elizabeth at knife point, p. 60. This lurid story was circulating as early as 1468, according to the Milanese poet Antonio Cornazzano in *De mulieribus admirandis*.
9 *See* Wavrin, *Anchiennes Cronicques d'Engleterre*, pp. 458, 459.
10 Commynes, who had seen both the King and Richard in the flesh, attests to Edward IV's striking good looks—'*fort beau prince.*' *Mémoires*, I, p. 197.

CHAPTER THREE: WARWICK UNMAKES A KING

1 No one really knows why Clarence turned against Edward—'George, Duke of Clarence, was for some secret, I cannot tell what cause, alienated in mind from his brother King Edward' says Vergil, p. 120.
2 For Desmond *see* 'Thomas FitzGerald, eighth [sic.] Earl of Desmond' in *Dictionary of National Biography*, *Complete Peerage*, IV, p. 247–8 and Richard's letter in *Letters and Papers of Richard III and Henry VII*, I, pp. 67, 68.

CHAPTER FOUR: THE WHEEL OF FORTUNE

1 *See* Myers, 'The outbreak of war between England and Burgundy in February 1471' in *Bulletin of the Institute of Historical Research*, 33 (1960), pp. 114–15.
2 '*lequel* [Montagu] *estoit très vaillant chevalier*'. Commynes, *Mémoires*, I, p. 214.
3 According to a later tradition. No contemporary account—including *The Historie of the Arrivall of Edward IV in England* or a letter from Margaret of York—makes any mention of Richard commanding the van at Barnet, despite Kendall's claims for his contribution to the victory.
4 Hutton, in *The Battle of Bosworth Field*, p. xxxiii, says that two of his squires—John Milwater and Thomas à Par—were killed at his side but does not cite any contemporary authority.
5 For a report of Richard being wounded at Barnet, *see* J. Adair, 'The Newsletter of Gerhard von Wesel, 17 April 1471' in *Journal of the Society for Army Historical Research*, 1968.
6 *See* J. D. Blyth, 'The Battle of Tewkesbury' in *Transactions of the Bristol and Gloucestershire Archeological Society*, 80, 1961.
7 At Tewkesbury Richard was undoubtedly in at least nominal command of the right, according to *The Historie of the Arrivall*.

CHAPTER FIVE: FIRST BLOOD

1 As Constable Richard had the right to condemn men to death out of hand for treason, without jury or witnesses. *See* M. H. Keen, 'Treason trials under the law of arms.'

2 For Fra John Langstrother, *see Dictionary of National Biography* and E. J. King and H. Luke, *The Knights of St John in the British Realm*, St John's Gate 1967.
3 Gairdner, p. 14.
4 Hanham, p. 116.
5 'hereunto King Edward gave no answer, only thrusting the young man from him with his hand, whom forthwith those that were present [which] were George, Duke of Clarence, Richard, Duke of Gloucester and William, Lord Hastings cruelly murdered.' Vergil, p. 152. Neither Professor Ross nor Professor Lander accept this 'later story.'
6 'he took it to so great despite, ire and indignation, that, of pure displeasure and melancholy, he died.' *Historie of the Arrivall*, p. 38.
7 '*tua de sa main, ou feit tuer, en sa presence, en quelque lieu à part ce bon homme le roy Henry*.' Commynes, *Mémoires*, I, p. 216. In September 1486, in verses addressed to Henry VII, Pietro Carmeliano, accuses Richard of having murdered Henry VI. *Memorials of King Henry VII*, p. lvii. Writing about 1500, Bernard André says that he did so on Edward IV's orders. Ibid., p. 23. However Ross agrees that Richard 'may have been the agent, not the director of King Henry's murder.' *Richard III*, p. 22.
8 'The continual report is that Richard, Duke of Gloucester, killed him with a sword, whereby his brother might be delivered from all fear of hostility.' Vergil, p. 156.
9 *See* Richmond, 'Fauconberg's Kentish Rising of May 1471'.

CHAPTER SIX: THE RIVALRY WITH CLARENCE
1 For Richard's illegitimate children *see* P. Hammond in *The Ricardian*, vol. 5, no. 66, 1979, pp. 92–6 and no. 72, 1981, p. 319.
2 For the heraldic significance of the boar, see Guillim, *Display of Heraldrie*, London 1638 (3rd edn), p. 188.
3 '*tres beaulx presens, comme de vaisselle et de chevaulx bien accoustrez*'. Commynes, *Mémoires* II, p. 67.
4 However some authorities believe that Richard's son was not born until 1476. *See* Hammond, *Edward of Middleham*, pp. 35, 36.
5 For Edward IV to have permitted such a marriage between Clarence and the heiress of Burgundy meant certain involvement in a potentially ruinous continental war with France and the Habsburgs.
6 For the drowning in Malmsey, *see* Mancini, p. 62—'*in dolium mollissimi falerni mersus vitam cum morte commutaret*.' And Commynes—'*Le roy Edouard fist mourir son frère, duc de Clarence, en une pippe de malvoisye*.' *Mémoires*, I, p. 533.
7 Commynes, however, heard that it was because Clarence '*se vouloit faire roy, comme l'on disoit*.' *Mémoires*, I, p. 533.
8 Hicks in *False, Fleeting, Perjur'd Clarence*—surprisingly favourable to Duke George— argues that no one benefited more from his death than Richard, who had plainly sold out to the Woodvilles. Even the cautious Ross admits that 'it seems quite inconsistant with what we know of Richard's character, and of his past relations with Clarence, that he had not condoned—to say the least—the carefully orchestrated overthrow of his brother in 1478.' *Richard III*, p. 34.

CHAPTER SEVEN: RICHARD IN THE NORTH
1 Richard was granted custody of silver mines in Northumberland in 1475; *Complete Peerage*, V, p. 740. *See also Victoria County History*, Cumberland, II, p. 343.
2 Richard maintained his own group of actors and minstrels who seem to have travelled all over England. 'In 1478 and 1480 the duke of Gloucester's players have been traced in places as far apart as Canterbury and New Romney in Kent and Selby Abbey in Yorkshire.' Lander, *Government and Community*, p. 164.
3 See 'Thomas Stanley, first Earl of Derby' in *Dictionary of National Biography* and *Complete Peerage*, IV, pp. 205–7.

4 *See* Scrope of Bolton in *Complete Peerage*, XI, pp. 544–6.
5 *See* Atthill, *Documents Relating to the Foundations and Antiquities of the Collegiate Church of Middleham*.
6 Commynes had a good opinion of him too—*'le seigneur de Hastingues, homme de grande sens et vertu et de grand auctorité.' Mémoires*, II, p. 240.
7 For the war with Scotland, *see* Nicholson, *Scotland: the Later Middle Ages*.
8 *See* 'John Howard, first Duke of Norfolk' in *Dictionary of National Biography* and *Complete Peerage*, IX, pp. 610–12.
9 For Assheton *see Dictionary of National Biography* and Wedgwood, *Biographies*, p. 26.
10 Uncharacteristically Edward decided not to lead the army himself, probably because of illness; it is known that rumours about the King's serious ill health were definitely circulating in 1481 or 1482. (Ross, *Edward IV*, pp. 287–8.) By this date Richard had therefore clear warning that his brother might die prematurely—and to lay plans.
11 *'tam elevatae mentis'*.
12 Bacon, most plausibly, describes Richard 'as having an expectation and a kind of divination, that the King, by reason of his many disorders, could not be of long life.' *History of the Reign of King Henry VII*, p. 6.

CHAPTER EIGHT: 'PROTECTOR AND DEFENDER'

1 Mancini is unequivocal. 'Indeed there were those who were not unaware of his ambition and cunning, and who had always had misgivings about where they would lead.' (*'Nonnulli tamen qui eius ambicionem et artem non ignorarent, semper dubitarunt quorsum eius conatus evaderent.'*) Mancini, p. 82.
2 For Buckingham, *see* 'Henry Stafford, second Duke of Buckingham' in *Dictionary of National Biography* and *Complete Peerage*, II, p. 389–90.
3 'It is sometimes forgotten now that the capacities of a twelve-year-old youth were much more highly rated, and extended, in mediaeval times.' Hanham, p. 4.
4 *See* 'Excursus. A note on the dating of Lord Hasting's execution.' Hanham, p. 24 *et seq.* Admittedly neither Professor Ross nor Professor Lander agree with her conclusions. Ross, *Richard III*, p. 84.
5 Mancini pays a terser tribute to Hastings which may well reflect the impression he made on ordinary Londoners— *'comes fidus et miles strenuus fuerat.'* Mancini, p. 88.
6 Probably about the same age as her lover Edward IV, Mistress Shore must have been in her early forties by 1483 if still very beautiful.
7 Mancini does not seem to appreciate that in England only the King wore purple when in full mourning, but its significance would not have been lost on English spectators. Mancini, p. 94.
8 The Crowland writer's actual words are *'in cathedram marmoream intrusit'*.
9 For Sir John Fogge *see Archaeologia Cantiana*, V, 1863, p. 125 and Wedgwood, *Biographies*, pp. 339–40.

CHAPTER NINE: 'KING RICHARD THE THIRD'

1 Even if Stillington's story was true, Eleanor Butler had died in 1468 and by the time the boys were born their parents' marriage was publicly accepted by both the ecclesiastical authorities and the English people as a whole—an acceptance quite sufficient to make it perfectly valid by the canon law of the period.
2 *'appert et prompt aux danses et aux esbats.'* But the chronicler's testimony is hardly strengthened by giving York's name as 'Georges' instead of Richard—perhaps confusing him with a younger brother of that name who had died in infancy. Molinet, vol. II, p. 402.
3 Writing of his coronation, just after the reign, the Crowland writer says 'From this day forward, as long as he lived, this man was called King Richard the Third'—*'homo iste'* is amusingly but not inaccurately translated by Gairdner as 'this fellow.'

4 Buck is incorrect in stating that Cardinal Bourchier attended the Coronation banquet—his traditional place on the King's right, as Archbishop of Canterbury, was filled instead by the Bishop of Durham.

5 For Richard Ratcliff, *see Dictionary of National Biography.*

6 *See* 'William Catesby, counsellor to Richard III' in *Bulletin of the John Rylands Library, Manchester*, xlii (1959). *Also* Tudor-Craig, *Catalogue*, p. 97.

7 *See* Ross, *Richard III*, p. 59 and A. J. Pollard, 'The Tyranny of Richard III'.

8 *For* Dr Argentine's career *see* D. E. Rhodes, 'The Princes in the Tower and their Doctor' in *English Historical Review*, lxxvii, 1962 and, by the same author, *John Argentine, Provost of King's: his life and library*, Amsterdam 1967.

9 *'le duc de Bouciquignant qui avoit faict mourir les deux enfans.' Mémoires*, II, p. 306.

10 *'Et feit mourir ses deux nepveux.' Mémoires*, II, p. 233.

11 *'receüt lettres du duc de Clocestre qui s'estoit fait roy d'Angleterre, et se signoit Richard, lequel avoit faict mourir les deulx filz du roy Edouart, son frère. Ledict roy Richard requeroit l'amytié du roy et croy qui'il eust bien voulu avoir cest pension dessusdicte* [i.e., to Edward IV], *mais le roy ne voulut responde à ses lettres ne oyr le messaige et l'estima très cruel et mauvais: car après le trespas dudit roy Edouart, ledict duc de Clocestre avoit faict hommage à son nepveu comme à son roy et souverain seigneur; et incontinent commis ce cas.'* [i.e., committed this crime.] *Mémoires*, II, p. 305.

12 *'Aspicite, quaeso, quidnam post mortem regis Eduardi in ea terra contigerit, eius scilicet jam adultos, et egregios liberos impune trucidari, et regni diadema in horum extinctorum, populis faventibus, delatum.'* J. Masselin, *Journal des Etats-généraux de France tenus à Tours en 1484*, Paris 1835.

13 *'le duc de Boucquinghen, lequel fut mecreu d'avoir estainct et occis lesdits enfants, à cause qu'il pretendoit avoir droict à la couronne.'* Molinet, *Mémoires*, II, p. 403.

14 The theory that Norfolk was the real murderer of the Princes in the Tower was recently revived by Melvin J. Tucker in *The Life of Thomas Howard, 1443–1524*, The Hague 1964. It was definitively disposed of by Anne Crawford in 'John Howard, Duke of Norfolk: A Possible Murderer of the Princes' in *The Ricardian*, vol. 5, no. 70, 1980, pp. 230–34.

15 For Sir James Tyrell, *see Dictionary of National Biography* and Wedgwood, *Biographies*, p. 889.

16 For Sir Robert Brackenbury, *see Dictionary of National Biography.*

17 The highly partisan Kendall has to admit that the Wardrobe accounts reveal that at about this date Tyrell rode from London to York and perhaps from York to London as well. *Richard III*, p. 479.

18 *See* Hammond, *Edward of Middleham, Prince of Wales.*

CHAPTER TEN: 'HIM THAT HAD BEST CAUSE TO BE TRUE'

1 Author of the chronicle usually referred to as *Vitellius A XVI. See* Kingsford, p. 191.

2 'a man possessed of great qualities for the crooked times in which he lived.' Gairdner, p. 108.

3 For the origins of the Tudors, *see* Chrimes, pp. 4–15.

4 For Buckingham's tenure of Penshurst, *see Victoria County History*, Kent.

5 Conway, 'The Maidstone Sector of Buckingham's Rebellion, October 18th, 1483' in *Archaeologia Cantiana* is often cited as the authoritative study of the rising, but is in fact ill informed and inadequate; the author does not even appreciate that Buckingham owned Penshurst.

6 'Nothing can explain the language of this proclamation except a kind of cynical hypocrisy' is Gairdner's view, p. 146. Professor Lander discerns 'an obsession with sexual morality and a morbid sense of persecution. Again and again he struck a shrill note of moral indignation . . . in accusations against the marquess of Dorset and Henry Tudor.' *Government and Community*, p. 329.

7 For the siege of Bodiam in 1484, *see Victoria County History*, Sussex, vol. IX, p. 551.

8 For Sir Henry Wyatt, *see under* Sir Thomas Wyatt in the *Dictionary of National Biography*, and Chrimes pp 127–262. The story of his imprisonment comes from a statement by his son during Henry VIII's reign, the fanciful tale of the cat from J. Bruce in the *Gentleman's Magazine*, xxiv, (1850), vol. II, pp 235–6.

9 For Sir Marmaduke Constable, *see* Wedgwood, *Biographies*, p. 212.

10 For the Parliament of 1484, *see* Wedgwood, *Register*, pp. 475–93.

11 For the text of '*Titulus Regis*', *see* Rotuli Parliamentorum, ed. J. Strachey, London 1767, vol. VI, pp. 240–42.

12 For a detailed account of the King's redistribution of southern lands, *see* Ross, *Richard III*, pp. 119–24. A. J. Pollard, in 'The Tyranny of Richard III', argues—unconvincingly, in the present writer's opinion—that in consequence a black legend of Richard grew up in the South, leaving a white legend in the North; his principal evidence for the latter is the testimony of Sir George Buck!

13 The oath is printed in Gairdner, pp. 165–6.

14 For Sir Gervase Clifton, *see* R Thoroton, *The Antiquities of Nottinghamshire*, Nottingham 1790, vol. 1 pp. 106, 107.

CHAPTER ELEVEN: THE DEATH OF RICHARD'S SON

1 The tomb's identity has not been established beyond all doubt. *See* Routh and Knowles, *The Sheriff Hutton Alabaster: A Reassessment.*

2 For Henry Tudor's companions in exile, *see* Chrimes, Appendix B., p. 327, *Also* Vergil, p. 200.

3 For Dr Urswick, *see Dictionary of National Biography*. He was later to be Henry VII's confessor and Court Almoner, and was almost certainly one of Polydore Vergil's oral informants—and possibly one of More's as well, since he lived until 1527.

4 For Richard and Scarborough, see *Victoria County History*, Yorkshire (North Riding), vol. II, p. 551. For his naval activities, *see* Richmond, 'English Naval Power in the Fifteenth Century', p. 14.

5 Whitelaw's actual words are '*Nunquam tantum animum Natura minori corpore, nec tantas visa est includere vires.*'

6 In Poppelau's words, '*König Richard drei Finger länger, doch ein wenig schlanker und nicht so dik als er, auch gar viel dürrer, hatte ganz subtile Arme und Schenkel, auch ein grosses Herz.*' *Scriptores Rerum Silesicarum*, vol. III, p. 365.

7 The letter to Desmond is in *Letters and Papers Illustrative of the Reigns of Richard III and Henry VII*, I, pp. 67, 68.

8 Lord Lovell's crest of a dog is on his Garter plate, still at St George's Chapel, Windsor. *See* St John Hope LXXXV.

9 Richard's letter to his mother is printed in Gairdner, pp. 189, 190.

10 For John Risley—significantly a former Esquire of the Body to Edward IV—*see* Wedgwood, *Biographies*, p. 717.

11 'supposing that her days were at an end, she went unto her husband very pensive and sad, and with many tears demanded of him what cause there was why he should determine her death.' Vergil, p. 211.

12 The rumours that Richard had murdered his wife even reached Commynes in France. '*Aucuns dient qu'il la feït mourir. Mémoires*, II, p. 234.

CHAPTER TWELVE: 'OUR GREAT HEAVINESS'

1 And overseas as well. Jean Molinet (1420–1507), Canon of Valenciennes and Historiographer to the Holy Roman Emperor Maximilian I was a mediocre poet and an even worse chronicler. But, if owing too much to an excessively vivid imagination, his account of Richard is nonetheless yet another contemporary testimony to the King's unsavoury reputation in Europe. '*Il regna en grand crudelité le roy Richard, . . . le plus cremu de tous les rois d'occident à cause de sa tyrannie.*' *Mémoires*, vol. II, pp. 404, 405.

2 The wooden panel on which the portrait is painted has been tree ring dated to about 1516. The portrait seems to have been in the possession of the Pastons—the letter writing family.

3 *Acts of Court of the Mercers' Company*, pp. 173, 174. Molinet had heard a garbled version of Richard's sensational public denial. *'Il fut accusé et déclaré par les portaux des églises avoir faict mourir la reine sa femme, pour ce qu'elle estoit grosse, et d'avoir desfloré la petite fille sa niepce.' Mémoires*, vol. II, p. 403.

4 For contemporary criticism of Richard's inefficiency in matters of administration, see Somerville, *History of the Duchy of Lancaster*, I, p. 420.

5 Lander, op. cit., pp. 329, 330. For the text of Richard's prayer, see Tudor-Craig (2nd edn 1977), pp. 96, 97. For cults of St Julian, see *Acta Bollandista*, 1945. (I am indebted to Dom Sylvester Houédard for this last reference.)

6 For Henry's letter to his supporters, see Halsted, *Richard III*, II p. 556.

7 *'avec peu d'argent du roy [Charles VIII] et quelque trois mil hommes prins en Normandie et des plus meschantz que l'on peüst trouver.' Mémoires*, II, p. 306.

8 *'une bonne somme d'argent et quelques pièces d'artillerie.' Mémoires*, II, p. 234.

9 See A. E. Conway, *Henry VII's Relations with Scotland and Ireland 1485–1498*, p. 6.

CHAPTER THIRTEEN: 'THE KING'S ENEMIES BE A-LAND.'

1 Molinet testifies to the numbing fear inspired by Richard—*'et n'y avoit prince en Angleterre qui osast susciter guerre ni prendre armes contre lui.' Mémoires*, vol. II, p. 405.

2 For Sir William Stanley, see *Dictionary of National Biography*.

3 Nonetheless, Ross regards his handling of his nobility as almost 'a model exercise of patronage.' *Richard III*, p. 158. For a precisely opposite interpretation, see T. B. Pugh's 'The Magnates, Knights and Gentry' in *Fifteenth-Century England*, p. 114.

4 For the Stourton family, see Lord Mowbray, Segrave and Stourton, *The History of the Noble House of Stourton*.

5 For Northumberland's treachery, see 'A Castilian Report on English Affairs 1486', ed. Goodman and Mackay pp. 92–9.

6 This strange story about a third bastard is only to be found in F. Peck, *Desiderata Curiosa*, London 1779, pp. 249–51.

7 The best account is still Gairdner's 'The Battle of Bosworth' in *Archaeologia*, lv (i). Also valuable is Williams, *The Battle of Bosworth*, although it contains certain errors. The account in Burne, *The Battlefields of England*, is similarly patchy. That in Chrimes, *Henry VII*, is too reliant on Polydore Vergil (whose own reconstruction—only fifteen years after the battle—has a number of serious mistakes).

8 In a characteristically confused account, Molinet claims that though Richard fought bravely and wore the crown, when he 'found himself alone on the battlefield, he fled after the others; his horse galloped into a marsh from which it could not extricate itself; and then one of the men from Wales came up and struck him dead with a halberd.' *Mémoires*, vol. II, p. 409.

9 No doubt this was Blanche Sanglier. He was probably called Robert Watkyns, since a 'herald-at-arms' of this name was attainted in the first Parliament of Henry VII. Wedgwood, *Register*, pp. 493 and 496.

10 *The Most Pleasant Song of the Lady Bessy* (a slightly different version of the ballad *Ladye Bessiye*). Gairdner, p. 319.

SELECT BIBLIOGRAPHY

CONTEMPORARY

Acts of Court of the Mercers' Company, 1453–1527, ed. L. Lyell and F. Watney, C. U. P. 1936.

André, B., *'Vita Henrici VII'*, in *Memorials of King Henry VII*, ed. J. Gairdner, Rolls Series 1858.

Arnold, R., *The Names of the Bayliffs Custos Mairs and Sherefs of the Cite of London*, Antwerp 1502.

Bosworth Feilde, in *Bishop Percy's Folio Manuscript*, vol. III, ed. J. Hales and F. Furnivall, London 1868.

British Library Harleian Manuscript 433, ed. R. E. Horrox and P. W. Hammond, Alan Sutton 1980–81 (2 vols).

'A Castilian Report on English Affairs 1486', ed. A. Goodman and A. Mackay, in *English Historical Review*, 1973 (lxxxvii).

Caxton, W., *The Book of the Order of Chivalry*, O.U.P. 1926.

Caxton, W., *The Golden Legend*, Dent 1900.

The Cely Letters, 1472–1488, ed. A. Hanham, Early English Text Society 1975.

Chronicles of London, ed. C. L. Kingsford, Oxford 1905.

The Chronicle of Calais, ed. J. G. Nichols, Camden Society 1846.

Commynes, P. de, *Mémoires*, ed. J. Calmette and G. Durville, Paris 1924–5 (3 vols).

Davies, R., *Extracts from the Municipal Records of the City of York during the Reigns of Edward IV, Edward V and Richard III*, London 1843.

Documents Relating to the Foundations and Antiquities of the Collegiate Church of Middleham, ed. W. Atthill, Camden Society 1867.

Fabyan, R., *New Chronicles of England and France*, ed. H. Ellis, London 1811.

Fortescue, Sir J., *The Governance of England*, ed. C. Plummer, O.U.P., 1885.

Grafton, R., *Grafton's Chronicle, or History of England*, London 1809 (2 vols).

Grafton, R., *The Chronicle of John Hardyng . . . Together with the Continuation* by R. Grafton, ed. H. Ellis, London 1812.

Grants etc. from the Crown during the Reign of Edward the Fifth, ed. J. G. Nichols, Camden Society 1854.

Great Chronicle of London, ed. A. H. Thomas and I. D. Thornley, London 1938.

Hall, E., *Union of the Two Illustre Families of Lancaster and York*, ed. H. Ellis, London 1809.

Historiae Croylandensis Continuatio in *Ingulph's Chronicle of the Abbey of Croyland*, trans. and ed. H. T. Riley, London 1854.

Historiae Croylandensis Continuatio in *Rerum Anglicarum Scriptores Veterum*, ed. W. Fulman, Oxford 1684.

Historie of the Arrivall of Edward IV in England and the finall Recoverye of his kingdomes from Henry VI, ed. J. A. Bruce, Camden Society 1838.

Journal des Etats généraux de France tenus à Tours en 1484, ed. J. Masselin and A. Bernier, Paris 1835.
Ladye Bessiye, in *Bishop Percy's Folio Manuscript*, vol. III, ed. J. Hales and F. Furnivall, London 1868.
Letters and Papers Illustrative of the Reigns of Richard III and Henry VII, ed. J. Gairdner, Rolls Series, London 1861–63 (2 vols).
Letters of the Kings of England, ed. J. O. Halliwell, London 1846.
Mancini, D., *De Occupatione Regni Anglie per Riccardum Tercium*, trans. and ed. C. A. J. Armstrong, Oxford 1969.
Molinet, J., *Chroniques*, ed. S. A. Buchon, Paris 1827–8 (5 vols).
More, Sir T., *The History of King Richard the Third*, in *The Complete Works of St. Thomas More*, ed. R. S. Sylvester, Yale 1963 (vol. ii).
Nokes, E. M., and Wheeler, G., (ed.) 'A Spanish Account of the Battle of Bosworth', in *The Ricardian*, March 1972.
Paston Letters, 1422–1509, ed. J. Gairdner, London 1904 (6 vols).
Rous, J., *The Rous Roll*, ed. C. R. Ross, Alan Sutton 1980.
Scriptores Rerum Silesiacarum, ed. G. A. Stenzel, Breslau 1847 (3 vols).
'The Song of the Lady Bessy', in *English Historical Literature in the Fifteenth Century*, C. L. Kingsford, Oxford 1913.
Sources for the Reign of Henry VII, ed. A. F. Pollard, London 1913 (3 vols).
The Stonor Letters and Papers 1290–1483, ed. C. L. Kingsford, Camden Series 1919 (2 vols).
Vergil, P., *The Anglica Historia of Polydore Vergil, A. D. 1485–1573*, trans. and ed. D. Hay, Camden Series 1950.
Vergil, P., *Three Books of Polydore Vergil's English History*, ed. H. Ellis, Camden Society 1844.
Warkworth, J., *A Chronicle of the First Thirteen Years of the Reign of King Edward the Fourth*, ed. J. O. Halliwell, Camden Society 1839.
Wavrin, J. de, *Anchiennes Chronicques d'Engleterre*, ed. E. Dupont, Paris 1858–63 (3 vols).

LATER AND MODERN
Armstrong, C. A. J., 'The Piety of Cecily, Duchess of York' in *For Hilaire Belloc*, ed. D. Woodruff, Burnes Oates 1942.
Bacon, Sir F., *The History of the Reign of Henry VII*, C.U.P. 1888.
Bagley, J. J., *Margaret of Anjou*, London 1948.
Bonney, H. K., *Historical Notices in Reference to Fotheringay*, Oundle 1821.
Buck, Sir G., *The History of King Richard the Third*, ed. A. N. Kincaid, Alan Sutton 1979.
Buck, Sir G., *The History of the Life and Reigne of Richard the Third*, London 1646.
Burne, A. H., *Battlefields of England*, Methuen 1950.
Burne, A. H., *More Battlefields of England*, Methuen 1952.
Cheetham, A., *Richard III*, Weidenfeld and Nicolson 1972.
Chrimes, S. B., *Henry VII*, Eyre Methuen 1972.
Chrimes, S. B., 'Lancastrians Yorkists and Henry VII', in *Fifteenth-Century England 1399–1509*, ed. Chrimes, C. D. Ross and R. A. Griffiths, Manchester 1972.
The Complete Peerage, ed. G. E. Cockayne and V. Gibbs, St Catherine's Press 1910–59 (13 vols).
Conway, A. E., *Henry VII, Relations with Scotland and Ireland 1485–1498*, C.U.P. 1932.
Conway, A. E., 'The Maidstone Sector of Buckingham's Rebellion', in *Archeologia Cantiana* 1925 (xxxvii).
Dictionary of National Biography, passim.
Dunham, W. H., 'Lord Hasting's Indentured Retainers', in *Transactions of the Connecticutt Academy of Arts and Sciences* (xxxix). New Haven, Connecticut 1955.
Gairdner, J., 'Did Henry VII Murder the Princes?' in *English Historical Review* 1891 (vi).
Gairdner, J., *History of the Life and Reign of Richard the Third*, Cambridge 1898.
Gairdner, J., 'The Battle of Bosworth' in *Archaeologia* 1896 (lv).

Green, V. H. H., *The Later Plantagenets*, Edward Arnold 1955.
Halsted, C., *Richard III as Duke of Gloucester and King of England*, London 1844 (2 vols).
Hammond, P. W., *Edward of Middleham, Prince of Wales*, Gloucester 1973.
Hanham, A., *Richard III and his Early Historians*, Oxford 1975.
Hicks, M. A., *False, Fleeting, Perjur'd Clarence*, Gloucester 1980.
Hope, W. St John, *The Stall Plates of the Knights of the Garter*, Constable 1901.
Hutton, W., *The Battle of Bosworth Field*, London 1813.
Jacob, E. F., *The Fifteenth Century 1399–1485*, Oxford 1961.
Jenkins, E., *The Princes in the Tower*, Hamish Hamilton 1978.
Keen, M. H., 'Treason Trials under the law of arms', *Transactions of the Royal Historical Society*, 5th series, 12 (1962).
Lander, J. R., *Crown and Nobility 1450–1509*, London 1976.
Lander, J. R. *Government and Community: England 1450–1509*, Edward Arnold 1980.
Lander, J. R., *The Wars of the Roses*, Secker and Warburg 1965.
Leland, J., *Itinerary in England and Wales*, Centaur 1964 (4 vols).
Kendall, P. M., *Richard the Third*, George Allen and Unwin 1955.
Mackie, J. D., *The Earlier Tudors*, Oxford 1952.
MacGibbon, D. *Elizabeth Woodville*, London 1938.
Markham, Sir C. R., 'Richard III: A Doubtful Verdict Reviewed' in *English Historical Review*, 1891 (vi).,
Markham, Sir C. R., *Richard III: His Life and Character*, Smith Elder 1906.
Mowbray, Segrave and Stourton, Lord, *The History of the Noble House of Stourton*, London 1899 (2 vols).
Myers, A. R., *England in the Late Middle Ages*, Penguin 1952.
Myers, A. R., 'The Character of Richard III', in *History Today* 1954 (August).
Nicholson, R., *Scotland: The Later Middle Ages*, Edinburgh 1974.
Peers, Sir C. R., *Middleham Castle*, HMSO 1943.
Pollard, A. F., 'The Making of Sir Thomas More's Richard III' in *Historical Essays in Honour of James Tait*, ed. J. G. Edwards, Manchester 1933.
Pollard, A. J., 'The Tyranny of Richard III,' in *Journal of Mediaeval History*, 1977 (iii).
Pugh, T. B., 'The Magnates, Knights and Gentry,' in *Fifteenth-Century England* (above).
Ramsay, J. H., *Lancaster and York*, Oxford 1892 (2 vols).
Richmond, C. F., English Naval Power in the Fifteenth Century' in *History* lii, 1967.
Richmond, C. F., 'Fauconberg's Kentish Rising of May 1471' in *English Historical Review* 1970.
Ross, C. D., *Edward IV*, Eyre Methuen 1974.
Ross, C. D., *Richard III*, Eyre Methuen 1981.
Ross, C. D., 'Rumour, Propaganda and Popular Opinion during the Wars of the Roses' in *Patronage, the Crown and the Provinces in Later Mediaeval England*, ed. R. A. Griffiths, Alan Sutton 1981.
Ross, C. D., *The Wars of the Roses*, Thames and Hudson 1976.
Routh, P., and Knowles, R., *The Sheriff Hutton Alabaster: A Re-assessment*, Rosalin Press 1981.
Rowse, A. L., *Bosworth Field and the Wars of the Roses*, Macmillan 1966.
Scofield, C. L., *The Life and Reign of Edward the Fourth*, London 1923 (2 vols).
Somerville, R., *History of the Duchy of Lancaster*, London 1953.
Storey, R. L., *The End of the House of Lancaster*, Barrie and Rockcliff 1966.
Storey, R. L., 'The North of England' in *Fifteenth-Century England* (above).
Stow, J., *A Survey of London*, Oxford 1908 (2 vols).
Stow, J., *The Annales or Generall Chronicle of England*, London 1615.
Tanner, L. E., and Wright, W., 'Recent Investigations Regarding the Fate of the Princes in the Tower', in *Archaeologia* 1934 (lxxxiv).
Tey, Josephine, *The Daugher of Time*, Peter Davies 1951.
Tudor-Craig, P., *Richard III*, Catalogue, National Portrait Gallery 1973.
Victoria County History, passim.
Walpole, H., *Historic Doubts on the Life and Reign of Richard III*, London 1768.

Wedgwood, J. C., *History of Parliament: Biographies of Members of the Commons House 1439–1509*, HMSO 1936 and *Register*, HMSO 1938.

Williams, D. T., *The Battle of Bosworth*, Leicester 1973.

Williamson, A., *The Mystery of the Princes (an Investigation into a supposed Murder)*, Alan Sutton 1978.

Wolffe, B. P., *Henry VI*, Eyre Methuen 1981.

INDEX